1 Possiplex

Possiplex

AN AUTOBIOGRAPHY OF TED NELSON

POSSIPLEX

Movies, Intellect, Creative Control,

My Computer Life

and the Fight for Civilization

First edition

POSSIPLEX: Movies, Intellect, Creative Control, My Computer Life and the Fight for Civilization, Bookstore Edition, ©2010-11 Theodor Holm Nelson. All rights reserved. ISBN 978-0-89347-004-3.

INTELLECTUAL PROPERTY NOTICES:
The following are current trademarks of Project Xanadu, either registered or claimed:
    Xanadu® hypertext; XanaduSpace™; the Eternal-Flaming-X™ symbol

    ZigZag® database and software mechanisms; the Zigfinity™ symbol; Illusium™ multidimensional viewdata– "The stuff that dreams are made of™". UltiDimensional™ viewing.

    Transcopyright™ permission doctrine, content delivery and sale method.

The following are trademarks for designs still offered under consultation by the author:
    Fantasm™
    Parallel Textface™ (broader generic: Transpointing windows)
    Walkie-Thinkie™
    Retrocorder™
    Ted Nelson's JOT™ [not to be confused with 'JOT' offered by others]
    Cinenym™
    HyperCoin™
    SoftWorld™
    LedgerDomain™
    FlapDoodle™, Pictrola™
    SpiralTime™

TRAC® is or was a registered trademark of Rockford Research, Inc.

The following are former trademarks of the author used in this book–
    "Vortext" was at one time a claimed trademark of the author, and is used to refer to a specific design in this narrative. It is now a trademark of someone else.

    "Unifire" was at one time a claimed trademark of the author, and is used to refer to a specific design in this narrative. It is now appears to be under use by several others, but possibly with no trademarks claimed.

Cover pic:
The author as he wishes to be remembered: clever, determined, defiant. (ID photo from Hacker conference, ca. 1998)

Possiplex

Possiplex

> There is too much to say and it goes in all directions.
> — TN
>
> My religion is human creativity and human freedom.
> — TN
>
> Everything is possible, nothing is easy.
> — TN
>
> I mistook a clear view for a short distance.
> — TN
>
> Everything is deeply intertwingled.
> — TN

> Ah, but a man's reach should exceed his grasp,
> or what's a Heaven for?
> — Robert Browning

Possiplex

AFORETHOUGHT

I am writing my history because they say that history is written by the winners, and I still intend to win.

This book is coming out just fifty years after I had my main ideas in the computer field. The anniversary is an accident. I've tried to tell the story before, but it's taken till now to clarify and package it reasonably.

Everybody wants to tell their story; I have special reasons. I have a unique place in history and I want to claim it. Indeed, I want it as a vaulting-pole, a lever still to move the world.*

> * Archimedes supposedly said: Give me a lever long enough and a fulcrum on which to place it, and I shall move the world. Conceivably this book could be both. (Every pole-vaulter creates a small Archimedean shift of the planet; I see a much greater shift as necessary and possible still.)

I also want to clear the air, substituting the true story for myth and misunderstandings about my life and work.

This is not a modest book. Modesty is for those who are after the Nobel, and that chance (if any) is long past. This is what I want known long after. Like Marco Polo and Tesla* in their autobiographies, I am crazed for people to know my real story.

> * If you don't know about Tesla, the true inventor of the modern world— I didn't hear of him in my youth either— there is more about him later.

What the hell gave me the background and temerity to think I could design the documents of the future, and indeed conjure a complete computer world, on my own and with no technical credentials, when no one else in the world even imagined those things? And why do I still stand against thousands of experts who want to impose their own worlds on humanity? And why do I think I know the true generalization of documents and the true generalization of structure, when they don't?

That's what this book is about: how I came to the visions, attitudes and initiatives which have driven me for the last fifty years, and drive me still to keep trying though at first I haven't succeeded.

This is not the autobiography I wanted to write—languorous, loving, literary, full of family and friends, atmosphere and philosophy, sparkle and sunsets, what the times were like, the powerful emotions we all faced. This is not that. This is far more urgent, a story about attitudes and designs—what I knew and thought about and designed and why, as I stumbled and clawed and thought my way through the developing computer world of these last fifty years.*

> * Here's how the book evolved: the languorous version, deeply intertwingled with thousands of interconnections of the world and my life, was going to be called *World Enough* (as in the poem by Andrew Marvell). But that got too big, and with its hundreds of threads and criss-crossing connection, would be impossible to follow unless it could be a proper hypertext, which is still impossible in today's software world, and impossible to write without a decent text system.
>
> So to get something done without a decent system, I got the idea of a slimmed-down autobiography, just about my computer and hypertext struggles, to be called *My Computer Life*. But that was too narrow, parochial and boring.
>
> The current volume combines them— the computer-hypertext story, augmented by aspects and connections of my life that contributed to that story. I had to cut and cut to make it interesting, but still it's much bigger than expected.

I am a controversial figure, which means those who know my name either love me or hate me, mostly the latter. Most seem to regard me as a raving, ignorant, unconscious, delusional dreamer who was strangely and accidentally right about a remarkable variety of things.

I was never ignorant and there was no accident— I knew ten times more fifty years ago, when I started in computers, than most people think I know now. I considered myself a philosopher and a film-maker, and what I knew about was media and presentation and design, the nature of writing and literature, the processes of technical analysis and idea manipulation, and the human heart. I also knew about projects, and why one dares follow the inner urgings of a project, going where its nature wants to go.

I saw in 1960 how all these matters would have to transpose to the interactive computer screen. And I have been dealing with the consequences, including both the politics and the technicalities, straight on through since then.

- For five years I designed documents and interfaces for the interactive computer screen without ever seeing an interactive computer screen, but I understood perfectly well what it would be like, imagining its performances and ramifications probably better than anyone else.
- For five years I worked on interactive text systems without knowing that anyone else in the world imagined such things.

- For eight years I worked on methods for ray-tracing and image synthesis, without knowing anyone else imagined such things. (Now the film industry revolves around them.)
- For at least a decade I was designing hypertext structure without ever seeing a working hypertext. But I knew perfectly well how it was going to feel.
- For fourteen years I believe I was the only person in the world who imagined a world of personal computing as a hobby, everyday activity and art form—all of which I presented in my book *Computer Lib* in 1974— months ahead of the first personal computer kit, which started the gold rush.
- For nearly TWENTY years (until I convinced five colleagues), I believe I was the only person in the world who envisioned millions of on-line documents, let alone on-line documents being read on millions of screens by millions of users from millions of servers and publishable by anyone. Not only did no one else imagine it, I could not *make* them imagine it, though I lectured and exhorted constantly.

You might think this would give me a reputation for foresight, but many consider me a crank because I haven't gotten on any of the bandwagons— Microsoft, Apple, Linux, or the World Wide Web.

Why have I not joined any of these parades? Because *they're all alike* (heresy!), *and I have always had an alternative.* I don't like their designs—what you see around you— and I still intend to get my designs running, so you can at last have a real choice. (Unfortunately most people don't realize the computer world has been *designed*, so that's an uphill battle.)

I believe my standing designs for a real alternative computer world— complete, clear, and sweeping— are better, deeper and simpler than what people now have to face every morning.

THE MYTH OF TECHNOLOGY

The world is totally confused—everyone uses the word "technology" for PACKAGES AND CONVENTIONS— like email, Windows, Facebook, the World Wide Web. These all *use* technologies but are themselves just collections of design decisions somebody made without asking you. I see humanity as unknowing prisoners in systems of invisible walls— specific conventions created by hidden tekkies, sometimes long ago and never questioned since, by anybody.* The myth of technology is the myth that the software issues are technical; whereas what matters is *communicating to the mind and heart of the user*, and that is not a technical issue at all.

*So many people see an oppressive interface and say "Oh, I don't understand technology!", when a more appropriate reaction would be: *The sons of bitches!*

I am certain my designs, in part and whole, as well as the story told here, will someday vindicate me (what a pisser! To have to seek vindication at the age of 73). But I can't wait till I'm dead to tell the story and I can't wait till I'm dead to make the software work; I want to implement these designs *now*, while they can still be done right (with my own detailing), and reduce people's computer misery and quadruple the usability of computer documents. I want to improve the world that is.

This is a multithreaded story. I wish I could tell it in a decent electronic document—a Xanadu document of parallel pages with visible connections--

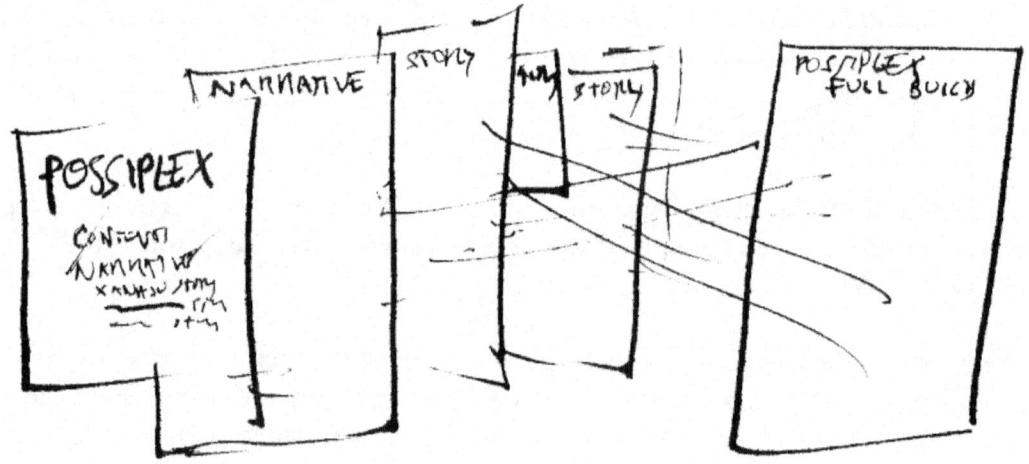

HOW THIS DOCUMENT OUGHT TO LOOK WHEN IT OPENS (links not shown, only transclusions).
A proper parallel hypertext in a possible opening view. The reader is able to read the full build (right), corresponding to this assembled book, or separate narratives and threads. Visible beams of transclusion show identical content among separate pages (stories, threads, and full build). Where are the visible beams of connection in Microsoft Word, Adobe Acrobat, the World Wide Web?

Unfortunately we have still not got decent documents working and deployed. (Part of the problem is that people don't understand why they need parallelism, let alone transclusion and multiway links.)

Trapped here on paper, I am simulating this parallelism clumsily. I'm using indentations and headings to thread the different stories, for example—

XANADU STORY——————————

FANTASM STORY——————

Personal Systems————————

CINENYM STORY

ZIGZAG STORY

If you have no technical interests, you can read the main story—the personal narrative—by reading only the parts that start at the left margin, and ignoring the indented parts. The indented stories above happen to be crucial. Among the many indented headings, the particular five above happen to refer to principal initiatives by which I hoped to achieve a financial foothold, creative resources and independence.

The first three of these ideas occurred to me in 1960 and 1961. There was no telling in the early nineteen-sixties which would bring money first; I may not have thought of the fourth until 1964, and the last not until 1983. All are valid, though no one has ever known it but I, and now these first four ideas have become four different vast industries. But in fact none of them brought anybody money for at least sixteen years after I thought of them.

Because there was no way to know which of these ideas would catch on first, I kept on with all of them. They took decades longer than I expected, and I was not on those trains when they pulled out. (If I had succeeded in patenting the first two, as I tried to, the patents would have expired by the time those things were commercial.)

The fifth, ZigZag, did not occur to me until 1983 (I first called it Unifire), and most people don't understand it or see its power even now.

But the most important problem I still face is to give the world decent electronic documents.

I do not embrace the World Wide Web, though many think it was my idea (my idea was better). Most people imagine that the Web is a wonder of technology, whereas I see it as a political setback by a dorky package. (As stated elsewhere, it is not technology, it's packaging and conventions.)

To me the World Wide Web is an unfortunate presence which must be dealt with, like the Internal Revenue Service. It's all right for shop-windows, but not for the precious documents and thoughts of mankind, which it smashes into sequence, hierarchy, rectangularity, fixed views, huge wasted screen-space and locked lines of text (usually far too wide and in faint unreadable sans serif). The Web offers no way to underline, no way to make marginal notes (let alone publish them), no way to make visible links between the documents, and other profound defects I won't get into yet. And it cannot be fixed.* The embedding of markup is a one-way ticket to hell.

> * Versioning (WEBDAV) cannot be combined with wikis, which cannot be defined with "trackback", etc.; and none of these cannot be combined with the

> annotations allowed by Kindle. All these things must be built into a design together. And have; see Appendix 1.

The alternative is still possible. And simpler.

The A-Word

There is an important word that has been little used in this book, because I've been talking about my experiences in the line of fire, and it was only a faraway concept in the background.

That word is Art.

Yes, I would like it if some day my designs are considered as art, for their minimalism and cleanliness and depth– and usefulness. (But in order even to be appreciated as art, they have to be implemented; nobody can understand them from the specs.)

It is still possible to help people out of the ever-more oppressive and silly world of today's computers.

People always think my designs are huge. They are as always small and clean, and my whole package can be created as a corrective level in existing operating systems. Disguised as an application, and turned on and off.

That might be considered art.

TECHNICALITIES OF THIS BOOK

Every word in this book is true to the best of my recollection, and can eventually be confirmed from my notes and diaries. I do not think I am retrodicting– re-imagining my thoughts of youth and middle age on the basis of what happened later– but that can some day be tested. Unfortunately these notes are scrambled into many cartons in different places, and I have had to write without their use. Some dates are probably off.

I use double quotes when I believe I am quoting someone exactly, single quotes if I am not sure of the wording.

I have had to omit a lot. I have had to drop numerous anecdotes, insights, threads, and people. There has been no time or space for more than a few illustrations. I wish I could have said far more about my grandparents and others I love. I am honoring the privacy of various relatives by leaving them substantially out of this narrative. And alas, a number of wonderful and fascinating people important to me could not fit into the main lines of exposition.

There are two special omissions in this edition. On the advice of legal counsel, because of an ongoing court case, I had to omit any reference to my biological mother. And I have entirely left out the chapter on my experiences at Brown University, pending two formal requests I made for an ethics hearing on how I was treated there. These matters are now closed, but the current edition is integral without them; on consideration, I shall leave it that way.

This is tricky writing. I am trying to maintain good relations with people like Larry Tesler, Alan Kay, Tim Berners-Lee, and certain of my former colleagues, even though I disagree with what they have done and deplore some of the consequences.

Before we start, my especial thanks to my sweetpartner Marlene Mallicoat, my eternal friend and former wife Deborah Stone, my son Erik, and other friends, well-wishers and patrons,* without whom I would not have survived.

> * My patrons– those who have given me financial aid, special aid or cut slack in my adult career– include (in rough chronological order) Jean and Theodor Holm, Norman W. Storer, L. Joseph Stone, Deborah Stone, Maurice G. Eldridge and Susannah Eldridge, Robert W. Fiddler, Robert Haavind, Leon Loeb, Bob and Ginny Levine, John R. Levine, Jonathan Fagin, Stafford Hopwood, Erik Nelson, Joseph I. Lipson, Sheila McKenzie, David C. Miller, Nancy Smith, Ray and Carol Dyda, Laura McLaughlin, Steve Witham, D.J. Cone, Sean Harmon, Steve Ditlea, Catherine Ikam, Bill Gates, Lauren Sarno, Marc Stiegler, Elisabeth Davenport, Marlene Mallicoat, David Bunnell, Andrew Pam and Katherine Phelps, Yuzuru Tanaka, Edward Harter, Bob Heyman, Kay Nishi, Mike and Krystyna Pikowski, Hajime Ohiwa, Kenji Naemura, Nobuo Saito, Laurie Spiegel, Yoshihisa Ogawa, Wendy Hall, Pierre de la Coste, Pierre Oudart, Alain Giffard, Xavier Perrot, Frode Hegland, Henry Lowood, Mike Keller, Helen Ashman, Tim Brailsford, Sellam Ismail, Brewster Kahle and Mary K. Austin, Douglas and Karen Engelbart, William Dutton, Arthur Bullard, Kuniko Kono, Duncan Whitmore. I hope none have been omitted. (I am not including family members, collaborators, employers, assistants, business associates or lovers *per se.*)

For Marlene—

    sweet,
    clever,
    tenacious,
    loving,
    magical.

    She kept it,
    and me,
    together.

18 Possiplex 18

POSSIPLEX

Chapter 1.
DIVISION STREET ERA, 1937-43

My Family

Our apartment in Chicago had wooden back stairs outside, like many Chicago buildings, but in front it was a regular stone-fronted apartment building. The living room– we called it the front room– I remember as sunny, though it faced north, so the sun could not have shone in directly. (My grandmother always wanted a "north light" for her drawing and painting; it was important that she was an Artist.) I probably remember it as sunny because I was happy there. I remember how beautiful my grandmother looked in that light, sometimes at her easel, sometimes combing her long blonde hair.

We lived, Jean and Pop and I, in Chicago, at 37 East Division Street, a short walk from the beach of Lake Michigan.* Frequently they took me to museums and the Aquarium, to the park, and to the beach. We saw movies at a wondrous, palatial theater, and we often went to a wonderful Chinese restaurant.

* Studs Terkel would later choose Division Street, Chicago, as a symbol of America.

I had been left at six months' age with my grandmother and grandfather, and named after him. These were entirely the right decisions. (I was Theodor Holm II, said a membership certificate on the wall).

Jean and Theodor Holm (I am calling him Pop) were an elegant couple. She generally wore high heels and a veil; in colder weather, furs. He was dignified, warm and thoughtful, and wore a fedora. Both spoke with what people mistook for English accents, but she was from Minnesota– in those days, many Americans spoke in a more English fashion– and he was from Norway, though no one could tell. They spoke elegantly and eloquently, with wonderful words.

My family was very cultured and loving. Ours was a home of culture. We were members of the Art Institute of Chicago-- actually *I*, in my crib, was the member; when my grandmother went to buy a membership for the family, the person at the desk suggested getting the membership in the name of the youngest member of the family, and I, the newborn, was it. So said the certificate on the wall-- the life membership in the Art Institute of Theodor Holm II.

Leonardo, Shakespeare, Shaw were our household gods; Shakespearean quotes were bandied about frequently. There were family tales of contacts with Gurdjieff and Tagore, and memories of a debate Jean had had with Emma Goldman. (By "debate", I assume what happened was that Jean asked a question at a lecture by Goldman, and then there was some follow-on banter between them. I bet I could even reconstruct it, plausibly, but that is another story.)

Jean and Theodor Holm at their grandest, possibly on their wedding trip to Norway.

I had four main grownups. I lived with Jean and Pop in Chicago. Jean's parents-- my great-grandparents, Blanche and Edmund-- were also present in spirit, though they lived far away in Brooklyn, but they would come to Chicago at Christmas, and we would spend the summer with them at our farm. Blanche, my great-grandmother, reviewed plays for the women's clubs of Brooklyn (unimaginable today!). Deeply affectionate, she ghost-wrote my first 'autobiography' when I was one, and read me numerous books when I was little.

The author's great-grandmother, Mrs. Edmund Jewett, née Blanche Eugenie Newell.

Edmund Gale Jewett, Blanche's third husband, was not actually my great-grandfather; she had been twice widowed before marrying Edmund, but we called him my great-grandfather out of courtesy and love.

*Smith and Jewett, *An Introduction to the Study of Science*, Macmillan (originally published 1917).

Edmund Gale Jewett (the author's great-grandfather, on the right) with his workmen at the Lain-Jewett Dry Kiln Company, ca. 1908. His beard was red then. We see the helical heating pipe being assembled. It says on the back, "High Point, 20 miles east of Seattle, Wash." We don't know much more.

Edmund was a science teacher, very reserved, with a white beard. He had invented the fundamental method of lumber-drying now in use, but the big lumber companies had stolen his invention and he got nothing for it. The 1920 edition of his science book,* still very good, is available for download (now copyrighted by Google).

*Smith and Jewett, *An Introduction to the Study of Science*, Macmillan (originally published 1917).

Edmund was to teach me about evolution, astronomy (his great love), physics, algebra. But he also wrote beautiful poetry. One of his poems about evolution, written in the thirties, is still precisely accurate within today's knowledge. My four grownups all treated me with great love and respect. In an early, hazy memory, I recall the four of us– Jean and Pop, Blanche and Edmund—in the lower cabin at the farm, perhaps on a summer evening. When I would speak they would all fall silent. By the way they listened, they told me that I was very clear-minded, that my thoughts were special and that I expressed them very well. That is how I first learned who I was.

Many children fantasize that their real parents are faraway, glamorous people. For me this was actually true. Like Harry Potter, I had magical parents who were not present, and like Harry Potter I have been greatly punished for it. But that is another story.

My parents were young actors who needed a divorce almost immediately they were married, but my grandfather made them stay married until I was born so I would be "legitimate." Away went my parents to their separate remarkable destinies, but each would visit, separately, a few times a year.

Jean and Pop already had a rich history. On the eve of World War I, she headed to Europe to document the coming war with her drawings, buying a ticket on the Lusitania. A friend, the great photographer Arnold Genthe, saved her, but that is another story. After the crash of 1929, Pop was offered a grand job and he quit the one he had, then the grand job offer was withdrawn, and there he was jobless in the depression; but that is another story. And they had friends among the moderately famous of those days, whom I often heard about; but that is another story.

However it may seem to you, I did not think I was having a privileged childhood. There was so much I could not have. And there was so much I did not like, especially school.

School

My school, the Bateman School, was in the old McCormick mansion, not far away. I hated it. I didn't hate the teachers, or Mrs. Bateman the principal; I hated the institution, and I remember wanting to burn the school down at the age of four or five. But that is another story.

I do remember the day I learned to read. I knew the alphabet, of course, and we had been learning to spell words, but it had never been all put together for us. And I had not been pressured on the matter. On this day Miss Ferlette, my lovely first-grade teacher, handed each of us a pamphlet with a different story. (They were photo-offset in dark blue, as I recall.)

Now the words were in a row, and I saw how they were put all together, and I read the story, and the excitement filled me.

Miss Ferlette was very pleased when I asked for another.

She was especially pleased when I asked for a third.

CYNICAL AND OUT FRONT: the author, 4, leads kindergartners debouching the school vehicle, ca. April 1942.

Love and Reading

Jean and Pop were not only elegant, but the dearest and most loving people I have ever known. Every night at bedtime one of them would read to me, sing to me or tell me a story. And we would read together—that is, Pop would read, while Jean would sit or sew; I would play with my blocks or kaleidoscope, or whatever. Pop read many books to us, including *Just So Stories*, *Swiss Family Robinson*, and a number of the Doctor Dolittle books. And my favorite early book, *Paddle-to-the-Sea*,* by Holling.

-------- A Note from the Present

> * My earliest visions of hypertext and hypermedia, in the 1960s, were closely related to *Paddle-to-the-Sea*. Each of its chapters has a text, a painting, an ink drawing, and a map. The reader (or the read-to) unites these in the mind, learning to connect different aspects of sight and story.

Pop had a beautiful voice and he would sometimes read for an hour or more. Those were happy times.

Summers at our farm, Blanche, my great-grandmother would read to me. I remember especially her reading animal stories by Albert Payson Terhune, and the Oz books that I so loved.

Media of the Nineteen-Forties

Every night, or so it seemed, we listened to the radio, and especially weekend evenings, with their concerts and comedians and fast talking, mischievous and dramatic.

Those were the glory days of radio. The actors spoke grandly, and their words were sauced with sneaky sound effects, of gloom, excitement or silliness. Announcers and commentators declaimed, news was delivered with sound-effects of telegraph code. Concerts were presented with majesty and elaborate introductions.

Forgotten today about radio then is *how people listened*—together, often making eye contact, sharing the atmosphere. Radio was a deep and shared experience, often the main pursuit of the evening.

We also had phonograph records that were like radio plays—"A Christmas Carol," "Treasure Island"– and we listened to them together, the same way. We always played "A Christmas Carol" at Christmas. It starred Ronald Colman.

------- A Note from the Present
Today people generally listen to the radio alone, using it for a pseudo-social environment.

Love and Words

We had a home of wonderful words.

I loved every new word. A new word was a gift, a lens, a construction piece. Words were my toys and my best friends. (I also had occasional friends among children, but most of them knew very little, though I would fall in love with the girls and have to hide it.)

We spoke the best English in our home. I became aware that most people did not. "It is I," we would say. The word "exquisite" had to be emphasized on the first syllable, as did "despicable". However, we considered "tomayto" to be an an acceptable variant to our pronunciation of "tomahto"; many aspects of words were matters of taste.

OUR WORDS

We often used old-fashioned and Shakespearean phrasings, like "Art thou hungry?" The words *thither* and *thence*, *whither* and *whence* were part of our everyday vocabulary. But only at home, between us.*

------- A Note from the Present
* Linguistic pride and conservatism ran in the family, it seems. Only recently did I learn that one of Pop's older brothers in Norway, Gerhard Holm, was the chief opponent of the official changes made to the Norwegian language in the 1940s. The made-up new language was in 1949 called "Lansmal." It has become the official Norwegian language, now called "Nynorsk" (pron. nu-norsk–'new Norwegian') but I believe Gerhard fought it all the way.

We talked about puns, spoonerisms, portmanteaux and teakettles,* euphemisms and paraphrases, idioms and clichés, synonyms and antonyms, malaprops and misspellings, old saws and epigrams, anglicisms and anglicizations and 'words which have no equivalent in English.'

* A teakettle was a token in a punning game, which I do not have time to explain in this edition.

Newly-coined words were always of interest, like someone a friend brings to dinner. I became aware that coining words was simply something one *did*, like naming children or pets.

I realized: Every idea needs a good word to swing it by.

The War Begins

Though I was only four, I remember the beginning of World War II. I was in Pop's lap, and we were listening to the symphony on our cathedral radio, when the program was interrupted with the news that the Japanese had attacked Pearl Harbor. Pop wept, saying "O my god, o my god."

After Pearl Harbor, Ralph, my father, instantly joined the service, eager to serve. Three weeks after Pearl Harbor he showed up in his uniform at our Chicago apartment, to join us for Christmas 1941.

Ralph Nelson, visiting father, dandles the author (left); probably spring 1943.

DEFINING MOMENTS
My First Movie, 1942

A little goddess was singing to me.

I was walking down the carpeted aisle of a movie theater in rural New Jersey. I believe I was four and Edmund was holding my hand, and I was transported by the smell of the Coca-Cola and the popcorn. And I looked up at the screen ahead, as we walked down the aisle, and there she was.

It was a religious moment: she was a goddess singing to me and we were in a kind of church. That moment and its magic are with me to this day.

I don't know who she was. (In later years I thought it was Shirley Temple but I have found no film of hers that fits with that release date.) But whoever she was, she was singing to my heart, and it was my heart that she captured. The love of her, and of the moment, and of the magical setting, have always stayed with me. And the movie theater, with its magic rays rippling above the audience and its changing façade of feelings and adventures, has been the closest thing to a church in my life.

Movies

In Chicago, Jean and Pop would take me to the movies. Our local movie theater was a great Art Deco movie palace, the Esquire Theater on Oak Street.

If I have had any religion it is movies, and the Esquire was our cathedral then.

It was there we saw "Bambi" and "Dumbo" and "Fantasia" when they first came out. "Snow White" and "Pinocchio" had already been around once, and I did not see them till later. ("Pinocchio" was the only Disney movie I hated, because of the horrible ending—he lost his distinctiveness, he didn't get to be an actor, and he had to go back to school.)

------- A Note from the Present

It is easy for people to think my obsession with movies and movie-making came from my parents' influence, but it absolutely did not. My obsession and reverence for movies and movie-making were in my soul from the beginning, entirely from my inner nature, long before either parent got into the movie business. Perhaps heredity is involved here, but I believe my parents' influence was only supplementary, adding sauce and whetting my sense of possibility.

Manuscripts

Jean's manuscripts were central and sacred. She would work on them from time to time. She had written, and privately published, poetry and several novels. Their contents did not concern me, but their importance to our family was clear.

Writing Together

I would hear Pop and Jean discussing letters as they composed them, writing to relatives and friends– trying wordings, reading them back and forth. Pop would propose a sentence and write it, Jean would ask him to read it again and suggest changing a word.

From this I began to learn the delicacy of the writing process.

CUT -- AND -- PASTE -------------
Sometimes they would rearrange. Jean would say, "I think that sentence should be at the beginning." They would discuss it, and perhaps that's where the sentence would go.

DEFINING MOMENTS

Flowers by Wire *(Data Structure, ~1942)*

I was five. Jean, my grandmother, often took me to flower shops in Chicago. Each flower shop had a sign outside with a picture of the Greek god Mercury, and the words FLOWERS BY WIRE.

How did they get the flowers down the wire?

I asked the flower-man how Flowers By Wire worked. He said, 'Oh, you wouldn't understand.'

The flower salesman wouldn't tell me, so I tried to figure out myself how they sent flowers by wire. I thought about it and thought about it. It was a hard problem.

Would they start with the stems first, or the petals? And what about the aroma?

I knew, obviously, that you could send a voice by wire; evidently flowers could somehow be sent as well.

I understood how phone calls went through the wire—there was something you talked into (I didn't yet know that it was called a microphone) that translated the speech into some sort of event (I didn't know the term "signal") that went all the way to the other end, and there was something else (I didn't know it was called a speaker) that translated the event back into sound. So I had a correct, if approximate, mental picture of telephony.

But how would that work with flowers?

You would have to have some kind of a device at each end, just as the telephone call had a device at each end.

I figured that the device at the starting end must take the flower apart, probably by grinding off a little at a time, and converting that into a signal which went down the wire, and then grinding till the whole flower was transmitted. And then at the other end there would be a device that reconstituted the flower fragments from the signals, and perhaps extruded the flowers like spaghetti.

But would they start with the stems first, or the petals? And what about the aroma?

These were difficult issues, but I felt I had a handle on the basics.

──────── A Note from the Present
I believe these were my first deliberations about data structure, and that the analysis was rather good considering the information I had—in fact, that's how many systems of scanning and transmission work today. But not for flowers.

If you had told me the real answer-- "How do they send flowers by wire? Someone at the first flower shop telephones the second flower shop, and asks the person at the second flower shop to deliver a bouquet to a specific address," I would have been outraged that the flower-man withheld such a simple, stupid fact.

Still, it was a thinking and learning experience.

Ideas and Their Expression

Truman Capote wrote somewhere that as a boy, it seemed to him that he had twenty times as many perceptions as the other kids.

That was my experience with ideas. The other kids had very few ideas and difficulty expressing them, and didn't understand many of the things I said.* Adults more often could, but not always.

> * I wanted to point out ironies and fascinating aspects, but it took so much exposition and argument that we never got to the ironies or fascinating aspects.

I was always flooded with ideas, new ideas shooting in all directions, and I could express many of them rather well, except the ones that were at the edge of the words and concepts I knew so far.

I now know that this is considered a pathology: 'Attention Deficit Disorder' means having too many ideas (as far as someone else is concerned), which are irrelevant (as far as somebody else is concerned), and that there are too many of them (as far as someone else is concerned). When you are supposed to be concentrating on one thing, a different idea—especially if it is fascinating—gets in the way of the agenda. But suppose you don't care about their agenda?

------- A Note from the Present

Much of my life has been about dealing with ideas and their flight: because the ideas that fly through my mind are important to me, and often the fast, evasive thoughts belong with something else I am trying to do or think about.

In college I began to take notes, trying to capture the profusion of ideas, sometimes very good ones, that would occur to me, frequently under inconvenient circumstances. Others with this condition— sufferers, they are supposed to be, of "attention deficit disorder"— supposedly get trained not to think of other things. I never went along with that. The sparks of mind go in all directions, some with deeply interesting trajectories, and unless you can catch them you miss some of the best.

DEFINING MOMENTS
~ MAKING MOVIES ~
Red River Dave's Studio (~1942)

I think my first two heroes were Disney and Tchaikovsky, but my next hero I acquired on my own– a cowboy singer named Red River Dave, whom I'd found by turning the radio dial. He invited listeners to come down to the Studio and see the show. At my request, Pop took me.

A Studio! Already, at five, I had gotten my idea of a Studio from the 20th-Century Fox opening title: a Studio had searchlights on top and 3D lettering. I was bemused to find that Red River Dave's Studio was a room in a downtown Chicago office building, with folding chairs. It did not match my expectation in the slightest.

But Red River Dave was very tickled that a five-year-old fan had brought his grandfather to see the show in person.

Though there were a number of folding chairs set up, I think the two of us were the entire audience. That was fine as far as I was concerned.

DEFINING MOMENTS
The Projector Gun (~1942)

I was four or five. In Pop's newspaper I saw an ad for a projector gun! What could a boy want more? The fusion of two key concepts! I think it cost $3.95. I pleaded for it. I imagined a full movie projector, with great undulating beams filling faraway walls, pointing wherever I chose.

The projector gun turned out to be a puny plastic object with a flashlight bulb and one battery, and a short strip of 16mm film (to be shown one unchanging frame at a time). It projected a faint image of the one frame that could only be seen on a wall a few inches from its lens. Pop tried to console me by showing that it did in fact project, but it only worked in shadowy places, and even then there wasn't much worth seeing.

This was perhaps my first media disappointment. It was not the last time I would be taken in by expectations of what media equipment would do.

-------- **A Note from the Present**

What I envisioned was very like today's DLP digital projectors. But those were far in the future, and still none is battery-operated, or the size or shape of a gun.

Comics

As soon as I had learned to read— that day I just remembered— I started reading comics. I loved them and studied them in every way—the stories, the characters, the jocund lettering (especially of the sound effects), the tiny dots of color (which my eyes could then see perfectly up close), even the smell.

I especially loved Ha Ha Comics (I had the first issue), "Walt Disney's Comics and Stories", Little Lulu, and Captain Marvel. The gruesome and detective stuff I did not like.

CUT--AND--PASTE-------------
Don't Touch My Noodles!

Jean, my grandmother, had a story about Tolstoy. She had once heard a lecture by one of his daughters, telling how Tolstoy would write. (I don't know if this is published anywhere else.)

Two of his daughters would transcribe. (There were no typewriters.) Tolstoy would dictate a first draft and the two daughters would each take it down, each making an identical handwritten copy.

Then Tolstoy would put one copy aside, for reference. He would then cut up the other copy and rearrange it, adding material and deleting, and eventually pasting the pieces and new notes into their new sequence.

He would then dictate again, from this new draft, to the daughters. One copy would be put aside, and the other would be cut up to make the next draft. And so on.

But in between, when the pieces were loose, they would be all over the floor in a current, tentative rearrangement.

Tolstoy would then go off for a long walk.

From the edge of the woods, he would call back:

DON'T TOUCH MY NOODLES!

My grandmother would often quote this jokingly, in various contexts.

------- A Note from the Present

I learned to write and rewrite when I was fourteen, and in my twenties I started keeping a carbon copy of each version for reference and cutting up the original. Only much later did I realize that I had rediscovered Tolstoy's method on my own.

And only gradually did I realize how central this issue is to all my work.

DEFINING MOMENTS
My Hand in the Water (~1942-3)

I trailed my hand in the water as my grandfather rowed. My grandmother was in the front of the boat, wearing high heels as always. I was four or five, and this was spring 1943 at the latest; we were still in Chicago.

Fuzzy shapes passed underneath. I studied the water's crystal softness. The water was opening around my fingers, gently passing around them, then closing again behind.

I considered the different places in the water and the connections between them, the places that at one instant were next to each other, then separated as my fingers passed. They rejoined, but no longer in the same way.

How is it, I wondered, that every instant's arrangement, in the water and the world, can be so much the same as just before, and yet so different? How could even the best words express this complexity? How could even the best words express what systems of relationships were the same and different? And how many relationships were there?

I could not have said "relationships" or "systems" then, let alone "particles" or "manifolds" or "higher-level commonalities," but those were my exact concerns. My questions and confusions were always exact, and fine distinctions concerned me greatly. They still do. In this book I will try to say exactly what I was thinking at different times: exactly, that is, in my vocabulary of now.

And how, you might ask, do I remember those floating swirling thoughts over sixty years ago? Because these are matters I have thought about ever since, in thousands of different ways, and I reconnect them even now with that early moment of floating crystalline study, rattle of oarlocks, sun-twinkle on the water, my grandmother clearing her throat, the thump of oars, my grandfather's earnestness; all with me as I write in the eternal Now and Then.

XANADU STORY
CONNECTION TO THE ORIGINAL (1)

That religious experience, the moment of my hand in the water, is with me always. Always I see the profusion of relationships, of connections, of ideas, of possibilities, as a great net across the world, across every subject, across everything.

All my philosophical thoughts since then derive from that insight in the rowboat, or perhaps some fundamental pattern in my mind that first projected into the water, some strip of mental film projecting outward from my inner center, from which that insight came.

The insight was sound. Profuse connection is the whole problem of abstraction, perception and thought. Profuse connection is the whole problem of expression, of saying anything. It is the problem of writing. It is the problem of seeing-- we see and imagine so much more than we can express. Trying to communicate ideas requires selection from this vast, ever-expanding net. Writing on paper is a hopeless reduction, as it means throwing out most of the connections, telling the reader only the smallest part in one particular sequence.

And this is what I have hoped to fix, or at least improve, through most of my life, giving the world a greater and better way to express thoughts and ideas. And that is what this book is about. This book is about the story of my life and thoughts, and of connections, and it is about the connections all-amongst life and thought, and how I have fought to bring about a better world of thought and its representation.

The Wonderful Future

My abiding interest was in the wonderful future and how great it was going to be. Everything would be all chromium and Art Deco; no longer would there be wood, or baroque curly decoration. Homes would be starkly rectangular. Robots would attend to our needs and whims. Automatic cars would take us everywhere on the ground, but rocket packs would take us further. Most of the time we would be off the planet, in spaceships.

Mainly everything would be different, and much, much better.

Chapter 2.
WASHINGTON SQUARE ERA, 1943-53

My God, I'm Six

Now we were in New York. I sat by the phonograph in our big living room, looking out on the treetops of Washington Square, and I thought, my god, I'm six! How time flies! And we've left Chicago, and I may never see Mary Ann again. This made me very sad, and I went on dreaming of her for years.

A da Vinci picturebook stayed on the coffeetable.

DESIGN INFLUENCES: da Vinci, when I was six
On our blue-mirrored coffeetable was a book that said "da Vinci" on the cover. It contained many of da Vinci's notebook pages. I realize now it was there for my benefit, and benefit me it did.

It told me that possibilities and designs for a better world were there for anyone to see, if you could just look through the way things are to what might be.

DESIGN INFLUENCES: The Theremin, when I was seven or eight

As a small boy I heard from Jean about two wonderful musical devices: the "Theremin-vox", and the Clavilux. She had seen them decades ago, I think in the nineteen-twenties.

I read about the theremin in the nineteen-forties, and later bought some 45s on which the theremin was played.* (This was before it was used in horror movies and Beach Boys records.)
                       * "Music out of the Moon" was the album.

The theremin was elegant in its simplicity: two hands played it. With your left hand (patting the air beside the device) you controlled the loudness; with your right hand (massaging the air above the device) you controlled the pitch. I later learned that it was elegant internally as well, based on heterodyning, but we need not go into that.

DEFINING MOMENTS

• **Interaction**
DESIGN INFLUENCES: Interface Horrors

The Exploding Pressure Cooker (~1946)

Pop loved his new pressure cooker, but one night he opened it without letting the steam off. My beloved grandfather was nearly killed as the heavy metal top flew past his head; his face was scalded by boiling-hot mashed potatoes; he would have been blinded except for his glasses, which were covered with boiling-hot mashed potatoes.

On the long drive to the country hospital, as my grandfather whimpered beside me in the back seat of our Model A Ford, I was filled with rage at the idiots who had designed that machine; even a nine-year-old—hell, even a five-year-old! could see how it could have been designed to be safe, making sure the pressure was released before you opened it. The designers chose instead to build a machine that could punish absent-mindedness by death. What fools! What bastard fools!

------- A Note from the Present

This was my searing introduction to interface design, and to the stupidity it invites.

The guys who designed that pressure cooker—or their spiritual heirs-- are in the computer business now.

DESIGN INFLUENCES: Frank Lloyd Wright, when I was about nine

By age 9 I was aware of Frank Lloyd Wright. I was hugely inspired by Wright's "Fallingwater" building. (I thought the stream went *through* the house, rather than past it—it would be fifty years before this misunderstanding was corrected.) I took the idea further, imagining an underwater house, and got rather excited about the idea. I wrote an essay about it.

DEFINING MOMENTS
I Become a Bohemian (1946)

Our home-room teacher in fifth grade was Mr. Vanderwall. We all loved him. He was playful and fastidious about language. If you asked him for a "piece of paper" rather than a sheet, he would tear off a corner and give it to you. He drilled us on the correct spellings of "supersede" and "surreptitious".*

> * How many fifth-graders today have even heard these words?

I was less fond of Mr. Bessenger, who taught us Geography for 15 minutes on Monday, Wednesday and Friday. (Mr. Bessenger was renowned for throwing books at students, but I never saw this.) All I remember of Geography was that Mr. Bessenger wanted us to recite the forty-eight states in one breath. I don't remember whether I made it. On Tuesday and Thursday, in the same 15-minute slot, Mr. Bessenger taught us Opera.

> * Now, you may think it strange that there was a course in Opera, and thinking back, so do I, but all courses are strange to kids, so who knew?

This consisted of having to learn the plots of famous operas. (I still have the little book of the 100 plots.) When we got to "La bohème", the book said it was aboht Bohemians. I asked, reasonably, "What is a Bohemian?"

"Look it up," said Mr. Bessenger.

Surprisingly, the school library had the original novel (in translation) from which the opera had been taken— *Scènes de la vie de bohème* by Henri Murger, as well as some history of bohemianism in .America.* I read these.

> * Apparently not the Parry volume of that title, since the book also made me a great admirer of Joe Gould, whom Parry treats disparagingly. The very best such history now is *Republic of Dreams*, by Ross Wetzsteon, but that was written much later.

The history said that Bohemians were free spirits who were uninhibited about life and sex, and unfettered by middle-class conventions.

I already felt very fettered by middle-class conventions— especially the tension in the elevator of our apartment building, where we had to discuss the weather with other people in suits— and this sounded fine to me.

I decided: *I'm going to be a Bohemian!*

The book said that the center of Bohemianism in America was a place in New York City called Greenwich Village. I wondered ardently where this Greenwich Village was, or how to get there, as (swinging my little briefcase) I wandered home to our apartment on Washington Square.

> * Some readers will be amused to recognize that Washington Square has always been the epicenter of Greenwich Village—however, it is the respectable part.

The Bohemian part started a couple of blocks away. I never found it directly.

DEFINING MOMENTS
XANADU STORY
I Begin to Doubt Libraries (ca. 1946)

We took a Field Trip to the New York Public Library. Somebody told us— I think it may have been our home-room teacher-- that they had every book in the world there. Perhaps she believed it, perhaps she just meant it as a way of being emphatic. But I needed to check.

To test this statement, I looked up the Oz books. I believe the New York Public Library had three Oz books besides the original *Wizard of Oz*. I was appalled: I think by that time I owned thirteen of the books in the series.*

> * I eventually got the first thirty-six, after which they got quite poor.

Obviously libraries were not to be trusted. You had to find the information wherever you could.

Clearly people were misled about libraries. They had lions of stone but feet of clay.

Bucky Says It All (1947)

DESIGN INFLUENCES: Bucky in 1947-8, when I was ten

It was 1947, when I was ten, that Buckminster Fuller made all the newspapers. He was trying to mass-produce his Dymaxion House, and there was a lot of publicity for it; I remember reading about Bucky in a number of different places, especially newspapers. (He must have had a very good publicist.)

Bucky Fuller believed we could have a new and much better and very different world.

This gave me something to hope for in a world I rather disliked. (I have always believed life should be completely different.)

He said the educational system was horrible—I totally agreed; and he wanted to fix the world by *design*—the design of his magnificent car, the design of his house that would come in by helicopter and be lowered on a pole.

Buckminster Fuller was my hero ever since.

Sophistication, Age 10

I believe that at the age of ten my favorite word was "ostensibly." I know I could recite Hamlet's "To Be or Not To Be" and a few verses of the Rubaiyat; I could sing, write out (and accentuate correctly), numerous songs from Gilbert and Sullivan, the first verse of the "Marseillaise" and all four verses of the Star Spangled Banner.

Such it was to be a literate child in the nineteen-forties.

COINED WORDS

I believe that at ten I could have told you who had coined the words "tintinnabulate"[1], "chortle"[2], "robot"[3], "serendipity"[4] and "dymaxion"[5].

[1] Poe.
[2] Lewis Carroll.
[3] Karel Capek.
[4] George Eliot, and I would have been wrong. Now I have learned it was Horace Walpole.
[5] Bucky Fuller, and I would have been wrong. It was coined by Waldo Warren, who also coined the term "radio".

I was not a prodigy. I had no special direction. I was just very clever, high-strung, interested in a lot of things, disgusted with school and middle-class life, and a lover of reading and movies and ideas.

------- A Note from the Present

No one could have known, least of all I, that this bundle of traits would define the direction of my life.

DESIGN INFLUENCES: THE TUCKER TORPEDO, ca. summer 1947 (when I was ten)

It was modern looking! It would go a hundred miles an hour! (Not being a driver, I did not understand the problems of such a concept, especially on the two-lane roads of those days.)

I pleaded with Pop to get a Tucker Torpedo. He scoffed.

We drove past an automobile showroom in Morristown, and there was a real Tucker Torpedo in the window, shining in red. I pleaded to stop but we didn't.

Pop did, however, later buy a Studebaker, which was the most radical car that was actually mass-produced.

DEFINING MOMENTS

YOU CAN'T KNOW (ca. fall 1947)

The teacher, I think it was the lovely Miss Johnson, said: 'Class, what's the next number in this series? Four, seven, ten—'

Kids started yelling 'Thirteen! Thirteen!'

I raised my hand. 'You can't know,' I said.

They all yelled at me: 'Can't you see, it's thirteen? You keep adding three—'

I was used to being ostracized. I stood up for the obvious.

'You can't know!' I told them again. 'You can't know the next number unless you know the principle!'

The kids said it was obvious that the principle was adding three each time. I said there could be other principles that generated the series of 4, 7, 10— where the next number would NOT be 13.

The students, and the teacher, disagreed with me.

------- A Note from the Present

Only much later did I find out that I was correct according to mathematical theory. But I was simply stating the obvious, except the other kids couldn't see it. The series 4, 7,10 could be produced by many different methods, with different next numbers. Not even Miss Johnson got it.

It was obvious. But not to them.

Television, the New Medium
The TV Studio at Wanamaker's

I often hung out at Wanamaker's Department Store, which occupied two buildings just south of my school. The nearer building had a great atrium and grand stairs, an art-deco snack bar, Maxfield Parrish paintings, and the stationery department. The larger building held the Wanamaker's bookstore (ninth floor), where I spent a lot of time; the Toy Department, in which I was losing interest; and, on the third floor, just above the Toy Department, was the Television Studio. It was a large square room. The floor had cameras which moved around, with their wire tethers. Above and around the camera floor were audience seats. (As I recall, if you went out the exit from the audience you would be in the fourth-floor Record Department).

They broadcast on Channel 5; it was called the Dumont Network. (The Dumont network probably rented the space from Wanamaker's.)

No one hassled me or my friends—well-behaved 9-year-olds with neckties— when we quietly looked in or sat down in the seats and looked down on the camera floor.

Various sets were permanently set up around the camera floor. I presume there was a control room but I don't remember seeing it.

There wasn't much to see at the Wanamaker TV studio. Nothing ever happened during the hours I visited, but if I had stayed around till five I could have watched the broadcast of "Captain Video," a silly low-budget space show, which was broadcast from that room. I think its sets were in a nook in the north wall.

DESIGN INFLUENCES: Corbusier, 1948, when I was eleven

In 1948 Corbusier's book *The Modulor* was published, and I browsed it in the Wanamaker's book section. I was impressed and in accord with his notion that a house was a "machine for living"—it cut through traditions and styles and asked how we wanted to live.

This accorded with my notion that we should redesign our lives radically.

✦ COINED WORDS

Pop's brother needed a word for his invention. Danckert Krohn-Holm was the brother just older than Pop, and he was an engineer in Oslo, and he had invented a new wheel for conveyor belts. It was shaped in such a way that the conveyor belt could bang against it without getting damaged.

It could replace two different units that conveyor belts banged against: the *guide* (a wheel that held the belt in place vertically) and an *idler* (a bumper wheel to hold it in place horizontally).

Since it was both a guide and an idler, Pop suggested to his brother the name *Guidler*. That is still its trademark today.*

> * It is now a U.S. company, Guidler.com, still based on Danckert's original patents.

Television, the New Medium
Ralph Becomes a Television Actor

Ralph Nelson, my father, was in New York now, having ended a marriage in Georgia and having fobbed off his dog on us.

About this time, when I was in fifth or sixth grade, Ralph became a TV actor. I don't think there are any records of it, but Ralph's most wonderful appearance as an actor—at least, that I ever saw—was on NBC on a show called "Berkeley Square".

It was a time-travel story by Henry James. The story concerns a young man of our time who somehow goes back to 18th-Century London and falls in love with a beautiful rich girl who lives on Berkeley Square. Then he is brought back to the present—unwillingly.

(In those days the cameras required so much light—and therefore heat— that the candles on the dinner table of the set would sag and have to be replaced every few minutes.)

My father's performance was magnificent. He was a wonderful actor. This was before videotape, although there was a filming method called "kinescope"—but I doubt that any copy has survived.

Television, the New Medium

Mr. Proom's Key

Mr. Proom, a nice man in our building, gave me a key to his apartment so I could watch his big-screen projection TV. (In those days television was of course black-and-white.)

Mr. Proom was away most of the time, and I spent many hours watching television alone. I watched a lot of the earliest broadcast TV—short live dramas, puppets and test patterns.

Mr. Proom thought I would want to watch "Howdy Dowdy" (as he called it), but Howdy Doody was for little kinds and my interest in it was purely technical. As with movies, I always watched both emotionally and analytically—how was it done? How was it done? There were no TV special effects in those days—it was all just scenery and music. But you can do a lot with scenery and music.

I liked the dramas best. I felt proud when a show came on called "Mr. Mergenthwirker's Lobblies"– I had was already familiar with the original, which I had read when it first came out in magazine form.

Television, the New Medium
Ralph Begins Directing at NBC

Then Ralph went into directing. First he was an assistant director at NBC (where I got to sit in the control room).

------- A Note from the Present
In the TV control rooms of NBC and CBS, I saw men working at screens and saw what it was like for a new medium to be born.

This undoubtedly prepared me to think about working at screens, and to know that media are born—not from history books, but having been there and seeing it firsthand.

I sat in the control room while Ralph worked on "Texaco Star Theater", which at that time was a huge national hit, starring Milton Berle. Berle was a madcap comedian, so sure of himself that his presence was godlike. (Ralph and I got in an elevator with Berle once; Berle's charisma pressure seemed to push me against the wall.)

At NBC, Ralph also took me to a rehearsal of "Howdy Doody". It was done without makeup and I couldn't understand who the sour-looking man following Bob Smith was supposed to be. Years later I realized it was Clarabell the Clown, in street clothes.

=== Summer 1948 (I turned 11)

The Worst Birthday

Now that he lived in town, I would see Ralph six or seven times a year, instead of two or three; but there was always some unpleasantness when I saw him; he would have to scold or embarrass me for something. He would often sneer at me. Perhaps he thought he had to make up for Jean and Pop's indulgence, perhaps he thought of fatherhood as being stern.

My eleventh birthday was the worst day of my life. When I left Ralph alone in my room, he went through my drawers and found my stash of Esquire calendars and naughty books, all pocket editions. As I recall, the drawer contained three novels by Thorne Smith (*Did She Fall*, *Rain in the Doorway* and *The Night Life of the Gods*), Margaret Mead's *Sex and Temperament in Three Primitive Societies* and *Male and Female*, a Signet (or Mentor) pocket analysis of the Kinsey report, and *Finistère*, a homosexual novel. Ralph scolded me (and seemed to think I did not know what was really in these books). Then he gave me a junk children's toy and we went to Coney Island. I was horribly depressed throughout the day and threw away the books when I got home.

Only years later did I think, *what the hell right did he have to go through my drawers?*

Television, the New Medium
Ralph Moves to Directing at CBS

Then Ralph moved to CBS. Their main studios—Studio 1 and Studio 2– were at Grand Central Station. Again I got to come and sit in the control room. The atmosphere seemed more friendly and relaxed than at NBC.

Ralph told me he changed networks because NBC would not allow the director to speak directly to the cameramen.* I would later witness intense consequences of this issue.

> * A few years ago I was told by a seat-mate on an airplane that NBC did not change its policy, and allow directors to speak to cameramen, until the 1990s.

=== Fall 1948 (I was 11)

Television, the New Medium
The Mama Show

Ralph was now a director at CBS, with a weekly family comedy called "Mama", though everyone referred to it as "The Mama Show". Ralph let me hang around the rehearsals and watch the actual broadcast from the control room. The actors and producers all welcomed me and it felt like a second family.

"Mama" was about a Norwegian-American family in San Francisco at the turn of the century. It was a family show on the inside as well as on the screen: there was a warm family atmosphere among the cast and on the set, and Ralph had a several-years' affair with Rosemary Rice, who played the older daughter. The show was "heart-warming"— the stories concerned members of the family, their aspirations and difficulties; all resolved at the end through the wisdom of the character Mama, played by Peggy Wood.

The first three days of the week, as I recall, they rehearsed in ordinary clothes in the garret of Liederkranz Hall, an old building on east 58th. (I would join these sessions during school vacations.)

Friday they rehearsed 'Mama' all day at Grand Central, and broke for dinner at six. Ralph and some of the men would have dinner and drinks downstairs at the Oyster Bar. (I would join them; that was where Ralph taught me to drink bourbon.)

The show went on at eight, and it went out live. There was no videotape in those days; whatever went wrong would be seen by a million viewers. Usually nothing went wrong; Ralph was a terrific director. His tastes were on the corny side, but his shows went off, live, like clockwork.

=== 1949 (I was 11)

DEFINING MOMENTS
Dropout and Atheist (Jan. 1949)

One day when I was eleven Mr. Blackett sent me from the classroom one time too many.

As I walked down the stairs I didn't know I would leave the building. As I left the building I didn't know I would leave the grounds. And as I left the grounds I didn't know I would go home. But as I walked home I realized I would never go back to that school.

On that walk my alienation galvanized: my boiling resentments of school, of middle-class stuffiness, of the inconvenience of life, of the shallowness and complacency of my classmates, crystallized into what would be my adult point of view.

I think my atheism happened as I went down the stairs; and my alienation grew as the walk proceeded.

It was a church school. On the stairs, and that walk home, I became a vehement atheist. The church, and its rituals, seemed ridiculous to me now, as was the belief in an afterlife; and my classmates seemed to me gullible clucks. I considered their silly legend of a vain, vengeful god (with a gender, even though he's alone!)– a god who is especially interested in one species that supposedly looks like him (how long is His, er... nose—and what's it for?); the silliness of what was said about Heaven, a pointless and impossible afterlife, flapping around endlessly in vacuous celebration of that egotistical man-shaped deity; all this against the evidence of the rocks and the fossils and the telescopes. It was asinine and not to be compromised with.

I would say now that my adult life started at that moment-- the completion of my cynicism, the galvanizing of my defiance, the alienation from conventional society, and a grimness that set in, knowing I would be forever apart from ordinary people, but grimly proud of it.

For no imaginable reason, there followed the happiest six months of my life.

DEFINING MOMENTS
XANADU STORY
CONNECTION TO THE ORIGINAL (2)

The Horrible Oz Movie (1949)

The most angry day of my boyhood was the day I saw the movie "The Wizard of Oz."

I loved the Oz books. My great-grandmother, Blanche, had read perhaps a dozen of them to me, and I was collecting them all.

In the original first Oz book, Baum's *The Wizard of Oz*, Denslow the illustrator-- the first Oz illustrator-- made Dorothy a chubby, unattractive girl of about eight. (How the book became a best-seller with those awful pictures I cannot imagine.) But in the second Oz book (*The Land of Oz*) through the thirty-sixth Oz book (my favorite, *Lucky Bucky in Oz*), Neill-- the second Oz illustrator-- fixed Dorothy at about twelve, gorgeous, thoughtful and clever-looking, with a blonde pageboy haircut. (She stayed that way because no one grows old in Oz, to which Dorothy migrated permanently around book six or seven.)

But Judy Garland wasn't eight or even twelve. She was a GROWNUP! She looked like a SCHOOLTEACHER, and the dopey coverup dress, trying to hide her womanhood, didn't help.

In the movie, the Cowardly Lion wasn't a lion any more! They made him into a manimal—a palpable actor in a costume-- and put actors' faces on the Scarecrow and Tin Woodman.

Worst of all-- at the end, IT WAS ALL A DREAM!* What a vile copout! (A term that did not exist at the time.) The whole subtext (another word that did not exist at the time) of the Oz stories was that Oz is a parallel world, an alternate reality (also terms which did not exist at that time). It's essentially a wrapper around the whole plot that changes the meaning and the point.

> * I think this ending, which the Oz movie added to the story, may have been taken from Eddy Cantor's "Roman Scandals" of six years before, which ended the same way—the hero's adventures in ancient Rome turn out to have been the dream of an obsessive.

I loved the Oz books and I despised that movie. I've mellowed over time and gotten to like it somewhat, but as an inferior derivative; while most people are unaware of the original book, let alone the sequel books which make up the *oeuvre* of Oz.

XANADU STORY
PARALLEL VERSIONS

So many movies are based on originals (usually badly). This was just one example of parallel versions, like and unlike their originals.

Which is inturn a special case of parallel documents.

CONNECTION TO THE ORIGINAL (2)

This horrible Oz movie, so unfaithful to the original, so popular to those who did not know the series of books, strengthened my belief in keeping derivative works connected to their original. *You have to be able to compre the original.*

The original of a work has special status, and must not be lost, though the offspring may be legitimate as well. This became fundamental to all our work on the Xanadu project.

=== Spring 1949 (I was 11)

Magical L.A.

Jean and Pop took me to California for a two-week stay with a relative who was in the movies.

It was magical. I fell in love with L.A. I kissed a girl in the moonlight in Beverly Hills. (We had been sent to find Angostura Bitters, which a well-known actor at the party thought necessary for his indigestion. In how many neighbourhoods can twelve-year-olds be sent to borrow Angostura Bitters from strangers?)

We visited the Fox Lot (since demolished and replaced by Century City), ate hot dogs at Tail O' the Pup, went to the Turnabout Theater. At home, we projected the movies *The Long Voyage Home* and *The Miracle of Morgan's Creek*. For the latter showing we were joined by with the leading actor (Eddie Bracken) watching it with us; he came to the house a couple of times.

I found L.A. to be heaven, and it was where movies were made. Immediately I wanted to live there. The snap of the L.A. air in the mornings still reminds me of that wonderful time.

=== Summer 1949 (I turned 12)

The Mauretania and the Midnight Sun

In June of 1949 Jean and Pop took me to Europe. We went first class on the Mauretania, a wonderful prewar Art Deco ship, and I had my twelfth birthday in mid-Atlantic. For the occasion, the chef made crêpes suzette at our table—not the Captain's table, but the next best—the Purser's. The Purser was surprised when I told him that my birthday was also the anniversary of the ship's maiden voyage, which I'd read somewhere long before.

We went to London (Pop took me to Lloyd's and I saw the Lutine Bell, which rings at momentous Lloyd's occasions.) Then we went to Norway.

Norway in June is glorious. There was a Holm family wedding, still remembered—over a hundred people sat down to dinner. Pop was the guest of honor, because of all the food and supplies he had sent over as soon as the war blockade ended. We walked home at 2 am, as I recall, in broad daylight. It was lovely.

DEFINING MOMENTS
Uncle Agnar, the Enthusiast

Because of my interest in puppets, we were taken to meet my uncle Agnar Mykle (pronounced Ognar Mik-leh).

He was the first really enthusiastic man I had met, and he immediately became my first role model in real life. (He later stayed with us in New York; he and I hung out and went to shows.)

We had a special connection, and I still can't quite analyze it, because nothing at that time suggested the mischief and defiance that it turned out we both shared.

------- A Note from the Present

> Norwegian readers may be howling with laughter at this point. Agnar Mykle became the bad boy of Norwegian literature. His scandalous novel *Song of the Red Ruby* got him put in jail for its explicit sex; but after a great deal of debate the Norwegian parliament abolished censorship over sexual matters, and thus began the Scandinavian Sexual Revolution, which reverberated over to the USA.

=== Fall 1949

Television, the New Medium

COLOR TELEVISION METHODS

For my science project in the fall of 1949, I did a presentation on the different proposed methods for color television.*

> * The RCA method won in general, but the other methods still have specialized uses.

I just copied diagrams straight out of a magazine, but I explained them to the class, and for that I got an A.

······ A Note from the Present

> In hindsight, I was on my wavelength even then-- interested in technicalities that support presentational effects. The important thing was not the technicalities but the presentation, but the technicalities had to be considered for whatever you wanted to present.

> **DESIGN INFLUENCES: Raymond Loewy, 1949, when I was twelve**
>
> Raymond Loewy was on the cover of TIME on Oct. 31, 1949. I read that article carefully. (Rereading it now, I see it as a big puff-piece).
>
> Loewy was a well-publicized designer of that time. He had even designed a locomotive to *look* fast and powerful. Loewy designed a 'radical' car, the Studebaker, that people ridiculed—but it turned heads.
>
> (Pop got one of those futuristic Studebakers, ca 1950, and learned to drive in his sixties.)

=== 1950 (I was 12)

Television, the New Medium
On 'Mama'

Ralph gave me a part on 'Mama' early in 1950. I spoke a line and was paid $15. I got my social security card on that day.

"TED! You were on TELEVISION!" called out one of the girls in my class on the next Monday. Otherwise life went on as before.

~ MAKING MOVIES ~
"THE CONQUEST OF SPACE"

For my science project in the spring of 1950, I told Mr. Saunders, the science teacher, that I wanted to do a movie. Mr. Saunders said that was too big a project for one person, so I asked Bob Civita if he would join me. However, I still did the project without him.

It was simple and stupid, but it was my first film. It was just pictures shot from a book,* playing Khachaturian's *Sabre Dance* in the background (which really pumped it up).

> * Chesley Bonestell's *Conquest of Space*— wonderful paintings that were deeply inspiring to many people.

My little film, "The Conquest of Space," was shown in the Bentley auditorium, I think as part of the usual Friday Assembly. It lasted only two minutes, but I stretched it out by an audio introduction that Civita and I had done on the school's wire recorder. Nobody could hear the wire recorder and the music and narration synch got mangled, but seeing a color movie from a student (even out of focus) created tumultuous applause. Mr. Saunders publicly gave us each an A+ on the spot.*

> *Bob's executive ability was shown by his getting a high grade for almost no work. This executive ability has been confirmed in the subsequent years, as he became a famous media mogul in Brazil.

DEFINING MOMENTS
Nexialist, 1950

I found a wonderful word in a science-fiction novel. In van Vogt's *Voyage of the Space Beagle*, he defined a nexialist as 'someone who finds connections.'

I typed up a business card

```
        Ted Nelson
        Nexialist
```

and filed it.

=== 1951 (I was 13)

Television, the New Medium

The Night Camera One Went Out

Just as the Mama show started one Friday night, Camera #1– the boom camera– stopped working. (That was the main camera that could go higher and lower than the other two.) I was sitting in the back of the control room with the producers and half a dozen support people. The atmosphere turned electric with tension and fear.

The show had been completely rehearsed for the moves of three cameras. Now there were only two and the plan had evaporated.

Ralph, with military composure and the ever-present cigarette, started talking on the intercom, with one eye on his script and one eye on the monitors that fed from cameras two and three. 'Camera three to the kitchen, focus on Mama... Hold it there, camera three. Switch to camera three. Camera two to the kitchen, focus on Nels. Switch to camera two. Camera three, go to the living room for a wide shot...' All of this as the actors moved around and the dialogue continued.

The actors knew at once what was happening, and that they had to stick to their planned moves around the set. They did their parts exactly in the places they had rehearsed, with cameras coming from unexpected directions, having to trust these unexpected movements.

In the control room we were all on the edge of our seats. No one knew if the show could make it to the end without some terrible fuckup—a scene going on with no camera to see it, or one camera seeing another.

Ralph talked them on reading ahead in the script and, giving directions with a fierce calm, even his mischievous confidence. Some scenes were done with only one camera, sometimes he was able to put in two for a cross-cut.

At the midshow commercial break, cutting to a filmed commercial, I think Ralph went on the loudspeaker out to the studio floor, saying something like– 'Great work, everybody—as you see, we're doing this show with two cameras now, but we're going to make it to the end. Stick to your blocking and god bless.'

Now it was the final stretch. Ralph talked the cameras back and forth, scene after scene, down to the final cup of coffee that always ended the show. We all held our breath as the announcer, on the studio floor, signed off.

The big main monitor cut to the network logo, and the control room erupted into a tumult of cheering. Ralph, famously the most reliable director in television, had done it. He had more than done it. Some hiccup, some accident, could have been forgiven under the circumstances, but there was none. Ralph had saved the show seamlessly. The thrill and pride for his achievement that night stay with me today.

DEFINING MOMENTS
~ MAKING MOVIES ~

LOW-BUDGET, WIDE-ANGLE CYRANO, Nov 1950

I had seen José Ferrer as Cyrano de Bergerac on Broadway, and I think we had gone back to meet him; but then he actually filmed the play. I read with excitement how they filmed that play on the cheap. (I had been thrilled with Laurence Olivier's *Henry V,* also a filmed play, but that had been hugely expensive.) Since I daydreamed of film-making, any way to do it more cheaply caught my attention.

To film Ferrer's Cyrano, they had used a small set and a new wide-angle lens, only just become possible. The lens was called the Cine Balowstar.

I studied the movie with fascination. I have liked wideangle ever since, though I'm not sure the movie caused that or not.

=== Fall 1952 (I was 15)

CUT -- AND -- PASTE -------------
Learning to Write

I wrote long papers for my courses at Bentley. There was always so much to say, and it was so hard to decide the order and the emphasis.

I learned the motto:

WRITING IS MOSTLY REWRITING
REWRITING IS MOSTLY REARRANGEMENT

I think I heard the first line from many people. I'm not sure where I heard the second; perhaps I figured it out.

Rearranging in my manuscripts took hours and hours, much longer than the actual generation of text.

DESIGN INFLUENCES: The Eamses, 1952, when I was fifteen

In early high school I became aware of Charles and Ray Eames, the principal designers for IBM. (I assumed they were brothers; I was not aware that they were man and wife.) In 1952 I got an Eames Chair, a desk-chair of bent plywood. Mine was black. It went with the new, grownup desk Pop bought me. I also got a canvas sling chair. I thought it would be great to sleep in. It wasn't.

But it was MODERN.

Chapter 3.
CENTRAL PARK WEST, 1953-55

=== Fall 1953 (I was 16)

A California Too Brief

I will skip largely over this period.

In the fall of 1953 I moved in with a relative in L.A. I had only one more year of high school and I wanted to get into the movie business when I got out, so L.A. was the place to be.

(Emotional aspects of this move are beyond the present telling.)

Central Park West

Unfortunately I was then told we were going back to New York, and I was made to take the eleventh grade again, and I was told not to contact my grandparents directly any more. This seemed to me wrong—I never wanted to hurt them—but I had made a huge new choice, burning my bridges, and I had to stick with the new life I had undertaken.

I was put in a rich kids' private school which at that time had very low standards. It was called Browning, and I had only six classmates. (Three of them had left the more prestigious school, Lawrenceville, under various clouds, as I recall.) A fire hydrant could have been first in my class, but the honor, meaning little, went to me.

I rode my bicycle across Central Park every morning. (Almost nobody rode bicycles in New York in that days, but I liked to do things new ways.)

If I had stayed at Bentley I would have been out of high school by now, but I was told I had to go to college. I just wanted to get to Hollywood and make movies, but I was told college was a necessary step. (This was bullshit; by most standards I was already well educated. But grimly I applied to college.)

The author briefly reunited with grandmother Jean, probably spring of 1954. This is perhaps the most candid photo she ever allowed.

DESIGN INFLUENCES: Bauhaus, 1953 when I was sixteen

I became taken with the story of the Bauhaus, the revolutionary group of architects and artists in the Weimar Republic-- who revolutionized typography, architecture and furniture.

It was MODERN.

Their notion of challenging everything greatly appealed to me.

I bought the Bauhaus book at the Museum of Modern Art.

DESIGN INFLUENCES: DADA, 1954, when I was sixteen

In early high school I went a number of times to the Museum of Modern Art, and mulled on the strange visions (and dubious value) of the venerated modern artists. But there was one school of modern art I loved: Dada. It was mischievous and humorous and did not bother with Beauty.

The central pieces were Duchamp's "Nude Descending a Staircase" and the commercial urinal he presented as a work of art.

(Later I learned that Dada was the origin of Cubism, Surrealism and much of the rest of modern art.) And later I also learned that Duchamp had been my neighbor in Greenwich Village; I could have called him up and talked to him! Sigh.)

DESIGN INFLUENCES: Rudofsky, ~1954

I don't know when I saw Rudofsky's wonderful book *Are Clothes Modern*, but I bought it at once. It challenged the conventions of clothing, cleverly and humorously, with many historic illustrations and nifty diagrams. (It had been a Museum of Modern Art exhibit, I believe in 1947, but I saw it much later.)

Rudofsky's notion of challenging everything greatly appealed to me. I wanted to redesign human life entirely.

DESIGN INFLUENCES: The Hammond Organ, 1955 (when I was seventeen)

I took high-school physics at Browning and loved it. There were just three of us: dear old Mr. Fitch, My classmate Ken Komito, and I.

One of the things we studied was the Hammond Organ. It was elegant in its simplicity: polygon wheels, spinning on a rod, generated sweet-sounding currents in a coil. I had heard the Hammond Organ in various places (I think the Christmas carols at Wanamaker's were accompanied by a Hammond Organ).

This kind of simplicity and elegance deeply appealed to me.

Applying to College

I was accepted by Allegheny (my safety) even before the college boards. Haverford rejected me, perhaps because I wasn't sporty. I got into Stanford but I didn't want to go to a junior college (I misread their logo).

Astoundingly, I got an honorary scholarship to Harvard.

However, my interview at Swarthmore had made a special impression on me, and I took the train back down to look over Swarthmore again.

I was shown around by the president of the Student Council, a beautiful, svelte young Senior woman named Judy Kapp. I was smitten— with her, and by extension, with the place. Swarthmore looked like a friendly, warm place, and I was tired of the bleakness of the big city, which I thought Harvard would continue.

I chose Swarthmore.

My World, End of High School

Here is how the world looked to me then:

I was a New Yorker. I was sophisticated. (The denizens of the midland states, like Ohio, I thought of as benighted and clueless.)

My favorite words were "concomitant" and "societal." These were not showoff words, you could only use them if you needed them and knew what they meant. I also loved jokey words I had found in the dictionary, "transpadane" (meaning "on the far side of the Po River") and "sternutator" (something that makes you sneeze).

The three pillars of my identity were:
• *The New Yorker*– deep sophisticated journalism far above what most people got to see.
• The Museum of Modern Art. (I think I paid eleven dollars for my annual membership when I was fifteen, and that even got me an extra Museum card "for my spouse"— which I gave to a young lady I knew.)
• The Rand Corporation, which I had heard about from Leo Rosten. I was deeply worried about nuclear war, and that is where they made the policy; I felt I might contribute. (I only found out decades later that due to their own snobbery, Rand only hired economists and physicists.) The Soviet Union now had thermonuclear weapons, and both sides were continuing to prepare for the unthinkable nuclear war. This was terrifying and I tried not to think of it more than a few minutes a day.

*One of the big magazines— *The Saturday Evening Post* or *Collier's*– ran an incredible issue about a hypothetical nuclear war, which I read carefully. It had a vaguely happy ending—though Washington was nuked, somehow we won. It was a grim fantasy that made vivid to many Americans the kind of dangers we didn't want to think about.

But to the New York sophisticate like me, the Soviet Union was not the enemy.

The enemy was Ohio.

=== Summer of 1955 (I turned 18)
Onstage with Name Actors

For the summer of '55 I went to a training theater in Ogunquit, Maine. It was a satellite of the main theater, the Ogunquit Playhouse. Both theaters ran a different show each week.

Ralph was also up there with his new family; he was directing a production of "Picnic" with Eva-Marie Saint. I played little parts at the training theater, but twice I was given parts on the main stage, due to Ralph's influence (I realize now). I was given a walk-on in "Member of the Wedding" with Ethel Waters, and played the court stenographer in "The Caine Mutiny Court Martial," with Gary Merrill.

I enjoyed being onstage, and felt comfortable, and loved the company of actors, who were in general outgoing, often boisterous.

But then college began, and that all was swept away. I forgot about the stage in the excitement of my new surroundings.

Chapter 4.
SWARTHMORE ERA, 1955-59

Seeker After Truth

Swarthmore was nothing like my previous experience of school. School, for me, had been horrible for fourteen years. I hated school from kindergarten through high school. (What does that say about the educational system? Why must the first years be horrible? I am sure they are for the majority of students.)

But now this was exciting. My mind was a bird set free. There were wonderful new words on every side, exciting conversations wherever you were, free lectures only a short walk away.

I could choose my courses, and was surrounded by smart kids on a beautiful campus with very nice professors you could get to know well. In the afternoons and evenings there were public lectures on everything—by visiting great thinkers, by the faculty, even by students-- most of which there was no time for. Anyone could give a lecture and have it put on the calendar! I once did.

What would Sam Hynes have said? 1955/2010

I recently [March 2010] visited Sam Hynes in Princeton. He'd been one of the two faculty members of the Swarthmore Creative Writing Club, which I'd enjoyed. I told him how at Swarthmore I became so excited by ideas.

"WE ALL WERE!" said Sam.

There was a legend at other schools— may still be-- that students at Swarthmore study all the time. This came about, I think, because weekend visitors to the campus saw the students studying. But that was the rhythm of Swarthmore life— weekends were for studying because the weeks were so busy.

At first I thought the campus would be one big happy family, but it was harshly divided into factions—the extremes being (on one side) the fraternities and the engineers, both well-stocked with louts from the sticks, and (on the other side) the sophisticates and bohemian intellectuals, many in the Mary Lyons dorms, who cynically flouted the rules about drink and sex. The girls were divided correspondingly between prissy-looking and promising. I had found my Bohemia at last.

──── A Note from the Present

Only later did I learn that nearly everyone on campus flouted the liquor and sex rules, but the girls on the Bohemian side of the campus did so more stylishly.

DEFINING MOMENTS
What would Courtney Smith have said? 1955

At the Quaker Meeting House, a place for solemn gatherings, our class came together in its first great assemblage, to be addressed grandly by various members of the faculty.

"Take a look at the person on either side of you, because one of you won't be here four years from now." I don't remember who said that.

"Those of you who arrived as Christians will leave as Christians, those of you who arrived as atheists will leave as atheists.' That was Larry Lafore, the lovable tubby cynic and atheist historian.

But one thing was said that really hit home. Someone said, "Be a Seeker after Truth." [Caps mine, since I didn't see the notes.] That hit a glowing spot inside me.

To find the truth was exactly what I intended.

I don't remember who said "Be a Seeker After Truth." I recently (2009-10) asked some of my classmates. None remembered but several thought it was Courtney. (Everyone referred to Swarthmore's president, Courtney Smith, as "Courtney" behind his back.) Courtney Smith was a clip-art college president: tweeds, pipe, thoughtful demeanor. He stayed aloof from student affairs, leaving dirty work to the deans, but at solemn occasions would always be impressively grave, gazing from on high.

Publishing A Magazine

I went to the organizational meeting for the college literary magazine, *The Lit*, and found the students in charge very pompous. They said they were going to have the highest, grandest editorial standards, and that the magazine would cost eight hundred dollars to publish.

I thought this was ridiculous. I was sure a magazine could be published for much less.

I went to a printer in Chester, Pa. They had a new kind of printing press called a photo-offset machine: you made a big layout of what you wanted, they would photograph it, shrink it down and print it on office-sized paper. Cheaply.

I figured to do a little magazine—a *very* little magazine—on one legal-sized sheet, both sides. (I would cut and fold it myself.) I was told that would cost $32.50.

I did the magazine with a friend, Len Corwin—he contributed an off-campus mailing address and I did most of the work. I solicited contributions; I wrote most of it; I laid it out on big sheets; and I paid Russ Ryan, the great Swarthmore cartoonist, to decorate the paste-ups with his pictures.

The result was much better than I had originally hoped for. It was whimsical, wild, and full of clever cartoons.

It was called *Nothing*, and sold for five cents. It was not just a little magazine, but a *very* little magazine, the size of the palm of your hand. (Third issue is illustrated, later.)

A lot of people liked it. The issue sold out and I reprinted it.

> * Eventually *Nothing* ran for three issues. (I later heard "three issues" cited as the criterion of success for a little magazine, but was not consciously trying to reach that number.)

DEFINING MOMENTS

NEGOTIATING POSSIBILITIES:
Nothing takes its own shape (~ Feb 1956)

I don't remember what concept I started with in my mind, except that it had to fit on both sides of one sheet of paper (that was given). Then I decided the cover (all four inches of it) should be blank. Then students from around the campus started submitting poetry! Some of it was very good.

Then Russ Ryan, Swarthmore's great sarcastic cartoonist, agreed to do illustrations. I don't remember what I paid him, maybe $10, maybe $25.

Ryan's cartoons perfected the ideat. (As they did for *Nothing* #3, illustrated later.)

If I had started with an exact conception and stuck with it, the magazine wouldn't have been nearly as good.

From this I learned: *be open to project possibilities as they unfold; be ready to steer the project to follow your vision as required, but take heed of where the project wants to go.*

What would Victor Navasky have said?   1956/1997

I ran into Victor Navasky, editor of *The Nation*, also a Swarthmore alumnus, around 1997. He said, "Not THE Ted Nelson?" I politely waited to find out what that meant to him.

"Not the Ted Nelson who published *Nothing* Magazine?"

Ah, what an inner glow that gave me.

In the following semester, my good friend Charlie Harris published a parody of *Nothing*. He called it *Something*.

What would Courtney Smith have said?   June 1956

In his annual commencement address, Swarthmore's president Courtney Smith took note that magazines called *Nothing* and *Something* had been published on campus. "Next we may expect to see 'Anything and Everything,'" said Courtney.

Well, that was too good to pass up. "Anything and Everything" HAD to be the name of my next big project.

A year later, when I got the franchise to write the annual musical, that is what I named it: "Anything & Everything," with an ampersand, and I credited Courtney with the title.

=== Summer 1956 (I turned 19)

The Good Grey Times

After freshman year, I got a summer job at my home town paper, the *New York Times*. I found it immediately boring. I had no desire to be a journalist; journalism offered little opportunity for creative imagination. I respected those who could do that sort of thing, but it was not for me.

I worked in the City Room, which was an area of the big third floor of the main Times building, not the little one on Times Square.

CUT--AND--PASTE -- -- -- -- -- -- -- --

My first job in the morning was to fill the paste pots. At 9 am, before reporters arrived, I would pick up all the paste pots—I think eight or ten paste pots-- from the city desk (actually a lot of desks arranged in a sort of parentheses, as I recall) and various stations in the big room. Each paste-pot was a glass jar about five inches in diameter with a lid, and inside the middle of each lid was affixed a brush, pointing down. There was a plastic tube down the center of the jar so the brush would not sit all day in the goo.

Each morning the old paste had solidified into chunky flakes. I would scrape each brush and jar clean, then open the huge golden can (20 gallons?) of luminous fresh paste, and butter that paste into each paste-pot.

The reporters would come in whenever they chose, type their stories, and then cut and paste them—that is, they would take scissors and cut apart the paragraphs or pieces, rearrange them, add new material in handwriting, and paste them down.

That is what *real* cut-and-paste meant.

Times Square had of course been named for the *New York Times*. While the company still owned the little building where the news went around in lights, the newspaper was actually produced in a big building half a block west from Times Square, on 43d street.

Moving Letters

Once or twice I was sent to the OLD Times building in Times Square, with the text (it was called "copy") that was to go around the moving sign that circled the building. The sign was composed of individual incandescent light-bulbs in those days.

Up a flight of stairs, as I recall, was the room in which they made the letters go round. The building was small and four-sided (not quite rectangular), and so was the room.

It was an amazing scene. Two guys ran it. The actual letters did go around, physical letters that projected outward to the light bulbs.

The letters were physical objects, plastic plaques about 3" by 6", to which were affixed the letter-shapes in metal (though each had its identity painted on the back, as I recall).

A horizontal array of conveyor belts ran around the periphery of the odd-shaped room, a pair of small conveyor belts with a lawn of little metal blades between them, pointing up like blades of grass. The letters went on them face down. As a letter passed along this meadow of metal contact fingers, its shape would slide across the different blades. Each blade closed and opened a circuit to a light-bulb outside. The letter, passing sideways, thus projected its moving shape to the points of light the pedestrians would see.

The type was set by hand. To set the type, the operators would slap the letters onto the conveyor belts. Each hour, I think, they would sort the letters back into alphabetical bins and set the next headlines.

Give Me an E!

When I expressed interest in how the system worked, the guys gave me a whole letter of my own-- a plaque with the letter E. The letter itself was made of Monel metal, corrosion-resistant. I kept it as a symbol of setting words on fire, or having one's name in lights.

Libertarians

I had a strange summer in New York. It was a hot summer, and there was much less airconditioning in those days. Times Square had been gaudy for decades, but it was gaudy in a far simpler way then. I think there was still a big cigarette poster with a man who blew smoke rings—that is, there was a picture of the man's head, and a big hole for his mouth, out of which a big smoke ring would come every three or four second. And a huge male and female figure stood at either side of a fifty-foot waterfall, which was cooling to look at.

I was fond of a sleazy fast-food restaurant called Grant's, at 7th Avenue and 42d street. I recall that they had a 15c hamburger (rather small) and a 15c hot dog, a 15c beer and a 15c slice of pizza. I think the old Laffmovie Theater, where as a boy I'd watched old black-and-white comedy movies and hours of cartoons, was still in operation.

Most important, that summer, I hung out a couple of times with a group called the Libertarian League. Some of them had fought in the Spanish Civil War. They called themselves "anarchists" but they were not bomb-throwers; they were some of the warmest people I ever met.* Other members of the Libertarian League were a science-fiction group calling themselves the "fanarchists," but I did not meet them myself.**

> * John Sayles' wonderful story "The Anarchists' Convention" gets the style of New York radicals exactly right, but not anarchists, I believe.
> ** This was apparently the beginning of today's libertarians, who are very much involved with the science-fiction community.

=== Fall 1956 (I was 19)

The Confession Blank, Fall 1956

My second year, responding to the evil new dean, I forged a fictitious "confession blank", seeming to come from the Dean's office but not quite saying so. It was a form inviting students to confess to rules they had broken. This had a marvelous multi-whammy effect, causing outraged students to invade the deans' office and complain, and causing others to fill out the forms—some sincerely, some mischievously. As I had calculated, the deans knew I had done it but did not try to punish me.

Now, however, I was a troublemaker.

Taking Charge of My Education

I was planning to go into Swarthmore's Honors program, which I would start in my third year. The Honors program was quite restrictive. I could then take only eight seminars in my last two years, of which four had to be in my major subject (ho hum).

That meant my Sophomore year was the last chance to study around. There were so many things I wanted to know about. Although sophomores only had to take four courses, I signed up for six that first term sophomore year— three at Swarthmore, one at Haverford and two at the University of Pennsylvania. I wanted to take the subjects Swarthmore didn't offer—Anthropology, Sociology and Linguistics.

The linguistics course set me on fire.

I had been excited by Whorf's hypothesis—that language fundamentally shapes the way people think. (I believe his famous example was that Eskimos have forty different words for snow, and thus think differently about it; but Whorf went further, conjecturing that this applies to grammatical structure as well as linguistic categories.)

I wanted to know more, but at that time Swarthmore had no linguistics course. I cast about in the catalogs of our 'cooperating institutions'—Bryn Mawr, Haverford and U. of

Pennsylvania—and found that I could take a linguistics course at Penn. I went to see Zellig Harris.

Zellig Harris was a cordial linguist, seedily dressed (like a student) as I recall; a reading course with him at the University of Pennsylvania would be assigned a graduate-school course number. (Harris later showed me the new book by his student, Noam Chomsky, called *Syntactic Structures*. This was the major leagues.)

I told Harris I was interested in the Whorfian hypothesis. He said okay, he'd accept me for the reading course I requested, but it would have to begin with basic linguistics; I said fine.

He had me read Bloomfield's 1942 *Outline Guide for the Practical Study of Foreign Languages*, I believe.

It was one of the two most exciting intellectual experiences of my life.

As I recall it, the book was intended to prepare the reader—likely to be an army corporal on a Pacific Island– to analyze the language and give it a writing system in two weeks.

- Phonemes! Every language had its own family of sounds, and they had to be heard for their own idiosyncratic music, not forced into comparison with Italian (as the 19th-Century linguists had done), Language evolves as a great flopping mass. The phonemes change in different directions, possibly following Grimm's law and possibly not.

- Morphemes! 'Word' was a misleading concept; the generalized concept was now *morpheme*, a unit of speech with meaning. (The notion of a *word*, a free-standing lump of meaning, didn't always work. In English, for example, the morpheme *-ing* has a meaning but is never free-standing. This makes it a 'bound morpheme', as distinct from a *word*, a morpheme which can occur on its own–a 'free morpheme'. Some languages supposedly have only bound morphemes, i.e. no free-standing words with independent meaning. This made no sense till the Bloomfield-Sapir revolution.)

- *Morphonphonemic shift* meant the change of a sound under emphasis, the way 'pronounce' is accented on the second syllable into 'pronunciation'.

It all made so much sense, and clarified so many questions I had had about language.

Most important, the notion of *linguistic correctness*, which had been at the center of my soul from earliest years, became revealed as a system of traditions only—traditions associated with education, class and power. (As expressed in the wonderful slogan, *A language is a dialect with an army.*)

=== 1957 (I was 19)
A Kite-Shaped Nothing
DEFINING MOMENTS

Later that year I put out the third issue of my little magazine. I made *Nothing* #3 quite tricky—kite-shaped, and you had to rotate it as you read it, and with two-color printing. (Again I went to Russ Ryan, whose great drawings had so enriched *Nothing #1*, and again he festooned it with marvelous, cynical cartoons.)

I showed a mockup to Ned Pyle, my friend the printer, before we started to make the negatives, and he nodded approval; but when we assembled the first real one he was astounded. I thought he had given me the go-ahead for my design, but in fact I had done it all on my own.

Nothing #3 was a turning point in my life. I found out by accident that I could do stuff on my own that nobody else could imagine.

Kite-shaped *Nothing* #3, showing principle of rotary reading (right). The author is still mortified at having misspelled "Weltschmerz" on the cover.

What would Roland Pennock have said? 1957

For introductory Political Science, we were supposed to attend meetings of local governing bodies and write them up. I sat in on the Borough Council of Media, Pa., since it was nearby. The meetings were tiresome and the people who ran them were rather stuffy and conventional.

I wrote the meetings up with a lot of atmospherics and verbatim quotes, and called the paper "Tedia in Media."

My professor was J. Roland Pennock, the department head. He was an affable and emphatic gentleman in his fifties.

The paper came back with a grade of C. Pennock's comment was that it would be 'fine for the *New Yorker*, but not satisfactory for political science.'

To say my paper was 'fine for the *New Yorker*' was meant as a criticism, but it made me quite happy for a few days.

=== Fall 1957 (I was 20)

The First Rock Musical

My Junior I found myself writing the college musical, after a mandated collaborator departed. I found a talented freshman, Dick Caplan, who wrote the music exactly as I asked—I wanted it to be rock and roll but to sound like Threepenny Opera.

I called it Anything & Everything. The show was actually three projects: the play itself (with too many acts and too many songs), a long-playing record (dreadfully recorded in time for sale at the show), and a big cartoon poster, studded with photographs, that was also the program, I managed to do all this with very little sleep, caffeine pills, Miltown, and the minimum of studying.

Like *Nothing*, my Hamburg show started as a general idea and crystallized gradually as production continued.

Scriv

Michael Scriven was unlike any professor anyone at Swarthmore had seen. Tall, dashing, handsome and driving a sports convertible (often adorned with a female student), Scriven cut quite a figure on the campus. We all referred to him as Scriv. (Later in the year, a female student asked me to convey a love-note to him; he thought it was from *me*. It all got sorted out, however, and she became the new passenger in the convertible.)

Scriven's seminar was the most exciting course I ever took.

Many did not find it so. One friend of mine, Starr Koester, referred to it as "intellectual rape." Scriven would give a brief lecture, speaking quietly from notes, disposing of a dozen points of view in as many minutes.

He covered more, and thought faster, than anyone

The usual soporific atmosphere of repetitive class discussion was swept away. This was a guy who could say a lot very quickly and incisively and with powerful arguments.

I worshipped him.

But here was the most important thing: *He understood every word I said.* No one ever had before.

He was the only person who understood every word I said. I found this a personal validation of the greatest importance.

This was a personal validation that meant the world to me. I have always been confident of my ideas, but in a sort of feedback vacuum: the ideas were my only comfort, because other kids couldn't understand me, teachers couldn't understand me; I was saying things they'd never heard before and couldn't process.

=== Spring 1958 (I was 20)

Due to the frantic previous semester, I had taken an incomplete for Scriven's course. Thus in the spring I had to hunker down and finish that term paper.

Working on this paper was the third intellectual thrill of my Swarthmore years, after Bloomfieldian linguistics (with Zellig Harris at the U. of Pa) and the Scriven seminar.

My mind was bursting with ideas I had many ideas about structure, and ideas, and representation. I couldn't say it all; I couldn't even keep track of it all in my mind, and I couldn't write enough notes to track all the ideas.

As with *Nothing* and "Anything and Everything", I followed the ideas where they led, into strange new territories. I expressed badly what I tried to say, but the insights were valid.

The paper is wacky and unintelligible. Yet the ideas behind it, I believe, were actually at the cutting edge. I believe it is an early work on what is called "knowledge representation", roughly parallel to what was going on at MIT and Stanford at the time.*

> * This is further discussed in my PhD thesis (*Philosophy of Hypertext*, Keio University, 2001).

Stated simply with my words of now, here are some of the main points:

- Everything can be represented as discrete models of units and relationships, or graph structures.
- We can imagine such a system of representation for large templates or individual connective components, snapping together.
- We can reduce all forms of knowledge and abstraction to such models.
- Processes of cognition, abstraction and scientific method can be represented as operations in such spaces.

But I could not say it that clearly then. Hayek expresses the same experience beautifully:

What would Hayek have said? (relevant to my 1958 paper)

The paper in which as a student more than thirty years ago I first tried to sketch these ideas, and which lies before me as I write, I was certainly wise not to attempt to publish at the time, even though it contains the whole principle of the theory I am now putting forward. My difficulty then was, as I had been aware even at the time, that though I felt that I had found the answer to my important problem, I could not explain precisely what the problem was.

-- Friedrich von Hayek, *The Sensory Order*, preface.

From time to time I have tried to stop thinking about these matters, because they are too broad and tangled, but I have continued anyway, and have many thousands of notes, which I pray I will be able to assemble and coordinate in the time that remains.

However, I will not discuss these matters further in this book. Considering how much trouble people have understanding Xanadu, my philosophical work would be too much.

=== Fall 1958 (I was 21)

Senior Year

I dropped out of the Honors program. It was an agonizing decision. If I stayed in, I would have to take several philosophy seminars I dreaded—the worst being Moral Phil, which I'd heard was a real bore (and as a committed utilitarian, I had no interest in hearing about Kant). By leaving Honors I could take logic, music, ethics, another reading course with Zellig Harris, a history course with Lafore. That was my decision, though it felt also like copping out. The main issue was not a Latin phrase after my degree, like "cum laude" (almost guaranteed if I stayed in), but my actual education. I dropped out and went back to Course.

Otherwise, Senior year started wonderfully. Tony Pool, my best friend, was my roommate, and in the room lottery we had drawn the very best room on campus— the one with its own back entrance (in Mary Lyons Three). And our huge "closet" actually could hold one of the two beds, for privacy. Surely we would be wallowing in women.

Even more excitingly, we enticed a $700 grant out of the Student Council's Green Card Fund, *to make a movie*. We started planning it. Tony would write it and I would direct. Ideas for the movie were bursting between us like firecraciers.

Then, without warning, Tony got a terrible chill. In the morning I took him to the college infirmary on my Vespa motorscooter. That night, when I got off a train from Philadelphia, David Baltimore was standing there to tell me Tony had died.

Tony's parents came down to Swarthmore for a memorial service at the Meeting House. It was tough for everyone.

We all had to start over. His parents, without their dearly loved son. I had lost far less than they, but he had been my best friend. I felt very alone.*

    * I later got a delightful freshman roommate and joined a fraternity. But that is another story.

The Twilight Zone

I did not hear of this until much later.

Ralph's friend Rod Serling—who had written the show that got Ralph an Emmy in '56—was going to have his own new TV series, on the spooky side.

He wanted a title for the series, which would start in 1959.

My father suggested a term they'd used when he was in the Army Air Corps. It was a term for not knowing where you were on the radio direction finder.

The term was "the twilight zone."

My father had not coined the phrase originally, but he switched its meaning from that used in the Air Corps, and Serling brought it to prominence in the titles of his show, with tingly music. It now forever suggests: matters of ominous and spooky uncertainty.

What would Richard Burton have said? ca. 1958

I have no idea what he was doing there. Ralph had taken me to see "The Music Man" on Broadway, and then we had gone out drinking with Robert Preston, the star of this clever but lightweight musical. But how the serious actor Richard Burton had joined the group I have no recollection. Perhaps he thought my father, as a director of television and the occasional play, would be a useful contact. But he said nothing, just sat, as Preston carried on in his leather-lunged voice.

(It is only in writing this that I realize: I was with three of the greatest male voices in the theater.)

The four of us were sitting in a circular booth at the Carousel Bar on Times Square. I believe Preston was nattering on in a showbiz sort of way. Ralph was listening and smoking carefully without speaking, as he generally did.

I was sitting next to Burton, who seemed immensely bored. (A serious actor indeed.) I suppose now he may have felt greatly superior to Preston, who was a fast-talking vaudevillean of little depth; Burton was a serious actor with an Oxford education. (Also he had not yet met Elizabeth Taylor and was perhaps directionless.)

I had not yet seen any of Burton's movies, but I had seen him off Broadway in "Coriolanus", and he had been magnificent. I thought of telling him how great he was as Coriolanus, but I thought it would be too fawning, so I took a different tack.

"Mr. Burton, I know your father," I said. (Philip Burton, whose name he had adopted, was a teacher who had brought him out of a Welsh mining town, seen him through Oxford, and prepared him for the theater. I knew

Philip as one of our dinner-guests whose recommendations helped me get into good colleges. Philip referred to Richard as his adopted son, though technically he was not.)

"Oh?" replied Richard Burton, without looking at me. In his grand upperclass British accent (learned from Philip) it was two long-drawn-out syllables, eh and oo, delivered with withering sourness. I said nothing further. I should have gone with Coriolanus.

Chapter 5.
NOW WHAT? (1959)

=== 1959 (I was 21)

College was winding down. My education was about to be interrupted by graduating.

I had used my opportunities to the hilt—pursuing every subject (except those for which I couldn't do the math), and mainly extracurriculars, where I had sampled everything and gotten the taste of creative control.

I had not found a wife yet. I was looking for a brilliant intellectual companion, a sexual adventurer, a wonderful mother to my children, and an Olgivanna* to my projects.

*Olgivanna Lloyd Wright, Frank Lloyd Wright's third wife, was a ferocious organizer and ally in his wrangles.

I would find them all, but not at the same time.

I was hyperambitious, but I did not know for what. I knew a lot about media (the term had not yet been popularized) and their creation. I was good at writing, photography, stage direction, calligraphy; I had won prizes for poetry and playwriting, published my own magazine and my first book, created a typefont (as paper cutouts) and produced a long-playing record. (I had not yet tried the one remaining medium, the one I loved most.)

I understood the different career ladders of authorship, show business, publishing. They did not immediately appeal. (I had a special talent for advertising, but that was absolutely unthinkable, the quintessence of Selling Out—and while I found it fun, certainly not interesting in any deep way.)

Most of all I knew about projects, and about momentum. New projects were my heart and soul, and I dared not lose momentum. I was supercharged, but I knew how hard it was to reach that level of energy and I knew that if I lost it, I might never get it back again.

My father had offered to start me on a career in acting, which I had wanted all my life until college. Now I saw a bigger world. Also, I wouldn't be that good as an actor. I had stage presence, but a horrible voice and deep acne scars. I didn't have great acting talent—Steve Gilborn, a classmate, was a far better actor. In the big world, there were great actors like John Barrymore and (later) Johnny Depp; I would be embarrassed to pretend to a place in that world.

I wanted to be the best, and to do something that had never been done before.

THE ACADEMIC OPTION

Of course I would be writing and doing media, I knew not what; that was given, and the opportunities were everywhere. But I could not leave the intellectual world.

The sheer excitement of all the world's ideas still filled me. And in these four years I had found my way to the new edges, the precipices of thought: Bruner in psychology, Whorf and other linguists (Bloomfield, Chomsky); romantic extenders of the linguistic ideal (Whorf, Edward Hall, Pike. What more new ideas would be out there? (Nothing that would get into the intellectual laymen's magazines like *Harper's* or the *Atlantic*.)

I had not learned enough, there were fields about which I knew little, and I dared not lose intellectual momentum. I had seen what happened to people who let their minds go to seed. And there were still so many things I had to know in courses I hadn't had a chance to take. Why couldn't there be a five-year or six-year bachelor's?* But in what field should I continue? In graduate school, the enforced next step, there was no such thing as an undeclared major, or General Studies. You had to pretend you were going to *be* something, and pretend to choose a field (though of course few people ever end up in the field they study there).

> * Answer: you actually can do this, especially at the larger universities. But it's not acknowledged as a valid educational strategy, and it's expensive. The main question is who pays. No one in my family would have backed it.

I thought I might get a doctorate, then teach for a while until my true vocation was revealed.

> * I did not realize what a doctorate took, but that is another story.

Meanwhile, anthropology interested me strongly. I had the rough notion that I might bring to anthropology a new analytic clarification, perhaps straightening out Levi-Strauss, the metaphysical and sweeping theorist, with new tools of analysis and description.*

> * To non-academic readers: for academia, this was a very ambitious thought.)

I had a long talk with Jean Herskovits* (a recent Swarthmore graduate and daughter of anthropologist Melvil Herskovits, one of the creators of the doctrine of cultural relativism). She was getting a D.Phil in anthropology at Oxford, and I impressed her. She thought I should go to Oxford in anthropology and would give me a strong recommendation; I agreed that sounded right. I had loved my anthropology course at Penn, and was taken by the romantic anthropologists like Margaret Mead and Francis Huxley (whose book *Affable Savages* made field work sound wonderful). And next to actors, cultural anthropologists were my favorite people.

                                                    * Later Jean Herskovits Kopytoff.

So Oxford in Anthropology was my next plan.

But deep down I thought I might invent a field that nobody had created yet.

CLOSET IDEALIST

I did not hang out with the big-time idealists on campus— the religious kids, or the disarmament guys. People thought I was just flippant and playful. In fact I had strong ideals, but because I was a total cynic I saw few hopes for the world. I was deeply worried about nuclear war, pollution, deforestation, the loss of books and libraries, the loss of native cultures and languages. (These causes have since all become fashionable, but they weren't then.) And I very much wanted a change in the sexual system. (In those days, unmarried women could not get contraceptive equipment and there was no pill; anything but straight intercourse was illegal in most states; group sex was spoken of in horror.) All this would change, I hoped.

But what I saw everywhere was shallowness, conventionality, pomposity and smugness— the Four Horsemen of Respectability.* I saw the world as run by the shallow, conventional, pompous and smug. Those in power were shallow, conventional, pompous and smug, and so were those who supported them.

————— COINED WORDS —————
                       * My term, used here for the first time.

There were so few possible hopes—

     • *Politics* was hopeless. It was always the same circle of tricks and speeches.

     • *Economics* was hopeless. Communism had been horribly tried, socialism was impossible, and our existing system (whatever you wanted to call it) had its nasty side; but there it was, unchangeable. I also believed that capitalism offered more hope for change and betterment than anything else. A man like Howard

Hughes, who could do what he damn pleased with his money, could take steps to improve the world that no official charity could hope to do. (Except, of course, he didn't. But a some do, outside official charities.)

• *Philanthropy* was hopeless. Official charities and foundations were palliative window-dressing, small attempts to adjust what could not be changed. Most important, they were really defined and hemmed in by the tax rules, which guaranteed that they had to be run by boards of conventional people and that they would always be shallow, conventional, pompous and smug.

But here was the one hope I saw: there could be a *cultural* revolution.* And I hoped somehow to put my stamp on a part of that.

> * This was long before the Maoists gave a Red spin to the term 'cultural revolution.' I had something very different in mind.

Especially, I wanted to change education. Why did the first twelve years of school—the ones most people got—have to be so horrible? Why couldn't the excitement of ideas I felt in college be available to everyone? Surely there would be a way to break open the educational prison and show how really interesting everything all was? Some way of making clear all the exciting connections?

BIZ STORY
Creative Control
My Setup/Creative Control (1959?)

(I don't remember when this vision crystallized, but I think it may have been in early 1959.)

Others want riches, 'conventional success'— grand mansions, showoff dinner parties, jewelry, fancy hotels. Golf. Boats.

At Swarthmore I got a taste of creative control. I worked with friends, soliciting ideas, but then I would pull them together and decide the final structure and finishing touches. In Hollywood they call this creative control, but people fight for it in every field.

In Hollywood they start with a script, and usually have to stick to it. This limits the possibilities. But by postponing such decisions to the end, not overplanning, you find out where the project wants to go. (Some call this procrastination, but I call it *late closure*.) A nice movie example: originally "King Kong" was going to be a documentary about hunting gorillas in Africa. It morphed nicely to another concept.

All I've ever wanted is to be able to do lots of projects with a staff of helpers, but without fighting all the time. What I wanted was my own studio, or as I sometimes called it, 'my setup.'

I have always had only one objective: independence! I wanted my own company, like Wright's studio or the early Disney organization, where I could do big creative projects and work through others, putting together a staff who could work with me.*

> * I was not thinking on today's scale, reached by Lucas, Jobs and Cameron.

I envisioned myself as being like Disney with his animators— warm-hearted meetings where I explain the objective and we would go over possibilities, or I would look at what they've done and tell them what to fix. Where I got this vision of Disney I don't know.* However, I had already had this experience in my stage productions. There are different situations that allow people to open their emotions. Working with people in this way—when they are working on my projects—opens my emotional sinuses and makes it easier to like and enjoy others.

> *I long thought I got this idea of how Disney worked from the film "The Reluctant Dragon" (the feature version, not the cartoon version)– but when I re-saw it recently, there was no such scene.

Not Narrow Down

Here is what they said as graduation approached: It's time to narrow down, Ted!

I didn't think so.

My strength was in *not* narrowing down, in doing something new and different every time.

And here were my central talents, which I'd come to know at Swarthmore: I believed I could analyze anything, show anything and design anything. And I could innovate, imagining what no one else could, and bringing that new thing forth through projects of new shapes.

But what? What should I analyze, show, design and innovate about?

There was no determinate answer. I was good at a lot of things but not a great talent at any one (except that my mind was very good). My uniqueness was in the combination of numerous abilities, and in my ability to see the big picture quickly.

I was a very clever fellow accustomed to picking up new technicalities as required, but I preferred to delegate technical details once I had decided them. I had had a taste of creative control and knew that I could not be an Idea Man on someone else's projects. Deciding the details and finishing touches was what life was all about.

I knew this would make it harder, but what the hell, I was Ted Nelson.

I would not narrow down. That would be giving up and giving in.

Cocteau, Whorf, Bucky

I had very few living role models. I applauded my parents' grand success, but I intended some much grander career, like various great names in history. I felt I was off to a flying start.

But at what? I was a writer and designer and showman. I saw myself becoming perhaps–
- a showman-intellectual,* like one of my heroes, Jean Cocteau.

———— **COINED WORDS** ————
* A recent nice term is *showman-penseur*.

- a theoretical explorer in some new area like my hero Benjamin Lee Whorf, an academic outlier (he was in the insurance business) who was nevertheless respected in academia, and created a field of his own.
- like my boyhood hero Buckminster Fuller, a "designer and thinker".

———— A Note from the Present
Looking back, I tracked on the wavelengths of these three men surprisingly well. But little did I know what this agenda had cost Bucky, or what it would cost me.

Perhaps I could create a field of my own, like Whorf and Bucky.

Egotistical, you say? Of course.

But I was going to bet my life on it.

Still a Chance to Make a Movie

My grades were fairly poor. I had gone for breadth, not depth, and I thought it was my own business to judge my achievement, not anybody else's. No one would care about my college grades in the afterlife of the so-called Real World. What mattered to me was studying what I chose, to the degree I chose, and pursuing the excitement of new ideas and projects.

So because of my slackness with regard to grades, and not having done nearly enough of the reading, I was worried about graduating.

However, something came up that was even more important than graduating.

Late in the year I realized: I still have a chance to make my first movie! I still have that $700 appropriation that Tony and I got! I can MAKE that movie! Tony would have wanted me to!

Exams were coming but I figured I could squeak by. This was far more important, a full-on chance to make a movie by myself. I knew other media moderately well; this would tell me whether I had any ability at film-making.

There was no time to write a script, and synching the sound would be an enormous problem, so I made the whimsical decision to have the actors just say "parp parp", and postpone writing the dialog. I would write the script later on the basis of the film as shot, and synch it as best possible to the parping. The parping would look like "Huckleberry Hound", where the characters just move their jaws vaguely to the script. It would of course look stupid but I thought it would be funny as well.*

> * It turns out most people can't stand this; they cannot accept such a movie as a genre, like "Huckleberry Hound" or fumetti. They can't imagine it as a foreign movie shot in Parpland. It hits a cognitive wall. I bet if some famous person told them it was okay or clever, everybody would flip their perceptions and enjoy it.

As the lead I chose my friend Jody Hudson, who had a very expressive poker face, like Buster Keaton—showing a lot of emotion with minute variations of expression.

I didn't plan, I just began. I would have to make up the movie as I went along. I would shoot whenever Jody and I were both available, and grab other actors and sets as best I could.

I had a story vaguely in mind, but I started with a classroom scene somewhere in the middle of the story. This was because it involved a large cast and had to be shot in an empty classroom, and so it had to be done on a weekend.

~ MAKING MOVIES ~
DEFINING MOMENTS

THE FIRST SLOCUM SHOOT

I rounded up actors at Sunday lunch-- whoever could spare an hour or two. I just went around the tables and asked who wanted to be in the movie. We went to a basement classroom in Trotter Hall. I arranged the actors according to when they had to leave: I would shoot the full-room shots first, then the kids in front could leave as I narrowed down to the back rows, where I put the actors who could stay longer.

So it had to be shot out of order, and there were two sequences to keep in mind— the sequence of the intended final story, and the sequence of who had to leave when, which governed the order of the shooting.

I made up the story as I went along, starting with this basic idea: the hero, in a boring class, makes eyes at a girl in the front row, and his chair falls over.

Fleshed out as I shot, it went like this: the lonely hero (Slocum Furlow, played by Jody) sits doodling at the back of a classroom. The class is an idiotic mix of philosophy, sociology and nonsense. As the discussion drones on meaninglessly, Slocum catches the eye of a girl in the front row (played by Carolyn Shields). They make eyes at each other. He leans further and further back in his chair till he falls over, very very gradually. Everyone leaves. The girl is gone.

The result of that shoot was electrifying.

Somebody New
~ MAKING MOVIES ~
DEFINING MOMENTS

Something happened to me as I shot that first scene of my film, that afternoon in Trotter Hall. My absent-mindedness and scattermindedness disappeared. I figured everything out in the moment, and made up the story as I went, keeping track with surprising clarity of what was done and what was not. I had never been so clear-minded. I still had to keep making notes on the back of my hand, but I was awake and alive in a new way.

As never before, I kept all parts of the problem in my mind, working very fast. I will never forget the clarity and the excitement of making up that scene as I fought the clock, positioned and directed the actors, took the shots, dismissed the actors, and narrowed down to only Slocum. I became a different person.

I HAD SUDDENLY BECOME THE PERSON I ALWAYS WANTED TO BE.

And I have always wanted to be that person again.

~ MAKING MOVIES ~
movie editing
DEFINING MOMENTS
The Ceiling Flies Away: Slocum Rushes, May 1959

I kept shooting "The Epiphany of Slocum Furlow"— a scene every two or three days— but it took a week for the first rolls to be developed. I called in some friends to look at what I had shot.

I didn't realize that most people can't see a scene out of order and understand it in their mind. Here is what they saw: strange repeated shots of people lounging around and saying (silently) "parp parp", and repeated shots of Jody falling down in his chair. Even though I explained the scene to them before running the projector, they were utterly mystified.

They didn't know.

But for me, the roof flew off the building. I heard a roaring wind. My destiny had found me.

What I saw was the finished scene as it would be.* The scene was atmospheric. It developed characters. It had a plot. It was moderately subtle. It was rather funny. And it was *warm*—more like a foreign than an American film, like the films of Pagnol or Satyajit Ray.

* The finished scene—"Slocum Furlow Scene 7, The Classroom" may currently be found on YouTube.

Most people don't like it because there's no lip-synch (as in Huckleberry Hound)– an unrecognized genre. If somebody famous said it was funny, everybody would suddenly appreciate it.

It was far better than I had imagined it could be, far better than I had remotely hoped.

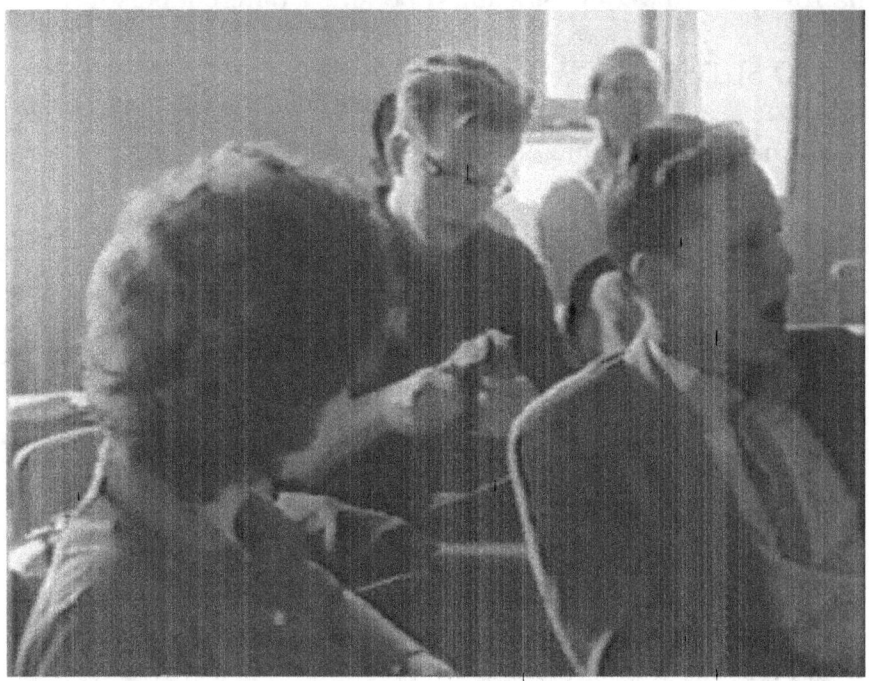

Hero Slocum exchanges glances with the girl in the front row. From "Slocum Furlow Scene 7 - The Classroom", currently on YouTube.

The question was not whether I could learn to make films. I already knew.

RESOLVE

I was a natural. This was what I had been put on earth to do. Partly to make movies, and partly to be again that person I was when I was shooting. This was no longer about being Best at anything. This was about my heart, which I had found.

The only problem was that I wanted to be an intellectual too.

Graduation Too Soon

It wasn't till my oral exam by the all the philosophers—that is, the members of the Swarthmore Philosophy Department— that I realized I had passed. (In fact, it was *fun!*) I graduated, as they used to say, not *magna cum laude* but *mirabile dictu*—miraculous to say. I was told later that many faculty members were surprised I made it through, let alone in four straight years as officially preferred.

They had given me a bachelor's degree. But my education was hardly over.

DEFINING MOMENTS
Darkness at Noon (June 1959)

Ralph Nelson, my biological father, did not come to my graduation. Soon after, however, he invited me to the Plaza Hotel for lunch. I had been under the impression that he had lined up a summer job for me. Instead things went very sour.

I realize now that Ralph had only three ways of being with me. He would either make pre-planned remarks, or he would smoke silently and block all conversation, or he would attack. But he would never listen.

This was an attack occasion. (By now I could see them coming.)

He started with his standard criticisms of my life: it had taken me too long to learn to tie my shoes, I hadn't been a Boy Scout, I hadn't been in a debating club, we hadn't kept the dog in the city after he foisted it on me, I shouldn't have been given a professional camera at 13. Then he said I was "conforming to non-conformity," which I found particularly shallow and irritating. I stifled the impulse to explain Reference Group Theory in social psychology. I stifled the impulse to say I was indeed conforming, but conforming to the spirit of defiant artists and intellectuals everywhere. I just sat there and endured it all.

I don't think I tried to explain to him that I hoped to be a major intellectual. (He thought my grades showed that I had no aptitude for the world of ideas, and I don't think be believed I had left the Honors program voluntarily.)

⸺ A Note from the Present

Now, decades later, I have realized that Ralph didn't like intellectuals, and he really wanted me in show business, and that in fact deep down he loved me, but I never had any sense of those things during his lifetime.

Ralph loved me but he disliked me and thought I needed to be scolded every time he saw me, I still don't know why. He somehow thought he could change me and my world-view by shouting in his great baritone. This only embittered me more and more. (I don't think he treated his other sons that way, but in any case they would have taken it more lightly; I take few things lightly.)

The best insight comes from Robin Morgan, the great feminist, who had been a child actress on "Mama." Robin says that James Dean was on two or three shows, standing in as Nels, and Ralph had hated him. James Dean and I had a lot in common, especially a cockiness and disdain for the conventional world that is now called "attitude." I always held it back around Ralph, and was always courteous and deferential to him, but I think he saw that underneath I was not in sympathy with the Respectability program. It may be this that infuriated him time and again.

Ralph repeated his offer to get me started as an actor, but not nicely. If there had been any warmth in his invitation, any sense that he looked forward to my being an actor, I might have responded differently. But the offer was dangled in a grudging and unpleasant manner, and did not appeal to me in any way.

Why didn't I tell him I wanted to make movies? Because there was never any point in trying to tell him anything; that would just have brought on another attack. (Ralph was not at the time a film-maker and I had no idea he was going to become one.)

But he had a punch line: there would be no summer job, and I would have to fend for myself for a year, after which I should come to him to get started as an actor.

I don't remember what I was expecting, but I think he had waited to throw this at me till my grandparents (Jean and Pop) were in Europe, so I had nowhere to turn, and in a bad economy as well. (Ralph liked to play harsh pranks.) I think he also thought this exposure to the Real World would change all my attitudes. (Lotza luck.)

▬▬▬ A Note from the Present

Now, what if I had gone with Ralph's plan and gone into acting? It was a highly credible offer.* Certainly a relative in show business is the best way to start, and anyone knows that going to Hollywood as an actor would have been an excellent starting-point for making movies. But I no longer wanted to be an actor, it would be a digression, and it would be at the price of being under Ralph's corrosive supervision, which I saw as absolutely intolerable. (I realize now it would probably have only involved being shouted at once a month— a cheap price for what was on offer, but more than I could tolerate from him.)

* He later started my half-brother, Ralph Nelson Jr., on what has been a long and distinguished career as a Hollywood still photographer.

I didn't know what to do. We had a second lunch at the Plaza again the next day, and I don't remember what was said, except for his final words: "Fuck you." They were final words because I got up unsteadily and left the table and did not look back.

RESOLVE

One thing was certain: I would never come crawling back to Ralph. We were through. I could succeed on my own.

But my life turned dark from his attack that day, and has never much brightened again.

Chapter 6.
ROCKET TO NOWHERE, 1959-60

=== Summer 1959 (I turned 22)

American Securities

Abruptly I could no longer go to the apartment on Central Park West. I moved into a cold-water flat on West 77th with two friends from college.

There were no summer jobs; I was able to get job only by going to an employment agency and signing up as a permanent employee; this meant that of my three months salary, one had to go to the employment agency, quite a docking. I was a typist in a securities cage on Wall Street. Surprisingly, I was able to type numbers with no mistakes by taking my time and not caring.

During the week I worked long hours in the securities cage. Saturdays and Sundays, that summer, I put in longer hours editing my movie.

~ MAKING MOVIES ~
movie editing

CONTINUITY: LEARNING TO EDIT MOVIES

On the weekends I went south seventy blocks to my old home on Washington Square, with my grandparents away, and cut my movie on the marbletop kitchen table.

I had thought originally it would only take a couple of hours. It took all the Saturdays and Sundays of the whole summer. (I'm surprised now that I managed to finish in that time.)

Movie editing is an agonizing business, and the more you care the more agonizing it is, because there are so many choices.

It's basically simple; you don't need anyone to teach you.

It's just like writing. You try something, you see how it looks, you adjust it or start over again. And again and again and again.

(As with writing, sometimes you have to walk away--go to another part-- while the previous impressions settle down.) Unfortunately, the more you care, the longer it takes.

The fact that I had shot Slocum without a script made it harder, because I was writing the script as I went along, from the final cut of the film, and it had no determinate sequence.

I hung a big plastic wastebasket all around the edge with bent paper clips and tumbled the shorter pieces of film into it, hanging from the paper clips. The longer pieces of film I rolled onto film cores (I had been taught about cores by a friend, Morrie Roizman, who lent me the viewer).

I had shot maybe two to one (ratio of film shot to used—pretty good!), but I edited 200 to one (ratio of editing time to running time). That's the problem with caring too much.

But it was worth it. I love that movie and its continuity. And in art, who is the artist out to please but himself?

=== Fall 1959 (I was 22)
Empty Niches (U. of Chicago)

The less said about my year at the University of Chicago the better.

The campus had a lot of empty statue niches, I don't know why. It was stupid, cold and squalid; the university had a few hundred women and thousands of men; and I constantly felt my father's curse like a sunlamp close to the back of my neck. I thought of suicide all the time, but I knew what that would do to my grandparents, and so I kept on. To purge Ralph from my life I seriously considered going back to the name I had lived under for ten years of my childhood, Theodor Holm II, but I knew it was too late; in college I had irrevocably become (i.e., become known as) Ted Nelson, and I figured that was who I had to stay.

I had gone to Chicago in sociology because I didn't want to be too far from my grandparents, and I thought U.Chi was the closest to the romantic anthropology I had enjoyed. I was thinking of William Foote Whyte's work there, decades before. But Whyte was gone and the atmosphere in the sociology department had completely changed, getting somewhat strange and stupid. Most of the graduate students in the department wanted to be social workers; I was interested in deep theory, and heard none. In fact, the sociologists of that department kept denouncing theory of any kind.

I had to leave that place. But after such an awful start in graduate school I had to get at least some advanced degree, so I applied elsewhere. I took a test called the Miller Analogies, and, amazingly, that got me a fellowship to Harvard for the following year.

Harvard at Last, 1960-62

Harvard is a state of mind: it feels like the center of human culture (unlike that crude place down Mass Avenue, called MIT, which Harvard people feel is lacking in culture). Who went to Harvard? Seven Presidents, innumerable authors, and, in the fall of 1960, a lot of beautiful young women with long hair. And I.

A key event that fall, indeed, was the election of one of our own: John Kennedy, the eighth Harvard president. (The cover of MAD congratulated him the next day— astonishing till you turned it over, where it congratulated Nixon.)

I was in a wonderful department: the (late lamented) Department of Social Relations. One day a week they had great free lunches for their members, so a lot of students and faculty turned up.

Soc Rel, as it was called, combined sociology, cultural anthropology, social psych and clinical psych. (There was another 'pure' psych department elsewhere.) The department was stocked with Great Names: Gordon Allport, David McClelland, Frederick Mosteller, George Homans. The anthropologist Clyde Kluckhohn had just died, but his widow Florence was still in the department.

Timothy Leary was in the department (he wore white suits at the time), and his colleague Richard Alpert.* It was clear they were up to something but I wasn't going to get involved, either as participant or whistle-blower.

> *I hated Alpert. At that time was a very snotty behaviorist, before he went through the looking-glass and became Baba Ram Dass.

The biggest name in sociology was also there, Talcott Parsons. He was my adviser, with the expectation that I would write a thesis in sociology. Unfortunately tings between us did not go well. He was the only professor in graduate school with whom I did not get along—partly because of his enormous pomposity, which once gave me the giggles. This was particularly unfortunate because he was my adviser.

But I did not feel deeply involved with my Department.

Again I had found my way to the precipices of intellect—Tom Schelling, and computers.

Schelling

I had heard Schelling speak at a meeting of the American Sociological Society (it was actually called that! in those days).* I was bowled over by his stunning brilliance on a subject I hugely cared about.

> * Parsons took great pride that in *his* tenure as president, the A.S.S. became the A.S.A., the American Sociological Association. No sense of humor.

I had long been concerned with nuclear war and the theory of deterrence. Unlike my friends in the Peace movement, I knew from intense personal experience that deterrence worked. I had independently discovered the theory of deterrence in my boyhood, and fine-tuned that understanding early.*

> * No time to get into that here.

Schelling was not the first person I had heard making sense on the of war and deterrence—at Chicago I had befriended Robert Osgood, "Limited War Osgood"—but Schelling put Osgood's ideas on a much deeper footing. Schelling was a man apart. His piercing lucidity and simple presentation were magnificent (he never said "uh"—his pauses were marvels of suspense). But most important, he smashed the standard silly game theory that had gripped academia.

The standard silly game theory, beloved of economists, assumes two perfect adversaries—what one wins the other loses—and no communication. This perfect rivalry is perfectly asinine, as Schelling demonstrated in his examples and tables, though he was much more polite about it. Real-life situations are always mixed; adversaries almost always have interests in common. Thus the most important things about conflict, said Schelling, are often the areas of mutual interest, and how adversaries communicate in real-life situations.

The supreme example, of course, hung over us: the perilous state of nuclear arms between the U.S. and the Soviet Union, each poised to destroy the other, and each almost certain that act would cause its own total destruction. This was not an idle theoretical exercise. This was life and death for everyone, global life and death, which Schelling analyzed in dry tones with clever examples.

········ A Note from the Present

I'll jump to the punch line. In large part due to Schelling's efforts, they put in a Hot Line between Moscow and Washington, so that the two frightened, gargantuan adversaries could communicate as much as possible at moments of stress; this lowered the temperature of near-nuclear confrontations, and we did not have nuclear war.

Schelling got the Nobel in 2005. In his speech he said, 'The most important event of the twentieth century is one that did not happen.' Partly thanks to him.

What would Thomas Schelling have said? (1) 1960

'You're my favorite student,' Schelling told me at some point during the course. This surprised me and made me feel very fine, particularly since I was not so happy with the Soc Rel courses I was taking.

Schelling's course, outside my Department, was one of my key Harvard learning experiences.

The other is better known.

Chapter 7.
THE EPIPHANY OF TED NELSON

In that first year at Harvard, 1960=1, I took a computer course, and my world exploded.

What would Freed Bales have said? 1960

Freed Bales (he didn't use the "Robert" socially) was a most amiable and pleasant psychologist in my Soc Rel department. His long-term research included a gut course that could be taken any number of times by undergraduates and grad students alike, in which they argued about interpersonal issues at any level of inanity they chose. Meanwhile, behind one-way glass, Bales' research assistants were taking down and coding everything that happened.

Bales made the most trenchant remark on computers I ever heard.

'The computer is the greatest projective system* ever created', Bales said to me. Meaning that anyone looking at the computer would think they were seeing reality, but would see something projected from their own mind.

> *A projective system is something which, like a Rorschach test, invites people to project on it their own personalities and ideas, often unwittingly.

For fifty years since then, I have marveled at how everyone projects onto the computer their own issues and concerns and personality.

I did too.

DEFINING MOMENTS
A Wild Surmise

> Then felt I like some watcher of the skies
> When a new planet swims into his ken;
> Or like stout Cortez when with eagle eyes
> He star'd at the Pacific--and all his men
> Look'd at each other with a wild surmise--
> Silent, upon a peak in Darien.
>
> *John Keats*

I was the first person on earth to know what I am about to tell you. I believe I thought of everything here in the fall of 1960, though some of it may have been in 1961, the second semester of that school year (before the summer of '61). I believe this can all be confirmed from my detailed notes of those days (though they will likely be telegraphic summaries and proposed articles to write explaining the ideas).

No one told me or suggested these ideas. I didn't read them, and there was no one to confirm them with. (A few conversations with computer scientists on campus made it clear they had other obsessions.) But I didn't need any confirmation. From all my background and daring, in media and in ideas and initiatives in many directions, I simply knew.* I saw the vastness of what I was facing, and the certainty of a new world to come.

* A longer list of reasons is given in Appendix 3.

A few words, a few pictures of people at computer screens, and the understanding that computer prices would fall—these gave me all I needed to know, a crystal seed from which to conjure a whole universe. And a good one. The only issue was how to shape the real world toward that good, because it could all go wrong in so many ways.

• They Had Been Lying

The public had been told that computers were mathematical, that they were engineering tools. This misstated things completely. The computer was an all-purpose machine and could be whatever it was programmed to be. It had no nature; *it could only masquerade.* The computer could become only whatever imaginary structure people imposed on it– onto which they would project their own personalities and concerns.

Therein lay the glory and the difficulty.

——— A Note from the Present

> This mathematical stereotype of the computer would continue to confuse everyone for decades—not just the public, but people in the industry as well, under the weight of their traditions.

The computer could handle text; alphabetical characters fit into the same memory slots as the numbers. Instead of adding and subtracting them, you could move them around. Text can be stored. Text could be printed. Text could be shown on screens. So far that was only done for technical purposes, but obviously there was no limitation on what text would be shown and how it might behave.

The computer did not contain 'knowledge.' Instead, it had to be programmed to simulate some unified arrangement of data. This data had to be represented by a lot of pieces of information placed in a lot of memory locations. Suitably organized, probed and updated, this collection of factoids could be made to appear as a unified body of information, but this too was a masquerade. (The term "database" did not yet exist.) The editorial problems for a collection of data—keeping it updated and consistent— were just like the editorial problems of a research paper, just more formalized and pretending to more rigor.

There was no magic to this simulation of knowledge. It just took diligence and a lot of work, and a lot of choices about conventions and standards and consistency and authentication. The implicit choices made all over the paper world—by librarians, office supervisors, clerks, everybody— had to be made explicit and locked into software.

• Computers Were Electric Trains; This Meant Personal Computing

INSIGHT: Computers were electric trains! Why did guys like electric trains? Because you can make them do things—plan them and build them and watch them go around!

The computer aroused all the same masculine desires to control and to putter.

I wanted a computer; that told me every guy would want one. (The one I lusted for at the time was called the AN/UYK-1, was highly reliable and was narrow enough be lowered into a submarine through its hatch, and cost $75,000. But obviously the price was going to come way down.)

> * Unfortunately this costfall took far longer than I expected.

And if every guy wanted one, that meant there would be a huge personal computer industry. When they got cheap enough, of course.

• The Future of Mankind Was at the Computer Screen

So much of modern life was about paper and its manipulations. But it wasn't the paper that mattered, it was what was *on* the paper, and that could be turned to data.

It was obvious to me that for all clerical purposes and for all information, the interactive computer would become the workplace of the future.

• Eliminating Paper

It likewise seemed obvious to me that paper would be completely replaced.

> ------- **A Note from the Present**
>
> The idea of "the paperless office" is widely derided and called an impossible myth. I totally disagree: it's entirely possible. But paperlessness is impossible the way they're thinking of it. Today's systems *imitate paper!* You can't have a paperless office unless you go to completely different representations and rich connective systems.
>
> We may compare simulating paper to the swimmer holding onto the side of the pool—there will be no progress without letting go of it.

But offices were hardly interesting to me back then. What mattered to me was how papelessness could contribute to the creativity, the understandings, the intellectual excitement of human life.

• Magic Pictures to Command

Diagrams, maps, history, every subject (and the connections between subjects) could all interact on our interactive screens.

The problem was working out the rules.

Everyone should be able to contribute to a great world of interconnection, but not to wreck it. How could this be set up?

• Unlosability

It would be vital to protect the user against losing content if the machine malfunctioned. Therefore, when a user entered an item, it would have to be stored immediately on tape—*and* printed out, for safety.

> **INTERACTION STORY**
> **------- A Note from the Present**
>
> It is amazing to me that even today's systems rarely respect the safety of user's content in this way. They all assume the hard drive will continue to function and they won't crash. Saving every change to an external flash memory would be the cheap and reliable equivalent to what I thought of then.

• The Same Notecard in Different Places

A fundamental idea came to me this way.

For three years I had been keeping notes on file cards, and I already had a terrible problem with these notes. Many of my file cards belonged in several places at once— several different sequences or projects.

Each card—call it now an *entry* or an *item*—*should be stored only once. Then each project or sequence would be a list of those items. Each entry would *seem* to be in each of its different projects, but it would only exist in one place, and the lists would point to it.

* Or in Doug Engelbart's terminology, a statement.

Of course, you would also want to see (from each entry) its different contexts—its different transclusions— and compare them side by side.

——— A Note from the Present

This perfectly reasonable premise—being able to see all the contexts of re-use– was to drive my work to the edge of madness, as recounted later. In hindsight, you could say that by bringing down the Xanadu project, this requirement can be said to have created the World Wide Web, in rather the same way that the assassination of Julius Caesar brought about Augustus.

——— A Note from the Present
COINED WORDS

This concept is now called *transclusion.*, referring to—
- re-use by pointer
- the same thing in many contexts, with access to the original
- content re-use with path back to the original

It is fundamental to my work.

But we've gone through so many words for it, trying to get the idea across—
- quote-window
- transquotation
•• various others I can't remember right now, and worst of all,
- *equolateration.*

The present definition: *content re-use with path back to the original.* It has many uses.

No conventional document systems (like Microsoft Word or the Web) will support transclusion.*

> * di Iorio and Lumley have done an excellent technical analysis of alternative methods of transclusion for the World Wide Web, and why they don't work. See Angelo Di Iorio and John Lumley, "From XML Inclusions to XML Transclusions,"

Proceedings of the Hypertext 2009 conference, ACM.

• Editing by Pointer

If you could have a list of pointers to file cards, you could cut it even finer: you could make a list of pointers to individual phrases, and build your document that way— just as pointers that would bring in the contents in the right order. It would be a *virtual* document, meaning it had no existence in a file, but that hardly mattered, since it could be reconstructed at the instant wanted.

------- **A Note from the Present**
XANADU STORY

This has been fundamental to the Xanadu design ever since.

XANADU TECH
------- **A Note from the Present**

EDITING BY POINTERS—WHY?

I wanted to use pointers, instead of moving the text itself, for a growing series of reasons—
- first I wanted to have the same file cards in multiple sets. Each of these sets would be represented internally as a list of pointers.
- second, this would make the content safe—if you store it and leave it alone.
- then, it was the idea that you could compare sets of file cards side by side to see which ones were in both sets.
- then came the idea of fine-grain editing by pointer.
- this meant full text documents could be compared side by side, to see what contents they shared (transclusion).

------- **A Note from the Present**
XANADU TECH

BILL DUVALL TRIES IT AND DISCOVERS--
EDITING BY POINTERS IS EFFICIENT! ca 1975

Much later (in the 1990s) I heard from Bill Duvall, a pioneer with Engelbart's group, that he had tested this method of editing text by pointers and found it was more efficient than the writing systems they were doing! (Such "efficiency" had not been my concern when I thought of it in 1960 or 1961. There were half a dozen other reasons (see above).) Duvall's has been the only test I know of this idea outside my own work, though undoubtedly there have been others.

Had he actually found the method to be efficient? I wrote to Bill recently (2010.03.29) to confirm this story. Here's his reply:

> what I actually did was to separate the content from the structure. This allowed a couple of really neat things, including:
>
> • The text was always intact, allowing easy processing by things like compilers, spell checkers, mail, and anything requiring clear text.
> • A document with a corrupted structure (remember how that happened?) was relatively easy to repair.
> • The same document could have multiple, different structures.
> • One was not bound to a single, hierarchical tree structure. You could slice it and dice it anyway you want.
> • It took much less space and processing to store and manipulate a document this way (this was once important.)
>
> The editor which I wrote originally ran on a Data General Nova in 8 KB (that's 8,000 BYTES), was lightning fast (complete screen refresh in well under 1/2 sec), and supported all of the entities used by NLS (statement, branch, plex, group, etc.) yet allowed there to be missing 'pieces' in the hierarchy, i.e. there could be missing branches on the tree. It also supported links, words, visibles, the keyset, and the mouse.

It had a useful life of over 20 years (it was ported several times and eventually ended up on the Alto, courtesy of Smokey Wallace, where it was called UGH (Uncomonly Good Hack).

There were not extensive text formatting features (mostly due to the state of the art at the time.)

Hope all is well in NelsonLand,

Bill

• The Simplification of Life

Because it would be so much easier to keep track of things, our lives would become simplified, and the drudgery of accounting and list-making and fact-fact-keeping would all be simplified.

Wonderful personal software would tie it all together and make our lives ever so much more enjoyable.

------- A Note from the Present

Are you laughing yet?

No one's life has yet been simplified by a computer.

Yet I believed that with my software designs I could make possible that simplification and clarification of life. And I still do.

• The Instrument I Had to Have

Obviously, well designed screen-editing systems would make writing far easier and quicker. Because my life was dedicated to projects with a lot of text (either text to publish or notes and scripts behind the scenes), that meant I would be able to complete far more projects in my lifetime, and do them better, too.

Being able to see different contexts for my notes would help optimize decisions, figuring out what to use where and knowing what had already been used.

In short, this was the fundamental writing system everybody needed, but especially someone with a lot of projects and notes to manage, i.e. myself. I often refer to it as the *fundamental* text system, or more simply as a *decent* text system, or even more simply by the trademark it later acquired: Xanadu.

So rather than try to complete other projects, I should build this system *first*.

──────── A Note from the Present

I could not stick to this plan in the short run, because I had no decent system. Then the short run got longer and longer, and there is no decent system yet.

• Splandremics
~~COINED WORDS~~ ─────────────

SPLANDREMICS *Presentational Arts, Structures and Conventions*
INTERACTION STORY ─────────────

I needed a word for all these ideas.

(It did not come soon. Sometime in spring 1961, I think, I came up with *splandremics*. By which I meant—
- the design of presentational systems and media
- the design of interactive settings and objects
- establishing conventions and overall frameworks for these designs

The place where you would work—your screen setup and computer, or whatever else it would contain—I wanted to call a *splandrome*.
Nobody could imagine what I was talking about.

> *It started with the "spl-" pseudo-morpheme, which connotes splintering, and splendor, and other outgoing situations. And "emics" from "phonemics" and "morphenmics." And it sounded good, I thought.

──────── A Note from the Present

In the nineteen-seventies, I came up with the word *fantics*, from the Greek root meaning "show" that also gives us "fantastic" and "sycophant." By which I wanted to mean "all aspects of the art and science of presentation." Nobody could relate to that either.

In the nineteen-nineties I started using the term *virtuality*, which correctly means the opposite of *reality*—the design and abstraction of imaginary worlds. My old* Webster's dictionary puts it this way:

> **vir′tu-al′i-ty** (vûr′tū-ăl′ĭ-tĭ), *n.* [Cf. F. *virtualité*.]
> 1. Quality or state of being virtual, or existing in essence or effect, but not in fact.
> 2. Potentiality; efficacy; potential existence. *Obs.*

Unfortunately Jaron Lanier's popularization of Artaud's term "virtual reality" has taken all the oxygen from the word "virtual"-- many people use the term "virtual" for 3D, literal 3D. This is an unfortunate loss of an important meaning.

* I think Merriam-Webster 1905; regrettably not on hand as I write.

• New Non-Sequential Tools

Being able to hold ideas in new structures meant we wouldn't have to make them just sequential or hierarchical any more. This had ramifications in every direction, and it created many more directions, too.

I wanted to make movies, but the idea of a fixed script pissed me off— so much happened while you were shooting, in the inspirations of the moment, and so many ideas might come later. What I wanted was a way of holding movie scripts that would show a number of alternative possibilities, and make it easy to rework the structure as scenes were shot.

-------- A Note from the Present

I had not at the time thought of the word *possiplex*.

• New Non-Sequential Media

We could have texts that branch and interpenetrate.*
* By interpenetrate I mean *transclude*.

-------- A Note from the Present

I had not at the time thought of the words *hypertext* and *hypermedia*.

Why should a movie have only one ending? If we could handle possiplexity, we could have movies that branch.

• Ideas in Flight

We could free text from rectangularity and sequence; this meant we could free readers and writers from the constraints of paper and of typesetting. (How silly it was to have 'space limitations' on an article, when it could go on and on! The point was to have some new way to organize it so the reader could grasp the whole in digest or overview form, then take a long or winding route depending. But there had to be a literary structure that made this clear.)

We would be freeing both reader and author. The author would not have to choose among alternative organizations; the reader could do that, choosing among the author's different organizations and perhaps adding his own. (What system of order would allow this was still not clear.)

We could also free up the educational system. If readers could choose their own paths through a subject, they would be far more interested (as had been my own college experience, skimming and flipping excitedly rather than slogging sequentially). The educational system could still have tests and strong criteria of learning; but we could give the student freedom to choose the *means and style* of learning a subject. This would be a very powerful motivator. (It had been for me.)

------- A Note from the Present

> Unfortunately, pre-college education as we know it (and inflict it) is a bureaucratic system for fulfilling lists– scheduling seats, classrooms, student movements, teacher movements, and tests. It is intrinsically and deeply hostile to what I am talking about here.

• Parallel Documents

While I was learning to write in high school, I had been boggled by the number of different possible ways to organize any piece of writing.

But in a suitably general new medium, the structure could represent those alternatives all at once, for different readers, and so the author would be freed from having to choose among many bothersome alternatives.

For instance, in a conventional history book, the author must choose a sequence to present events which were actually happening in parallel. In conventional writing, these go into different chapters, or have sentences that effectively point to the different event-streams. But if we can have parallel document structure,* the different event-streams can be in different text streams, coupled sideways; this structure should make clear all the relationships to the reader.

> * I am not sure that the genre of parallel documents occurred to me in the 1960-1 period.

• The Manifest Destiny of Literature

Obviously, writings like this would be far superior to ordinary writings on paper, and nobody would want the old forms or writing any more. But of course the old writings themselves could be brought forward as re-usable content for this new genre.

Nonsequential writing—the term "hypertext" had not yet been coined—was obviously the manifest destiny of literature.

I foresaw a sweeping new genre of writing with many forms of connection; and of course that was the genre in which I would want to create all my own works of the future.

-------- A Note from the Present

> Any reader who still thinks these ideas have any resemblance to the World Wide Web should probably take a hot bath.

But it was vital that this new literary genre would have to be simple, clean, elegant and powerful.

I saw this as the manifest destiny of literature.

I still do.

-------- A Note from the Present

> In case the reader doesn't get to that point in the book, I would like to acknowledge here that this design was finished, or perfected, by Gregory, Miller and Greene in 1979-80.

Because of numerous political setbacks, described later, I have had to abstract out a simplified version, which is the present Xanadu design—implemented in 2006 as XanaduSpace, and (at this writing) pending implementation in a client version in Flash or Silverlight.

• The Vast Publishing Network

Obviously, the future of publishing would be publishing on line.* A publishing house would have a system of servers (a term not then in use) and vast storage to hold its offerings.

---- COINED WORDS ----
* I don't think the term "on-line" existed yet, or even the concept. However, "data communication" at that time was already in use by the military and for air traffic control, so the idea seemed obvious to me.

A request for a particular document—or *part of* a document— would have to go to the publisher of that document. There would have to be some system of payment, whereupon the content would be delivered.

(Some, like a certain vicious journalist, have implied that I could not have known in 1960 that a world-wide electronic publishing system of interconnected documents could ever be possible. That is ridiculous. Data transmission was in the air, it was discussed everywhere. It was not standardized or generally available, but it was going to happen in some form, and whatever form it came in, I intended to use it.)

• Self-Publishing

I believed passionately in self-publishing, and still do. The publishing industry has always catered to, and been run by, the shallow, conventional, pompous and smug, with attitudes generally obtuse and behind the times. I wanted to free authors to publish on an even footing with big companies.

My great-grandfather self-published his poetry. My grandmother self-published her poetry, novels and drawings. I had self-published in college and intended to go on doing so, but this would be the real way to do it.

-------- **A Note from the Present**

(I have generally self-published out of choice [various bitter anecdotes omitted]. If self-publishing was good enough for William Blake, Samuel Taylor Coleridge, Richard Burton the explorer* and T.E. Lawrence, it's good enough for me. The revenue is a lot less but I there's no need to fight with editors, to compromise or dumb down.)

* Richard Francis Burton.

• Copyright and Royalty

This system of on-line publishing could not be free. Publishing has always been a system of commerce (what's the alternative, the government?)

I already knew a thing or two about copyright, principally that
- it was a pain in the neck to get reprint permission
- copyright would not go away, being thoroughly entrenched in the legal system.

The question was how to transpose copyright to this new world of on-line electronic documents, and whether this transposition would be beneficial and benign, or ugly and clumsy and forbidding.

A micropayment system would be needed— not just for whole documents, but for little pieces of documents. Why should you have to pay for a whole document—especially since documents might go on forever, since there were no space restrictions?

• Publishing the Pointer-Based Document

The virtual document I foresaw would be stored as a set of pointers, and the content it pointed to could be anywhere. Why not, then, point at content from various publishers? Then each publisher would sell a small piece to anyone who needed it to fill out a specific document. It would all add up: everything would be fairly paid for and attributable.*

* Note: Tim Berners-Lee said I proposed a *link* to every quotation (see 1999). That would be impossible and just as ridiculous as he seems to think. The way to do it is through transclusion of the quoted content, so it is delivered to the user from the original and the transaction of paying for the quotation is with the server of the original document.

This would settle the issues of permissions, and plagiarism, and context, all in one fell swoop. (And since you'd be able to look from any quote to its origin, nothing would be out of context—in this new sense of 'context' being another document zooming up* next to the quotation.)

>*This is the present visualization, as recently implemented in XanaduSpace, the most recent version. I do not remember what I visualized in 1960, except that I was thinking in about far less powerful screens.

HERE IS THE POINT: by this system, all content could be made easily re-usable with complete fairness. Everything would be paid for to its source publisher, and it would all add up correctly if each user's system buys each tiny portion as delivered from wherever.

Moreover, the original context of quotation would be available immediately, clarifying issues of
- author's meaning and surrounding issues
- credit and "moral right" (a term I did not know at the time)
- plagiarism— indeed, extensive offhand quotation would become legitimate

Conventional publishers would not have to join this system—they might resist it at first— but soon they would want to.

------- A Note from the Present
The elegance, clarity and power of this vision have driven me to continue fighting for it for the last fifty years.

COINED WORDS
I later coined the word "micropayment" for the miniscule payments I foresaw. Purchases of thousandths of a cent, or less, should be possible; I have been aghast to see people recently use the term "micropayment" for payments over a cent, even up to a dollar.

• Continual Change / No Forced Completion / Radical Revision / Staying Organized

Published documents would not have to have "revisions." They could be *continually* revised at the whim of the author, one edit at a time if desired. If you'd made a marginal note on one version, that marginal note would be in place if that same content were in the next version; and any two versions could be compared side by side.

This meant publishing without deadlines and without crises. What an improvement!

This also meant there need be no forced completions, no false pretenses of completion. Some works are indeed finished, an author's or committee's final version;. But many works never are ("art is never finished, just delivered," goes one saying.* *Any* *document could remain a work in progress,* published and continually changing, without breaking any of its connections (except where the ends were fully deleted).

Inded, not merely small changes, but radical revisions, could be accommodated. Instead of having to start fresh and throw away a previous document, it could be brought forward, radically revised and still connected. It could evolve as need be without losing its connections.

Almost every living document needs repeated revision. Indeed, the tradition of completion in publishing is fundamentally based on two things–
- the nature of the printing press and *print runs,* which all have to be the same;
- the nation of *canonical versions* in literary analysis. In this structure, the canonical version can be the whole docuplex of versions.

• Captive Content—Reusable and Linkable

All content would be
- reusable
- linkable
- annotatable

I foresaw a client-server system, though the term did not exist then. Content would stay on the servers and appear on the screens; it would not be downloaded to the user. (The terms "upload" and "download" did not exist then either.) If a user purchased content—in any amount, even a sentence— it would stay on the server, but now that sentence would be registered as belonging to him, so he would not have to purchase it again. If a user bought part of a document, a table would be created for that user of exactly what parts of it he owned and could re-access at any time.*

* This was implicitly the design from 1960-1, though I'm not sure when it became this definite.

But because everything in the system could be rearranged and recomposed by pointer—the awful term 'mashup' did not then exist—you could re-use anything once you owned it! This is because you could include it in your own document, as a pointer to whatever original you knew about it. (You could, in principle, also re-use original content you didn't know about, but how could you point at it?)

------- A Note from the Present

In some ways this resembles the systems of captive content that are now available, for example at the *New Yorker* website, where a subscriber may view any content from the *New Yorker.* Over the years.

But you cannot recomposite, link, annotate, underline these captive contents.

My fuller vision seems far more beneficial to everyone.

The elegance, clarity and power of this vision have driven me to continue fighting for this for the last fifty years.

Publishers would not have to join this system—they might resist it at first—but soon they would want to.

• What This Could Do for Education

The ghastly system of education, so oppressive to most kids (me anyhow, from kindergarten through high school), is a form of imprisonment and lockstep. A new explorable document world could create choices to energize students' minds.

Others try to create better curricula, but the problem of education is having a curriculum itself!

What does "curriculum" mean in Latin?

Racetrack.

As soon as you have a curriculum, some people are "ahead" and some people are "behind," and nobody can slow down to enjoy the parts they like or speed over what they understand already.

As long as there is a fixed schedule and path of learning, education cannot be improved. Having to do things in one sequence, with no variation for personal interests, is what makes school horrible.

Now, in our new document world, we would fix that.

Or so I thought.

• New Kinds of Anthology

The heartbreak of intellectual life is that there is no time to read everything. Since boyhood I was sad that there was no time to read everything— and so many wonderful books and articles, more every day.

Textbooks and anthologies try to help. They show us see quotations, and excerpts, but we get no sense of the whole documents they were excerpting. Every quote is cut off from its original.

But now, in this new world, anthologies could be different. Every excerpt would stay connected to its original context! Whenever you wanted, you could step from the excerpt to the original!– and browse, and delve.

This would be a total change in study and learning, especially of history and literature. It could deepen our understandings of everything. We would think less in stereotypes.

• A Movie Machine!

The computer was obviously a movie machine.

What are movies? Events on a screen that affect the heart and mind of the viewer. What would the computer present? *Events on a screen that affect the heart and mind of the viewer—AND INTERACT!* The movie screen would fly into this new dimension of interaction, but the fundamental issues were the same: *the heart and mind of the viewer.* And who knew these better than a movie director?

Interfaces and interaction are not "technology." They are movies.

This was not about technicality; it was about the user's experience, to which all technicalities were subservient.

------- A Note from the Present

Many tekkies want to believe that "interfaces" are a branch of computer science. They are not. They are a branch of movie-making, because they are all about what the user thinks and feels, and inviting the user to think certain ways (understanding menus, for instance) and feel a certain way (excited and participatory, rather than oppressed).

COINED WORDS

Only lately (ca. 2009) has the true issue been made manifest in the computer field, with a new slogan expressing my views of the last fifty years: *User experience design.*

• A Philosophy Machine!

The computer was obviously a philosophy machine.

What is philosophy? *The search for the best abstractions.*

What was the fundamental problem of the computer? *The search for the best abstractions.* Everybody in the field was taking initiatives in different directions, looking for the best fundamental units, the best fundamental methods. It was philosophy written in lightning.*

* I allude here to a famous remark on seeing Griffith's "Birth of a Nation": 'It is history written in lightning.'

This is not a technical issue, but rather moral, aesthetic and conceptual. Finding the right abstractions is the deepest issue, and computer scientists wrangle endlessly over it.

It is also a political and marketing issue: because eventually the different abstractions— call them, say, "Macintosh" and "Windows"—fight it out in the marketplace. This is marketing and politics.

-------- A Note from the Present

I thought that with my training in philosophical analysis I was especially well-prepared for this issue, and perhaps I was, but getting political leverage was quite another problem. I knew it would be but that did not help.

• Doing it Right, on the Cheap

I had the mentality of a low-budget filmmaker: the right way to get this going was without backing, because backers want to change things and it's always a fight. (I had seen this personally in my father's fights with sponsors over the details of TV shows, right up till air time.)

But there is nothing more powerful than an idea. Everybody said this and I believed it. The problem was to get the idea across, and the way to do that was to get it working.

• A Complete Literary System

This software had to be an entire literary system– not just a document format or a transmission format, but it had to have –
• ownership (ownership of copyright and ownership of copies)
• well-defined literary forms of connection
• a complete system of commerce.

• The Posterity Machine

This would obsolete libraries. It meant that the heritage of humanity would be stored on many computers in many places. This had many problems.

• Literary Structure as a Moral Issue

The point had to be: to make all contents interweavable—linkable, annotatable and re-usable, with every context of origin visible.

> **------- A Note from the Present**
>
> Note that things have gone in the opposite direction, with today's nightmare of incompatible document formats, and no proper generality of linkage or permitted vast quotation.
>
> This is still a moral issue, not just technical.

Many would oppose such a system for selfish reasons, but mankind had to have it. This plan could not be hostage to narrow concerns of different interest groups.

• Simple, Elegant Design
DESIGN INFLUENCES: *IT ALL LED HERE.*

From influences on every side since my boyhood, the idea of simple, elegant, minimalist design had become part of my soul. Clean design without exceptions was my ideal. There will always be temptations to make special cases and tangled design, but obviously these were to be avoided wherever possible.

Here were some examples of clean design and structure stamped on my soul–
- Frank Lloyd Wright
- the Theremin
- the Hammond Organ
- heterodyning
- Le Corbusier
- the Bauhaus
- my grand-uncle Danckert's "Guidler" invention
- the Bloomfield-Sapir revolution in linguistics, which unified all language into a few simple concepts, with no special cases
- a negative lesson: the unfortunate overdesign of my rock musical, "Anything and Everything," in college, with too much cumbersome loose stuff

- Russell and Whitehead's *Principia Mathematica,* which tried to assimilate all mathematics to a couple of simple concepts, with no special cases
- the Sheffer stroke function in symbolic logic, reducing the Russell-Whitehead model to a single concept

One reason to seek such elegance was making things clear to the user.

Another was just as important: *clean implementability*.

——— A Note from the Present

(This was before Dijkstra's Structured Programming and the Nassi-Schneiderman diagrams created new simplicity, and before Object-Oriented programming created new complexity.)

• How Improve on Paper?

I tried to imagine the best generalizations of documents and literature.* What forms of connection would we need, and how present them?

* Inspired by the best forms of generalization I'd seen—Bloomfield and Sheffer.

One thing was clear: we certainly did not want to imitate paper on the computer screen. Nothing could be more stupid or retrograde. The prison of paper, enforcing sequence and rectangularity, had been the enemy of authors and editors for thousands of years; now at last we could break free.

——— A Note from the Present

I could not have imagined that two decades later that others would *imitate* paper, or that the imitation of paper would become the center of the computer world!

The Macintosh, in 1981, brought font play to the masses; and two projects coming out of Xerox PARC (Project Bravo and Interpress) were brought to the public as Microsoft Word and Adobe Acrobat. Now the world thinks electronic documents should look and act like paper—*paper under glass*.

• Politics of the Future

It was clear that there were many dangers. The heritage could be wiped out by electrical glitches or well-placed bombs. Governments would try to censor. Special interests would try to control information, as they always have. There would be bad guys.

This was where my idealism faded and my anger kicked in.

• A Feel for It

From the beginning I could *feel* the way things would look on the screen. I could *feel* my interactive designs.

INTERACTION STORY
SPLANDREMICS *Presentational Arts, Structures and Conventions*
──── A Note from the Present

I have generally had absolute confidence about the way my designs would feel, and I have generally been right. Indeed, I have designed backward from the feel I wanted to achieve.

According to conventional wisdom, this is impossible. They say that you can't know what software (or an interface) will be like until you try it.

Ah, but you see, there are people with special talents. My favorite example is this: *Hitchcock did not look through the lens*. He knew how a shot would look, from a certain angle and with a lens of his choice, *without having to look*. (I have not heard this about any other film director.)

It has been the same with my software. Shaping the design in my mind (sometimes wiggling my fingers on an imaginary keyboard), I can imagine each variant and what it will do to the feel.

This is not to say I can imagine *other* people's designs from a description; only that I can work out the feel of my own in advance.

As explained in Chapter 20, I consider interactive software to be a branch of film-making. I think my talent in this area is somehow related to Hitchcock's, and the fact that I had been thinking about film-making all my life before I met the computer.

• My Own Renaissance

I came out of Swarthmore determined to be a Renaissance man– generalist, showman, designer, author, Thinker. But I would still have to fit somehow into the so-called Real World– the world of money, publication, film distribution, occupational structure and society that were already there.

But now, I thought, this would turn the tables and change the game completely. All those things were going to change in this new world. I was going to design and build my own Renaissance.

• The Sword in the Stone

In the legend, young King Arthur comes upon a sword-handle sticking out of a stone. He pulls it out because it his destiny. It is his destined instrument. The rest follows. The sword is called Excalibur.

I saw these discoveries as my Excalibur—beyond calibration!—with which I would carve the future; and with which I would slay the dragons of evil, shallowness, conventionality, pomposity and smugness.

RESOLVE

All Conflicts Gone

I had been waiting for a sign. I had been for I knew not what, but somehow I had expected a revelation. I had expected some life mission to reveal itself to me, though I was expecting something more along the lines of an intellectual discovery. What now was all this? Fate was daring me to do something entirely different, something unheard of, something very important that only I understood and only I could do. Where was that unique intellectual life whose revelation I had been awaiting?

But then, wasn't this an intellectual discovery? O my god! THIS WAS IT! This was everything I was searching for!

I knew a handle sticking out of a stone when I saw one.

I had thought earlier there would be a great philosophical revelation, or some great film to make, or that I could somehow fix education. This could be all these things and more. All my conflicts of long-term goals were resolved.

I had felt a conflict between being an idealist and making money. (Not an uncommon conflict for a young man.) No more. This would make the world a far better place and make me tons of money on the way. Here was a single path to everything I believed in and wanted. What more worthy goal could a brash young man choose, than to rebuild civilization anew?

I figured that programming the system, deploying it and revolutionizing the world would take about two years. I was impatient to get done with that. Then I could get back to movie-making, and I would be able to finance my movies myself without having to deal with backers.

There has never been any other plan.

I wanted to be the Gutenberg of this new medium that only I imagined. And the Griffith and the Disney. Especially the Gutenberg.

Little did I know that Gutenberg had gone bankrupt.

INTERACTION STORY

INTERFACE IDEAS

I had a lot of ideas for interfaces, right off the bat.

The feel of the interface was crucial. Interfaces should be swoopy and offhand, more like bicycles than typewriters. I wanted to use light pens, but also Theremins and hand-puppets.

I came up with an input language I now call Zorro-language, where the user would flick at the screen like that movie swordsman, in curving movements that crossed each other.

I soon thought of moving text on the screen (now called scrolling), which I realized could go up and down *or* sideways. Then I realized that text could also scroll *diagonally*, which was also equivalent.

The main thing was for interfaces to be cinematic and swoopy, not niggling and fiddly and boxed-in.

But beyond that—the issue was not just "interface", a term which assumes a structure that is already decided and being interfaced *to*. The real issue is designing a clean structure behind the interface that the user could understand. (The conceptual structure and the interface together I call the *virtuality*.)

········ A Note from the Present

Alas, "niggling and fiddly and boxed-in" characterize the interface styles popular since the PARC User Interface ("the modern GUI").

~~XANADU TECH~~
ASSEMBLER NIGHTS

The IBM 709, which our course finally focused on, had an assembler language called FAP.

I set about trying to write the code for my text system. After a few evenings, writing many pages of instructions, I realized--

- I'd have to figure out document structure from the users' point of view, as a clear set of abstract concepts
- (the document structure would have to be extremely detailed)
- There would have to be visualizations and interfaces that were very clear
- I'd have to map all that structure to computer files (I was planning to use tape; it's what they had in those days)
- I'd have to map this also to transmission, which was another level

So simple in principle, this problem was going to take a lot longer than I thought.

········ A Note from the Present

How long it would take I could not have imagined. I did not think I would live as long as I have.

"Soon we'll be reading and writing on computer screens," early 1960s

In the early sixties I tried to tell everybody my vision--
>'Soon we'll be reading and writing on computer screens.
>'And there'll be new forms of publication for the screen.
>'And you'll be able to call up any document out of millions.
>'And everyone will be able to publish in this new medium.
>'And there'll be many new kinds of connection among them.
>'And you'll be able to see every quotation in its original context.
>'And you'll be able to quote without limit without permission.
>'And there'll be an automatic royalty to each author for the part they wrote.'

And in the early sixties the general reaction was--
Blank look.

BIZ. STORY
THE GENERAL CREATIVE CORPORATION

I envisioned a computer company I would head. I thought I would call it the General Creative Corporation.

> **------- A Note from the Present**
> My image of this company in 1960 was very like what Apple is now, and I expected to do what Jobs has done, except with ideas of my own, rather than received from others. Jobs' genius has been to make received ideas seem radical and exciting.

Later, after I got the idea for Fantasm, I thought the company should be called "General Fantastic" (cf. General Electric). Nobody liked that.

Not all of my first ideas were good, but most of them were entirely correct.

XANADU STORY •
BIZ STORY --------------------------------

I was fixated on the idea of a Rearrangement service in Harvard Square. This would be a walk-in service for authors and professors to help organize and rearrange large-scale projects. (Actually, to be charitable, this is rather like Kinko's rent-a-computer-seat services now, but what I had in mind then was very unlikely to succeed.)

I actually found a first backer. He was a Harvard student named Graham Gibbard, who thought he could put in ten thousand dollars. I said I'd get back to him when I was ready to take the money. (I haven't yet. It looks like he got away clean :)

What would Thomas Schelling have said? (2) 1960-1
~ MAKING MOVIES ~

Sometime during the strategy course, Schelling told me he had just had lunch with director Stanley Kubrick and they had tried to start World War III.

'It's harder than you think', Schelling told me. (Since I worried constantly about World War III, I found this remark somewhat reassuring.) Schelling also gave me a copy of a pocket novel called *Red Alert* by Peter George, which he said Kubrick was working from-- it was the closest thing to the way a nuclear war might start.

Those deliberations of Kubrick, Schelling, Peter George and Terry Southern led to the film "Dr. Strangelove", which I consider the greatest movie of all time.

=== 1961 (I was 23)

FANTASM STORY 1961: The shock insight crossing Cambridge Common

In a famous incident, Bertrand Russell was walking along tossing a tobacco tin in his hand, and while the tobacco tin was in midair, it occurred to him: 'My god, the ontological proof is valid!' (I don't think he held to that belief, but the event is a classic story among professional philosophers.)

I had the same sort of shocking insight as I was crossing Cambridge Common in early 1961. I don't remember if it was day or night, but I remember the shock.

It occurred to me: you could simulate photography by computer!

First I was thinking about cartooning by computer in two dimensions, and how you might represent that. [Many such systems exist today.] But my mind went on immediately to the next thought: could we do graphics in three dimensions? The equivalent of Puppetoons, photographed as if they were real?

And I realized that it could be done.

A half-tone printed photograph is made up of dots, I thought; we just have to find the color of each dot*.

───── COINED WORDS ─────
*I don't think the term "pixel" had yet been coined.

First you create a 3D scene as a computer data structure (I'd figure out how later), and place a camera inside that same 3D space (I'd figure out how later). Now, starting out from the camera lens, consider a line toward the scene at a specific angle in X and Y. Now look along that line from the lens into the scene, and see where the line hits. What color is it at that exact point? That's the color of your dot for the corresponding position in the picture.

Do this for each dot of the picture, at the appropriate X-Y angles from the camera, and you have a photograph of the imaginary scene.

It was SIMPLE! In principle.

(It would take me years to work out the details. It would be some years before I learned that anyone else was working on the problem. It would be twenty-three years before it was first commercialized— I think with the film "The Last Starfighter," in 1984.)

What would Isaac Asimov have said? 1961

I was at a party given by John W. Campbell in a Cambridge hotel. John Campbell himself, the editor of *Astounding* !* It was like a dream-- I was at a Campbell party! With Hal Clement and Isaac Asimov! Also present were Mrs. Campbell, an audio guy named Wayne Batteau, and myself. I asked if my friend Charlie could join us, and Mrs. Campbell said yes. I think that was it, just the seven of us.

> * Originally *Astounding Science Fiction*, the title of the magazine had just become *Analog Fact Ã Fiction* (I use the symbol Ã for a symbol Campbell had devised for "analogy").

It was like having gone to Heaven, or rather, what would have been Heaven ten years before, when I was avidly reading *Astounding* in my youth. How had I gotten there? Freed Bales, my faculty friend in the Soc Rel department, told me once was enough for him, and he passed the invitation on to me.

There we were in the front room of the Campbells' hotel suite. Campbell was holding forth, reciting his own old editorials from *Astounding Science Fiction*. (I recognized them, having read them nine or ten years before at the age of twelve or thirteen). Clement and Batteau were listening politely, but Asimov was extremely bored, conspicuously expressing his boredom by his posture.

I got a chance to speak to Asimov, I think by the dry bar, when Campbell had paused in his speeches.

I said, "Mr. Asimov, soon we'll be reading and writing on computer screens."

"Yeah, *sure*," said the great futurist. Sarcastically.*

>*And as it happened, Asimov was a late adopter. It is my understanding that he refused to leave his typewriter for a personal computer until Tandy gave him a TRS-80. To that machine he became loyal until he died.

"Soon we'll be reading and writing on computer screens," (Asimov, 1961)

In the early sixties I tried to tell everybody my vision--
   '**Soon we'll be reading and writing on computer screens.**'

That's as far as I got with Asimov.

Architects Calamitous

I moved out of the grad-students' dorm into a wonderful little cooperative. It had a blue door that said ARCHITECTS CALAMITOUS. (This was a parody of the Architects' Collaborative, also in Cambridge, run by Bauhaus alumni.)

It was an exceptionally happy atmosphere. We cooked by rotation, announcing the menu; you could invite as many people as you like, the cook would buy enough groceries on the day for everyone signed up, and you would be billed according to the number of your guests in the kitchen accounting. This facilitated many happy dinner parties with people from all over. (You could also snack freely– in the sense of free speech–, billing yourself for the value of whatever you ate, provided you did not snack from the planned dinner provisions.) The system worked amazingly well, social engineering at its best.

FANTASM TECH 1961: Simple scenes

I continued scheming at my system for simulated photography.

I saw the scene and the operations spatially, not mathematically. (My algebra was lousy, but my spatial sense was good.)

I knew from highschool algebra that you could find where one line intersects another.

Obviously this could be generalized: you could represent a plane in 3-dimensional space and find out where a line intersected with it.

That line could be coming from an imaginary camera. A grid of lines radiating from the lens of an imaginary camera, and finding the colors of the surfaces they hit, would make up the dots of a picture.

So all you had to do was represent the scene as a set of planes, and search from the camera-point (I soon called it a Vantage) to the scene. (Years later this would be called *ray-tracing*.)

Of course, a scene made just of planes wouldn't do. The objects would have to be curved, like objects in real life. But thinking first about planes was a start.

FANTASM TECH 1961: Triangles for curved surfaces

As I thought about it, I realized that you could break up any curved surface into triangles as an approximation. (Nobody told me.) Then the problem was to *curve over* the triangles to get the surface right, and find where each ray intersected the curved surface.

I fiddled about with diagrams and blundering algebra trying to find a function for curving over the triangles. (I called this a curvaceous function, or fairing-function.) Eventually I got it from a mathematician.

FANTASM TECH 1961: Lights were like cameras

I had a surprising revelation: cameras and lights were isomorphic! That is, the imaginary camera lens was a point source for rays through the scene; so was a point source of light! Except that the rays from the imaginary lens were exploratory, probing the scene for its appearance, and the rays from the imaginary light were illuminative, changing the brightness of the points they hit.

This knowledge didn't help my calculations a lot, but it definitely was inspiring.

FANTASM TECH 1961: The Flat Map

The objects in the scene had to have colors, but they could also have patterns of color. This could be represented a number of ways, by table or picture; whatever the representation, I called it a *flat* map. (Later others would give it the strange name "texture map".)

What would Henry Kissinger have said? 1961

While I was taking Schelling's course on strategy, he announced that a certain seminar in the Law School might be of interest, so I went there one afternoon. The seminar was given by someone named Kissinger, whom I don't think I'd heard of at the time. It was in the Roscoe Pound Room of the Harvard Law School, and we all sat around a huge oval table of blond hardwood—perhaps forty law students, Kissinger, and I.

(In my notes I believe I wrote: "Why isn't this guy in Washington?")

I don't recall the whole seminar, but there was an unforgettable exchange at the end.

A callow student asked in what I remember as a whiny voice, 'Why don't we just *assassinate* Castro?'

Kissinger replied drily: 'Led us zay, for moral reasons.'

The whole room broke up in laughter.

=== Summer of 1961 (I turned 24)

That summer I worked on a dreary sociology project at Harvard's Widener Library. I also wrote a draft of a Schematics book and studied enough statistics to squeak by at the Master's level.*

> * I bought a teaching machine, which greatly helped by reducing distraction and making it into small steps. That sort of thing that should be far more easily available to floundering students, especially those who hate math homework.

=== 1962 (I was 24)

Meanwhile, Back at the Department

It became clear I wasn't going to get a doctorate in Soc Rel.

I did not pass the prelims, nor was I offered a second chance. My crazed interests were known to everyone. I was not on their planet.

What would Herman Kahn have said? 1962

One of the places I applied for a job that spring was The Hudson Institute, a new think-tank concerned with issues of strategy.

Herman Kahn was there. I had heard Kahn speak a couple of times, and respected him in his craziness. David Riesman called him "the Danny Kaye of the arms race"*, but Kahn was looking at what no one else dared think about. Kahn talked about nuclear war in a chummy way, as if it were always present in the room, which it was. My fascination with general strategics had been honed sharp in Schelling's course and I was concerned with these issues as always, so I applied to the Institute.
* David Riesman, personal communication.

I don't remember the interview in particular. But I do remember a ride in Max Singer's little car. Singer was the head of the institute, and was driving. Kahn was in the passenger seat, and with his weight—perhaps three hundred pounds, perhaps more—the little car sagged far to the right.

Kahn kept making interesting assertions and conjectures on a wide variety of topics, estimating all sorts of numbers, and would always close the sentence with "figures on that order." How did he know? Ah, but that was the meta-gamesmanship of nuclear gamesmanship.

A key point about Herman Kahn: he was one of the few people who predicted that the Soviet Union would implode from its own internal problems. That outcome almost everybody. And his thinking contributed to everyone's facing reality about nuclear weapons. This may have helped Schelling put in the hot line.

Ca 1962
FANTASM STORY *What I called it first: Fanfasm*

I was going to call this my pseudo-photography system system "Fanfasm," named after a tribe in the Oz books. (In my notes I therefore gave it the tag FNF.)

When I tried to tell people about the system, however, they found the name "Fanfasm" challenging. I switched the name to Fantasm (with the tag FSM).

Ca 1962
FANTASM STORY *Puppets, that's what they were*

(I had loved puppets as a boy, and Puppetoons, which unlike Disney animation were photographic and thus, I thought superior.)

I thought of the characters in Fantasm as "puppets," even though they would eventually be realistic.*

COINED WORDS
* Later, someone else coined the wonderful word *synthespian*.

Chapter 8.
TO NO GOOD PORPOISE, 1962-3

=== Summer 1962 (I turned 25)

Porpoise versus dolphin, alligator versus crocodile—these are unimportant distinctions overemphasized in popular words. Porpoise differs from dolphin and alligator differs from crocodile basically in their teeth; the distinction hardly matters.

The main point most people don't understand is that porpoises and dolphins are small whales (technically, cetaceans).

The dolphins were wonderful, personable, boisterous, moody, loud. They were wonderful company and I loved them. But that is another story.

After my first day on the job I came back home exhausted, but I made a full page of drawings of all the things I had seen. I'll put that in a later edition if I ever find it. I saw more on that day than I saw in the rest of my time down there.

How I wish I could spend time on the atmosphere of the lab, the personalities of the different dolphins and us who held them prisoner. That is another story.

I had suggested various research directions to Lilly, but when I got to the reality of the place it became clear that hardly any of it could be done. So much effort had to go to keeping the animals alive, and keeping Elvar from pulling oscilloscopes into the pool, that there was scarcely any opportunity for research. In my year there I only saw one research study done (by Peter Morgane). But before I came, they had already discovered that the dolphins only sleep on one side at a time.*

> * This appears to have been rediscovered only recently.

The atmosphere at the lab wasn't great. Lilly was away all the time, and the person in charge was an extremely unpleasant woman. My bad relations with her started immediately.

It became clear that this wasn't going to be a career, it was just a job, but I was going to stick with it for at least a year as a matter of pride.

=== Fall 1962

Personal Systems
INTERACTION STORY
BIZ STORY

THE WALKIE-THINKIE

I was very tired of writing my notes on file cards. Knowing that personal computing was coming, the question was how I would get the notes in. The pile to be transcribed got higher and higher.

What I really wanted was to capture my notes in digital form the moment I thought of them. I wanted a portable keyboard. But it should be a one-handed keyboard, so I could use it walking down the street or holding on in a bus.

First I thought It should be a Morse code key, and so I learned Morse code. But then I realized it would be possible to type ASCII with one hand as a parallel chord, and that would be much better.

I called this idea the Walkie-Thinkie.

A bright highschool student, Richard Devore, wanted to work on it, and we had several meetings. I don't know if he could have done it or not. He was a swell kid.

──── A Note from the Present

I didn't know at the time that Doug Engelbart was doing the same thing, typing ASCII with a five-finger keyboard.

How I wish we had built that, half a million notes ago. There is now little hope of getting my notes into digital form. (The tekkies imagine that pattern recognition can read my writing, and that voice recognition works. These are myths.)

My design for the Walkie-Thinkie has gone through several variations since then. What's important is to use standard components, not fiddle with specialized hardware.

=== 1963 (I was 25)

~ MAKING MOVIES ~
THINKING ABOUT MY BREAKTHROUGH MOVIE, 1963

I was always planning my breakthrough movie, the low-budget feature that would get me backing for other movies (everybody knew the rules).*
I had a script working, meant to be comedy-exploitation, called I Was a Teenage Beatnik, but that morphed into the idea for a comedy-horror to be called I Was a Teenage Beatnik Twist Monster.*

> * Note that "Blair Witch Project," successful in theaters, was done for a budget of essentially zero-- shot with video cameras which they returned to get their money back.

Then a better possibility came along.

~ MAKING MOVIES ~
Starting the "Man and Dolphin" Film, Late 1962~3

I proposed to Lilly that we make a low-budget film under the title of his book, *Man and Dolphin*. The occasional romantic documentary shot in 16mm has worked in theaters: I was particularly thinking of "Kon-Tiki", a cheap film made by Thor Heyerdahl on his reckless Pacific voyage, which was insubstantial in footage but very successful in theaters. I figured on shooting a lot of closeups of Elvar and the other animals, of Lilly directing work, and a narrative that pumped up scientific hopes. People were fascinated by dolphins and a simple-minded little documentary could get distribution. I could do the whole thing with Bolex, Kodachrome, voiceover and cheap music from someplace.

We already had a Bolex Rex. This was a fine 16mm camera; I believe that the very successful "Kon-Tiki" had also been made with a 16mm Bolex.

Lilly was very interested and asked me to work out a budget.

I actually took a first shot for it—a pan across the lab, I think during a storm, showing the various oscilloscopes with jumping traces on their screens, and the grave expressions of my lab-mates. It was a clean, powerful shot and fully worthy of the big screen, I thought. I may still have it somewhere.

=== Summer 1963 (I turned 26)

What would David Crosby have said? 1963

Besides reading, my only recreation in Miami was going to coffeehouses, which in those days meant folk singing. There were two coffeehouses, owned by two brothers, and a dozen or so folk singers who worked both venues. (The term "venue" did not yet exist at that time, I believe.)

I went on with my banjo on one of the open evenings, and after a few appearances I was offered $10 a night, cash, as a "folk comedian". This made up for the lack of intellectual companionship, and put me into a circle of friends.

The singers were a warm group, led by a charismatic guitarist-singer named Vince Martin. The high point of the week was the final set, when all the folksingers would get onstage and sing "Guantanamera."

I got friendly with a thin fellow my age named Dave Crosby, who sang with a guitar. He bobbed his head from side to side as he sang, but his manners were more ordinary and macho offstage. (On a wild guess, I asked him if he were related to Floyd Crosby, the cinematographer; turned out he was his son. But Dave hated the film business and L.A.)

Dave and I hung out a few times, sometimes reading girly magazines side-by-side at the drugstore in Coconut Grove. On one occasion he gave me a copy of Heinlein's *Stranger in a Strange Land*, saying it contained great wisdom. I never managed to get through it.

— COINED WORDS —

I did, however, like the word "grok" which the book introduced.

One Saturday or Sunday, Dave came by my place with a friend. (I had a nice little two-room apartment above a garage.) I may have been crabby because my working time on weekends was so precious to me, and this social interruption knocked out my plans.

Dave and I had joked about nuclear war a couple of times, as boys do. But then he found Herman Kahn's *On Thermonuclear War* on my shelf. He gave me a very dirty look, as if the subject was okay to joke about but not to study.

Last I heard from Dave Crosby, word reached the coffeehouse that he was looking for a name for his new singing group. They later chose "The Byrds."

For all too short a time I had an illustrious office-mate named Gregory Bateson. Famed anthropologist and psychological theorist, he was exceptionally warm and pleasant. He smoked his cigarettes to very short stubs and swore frequently but charmingly in a way that American academics did not, in those days. "Oh, fuck! Fuck and damn!" he would say, most charmingly. His very wrinkled face may have had to do with the smoking. He and the Lillys once came to dinner our over-garage apartment (by this time I was married).

I wish I had known how little time I had with him. We had only a couple of conversations. I once spoke of Margaret Mead, his ex-wife—"Oh, Margaret!" I remember him saying, with great enthusiasm for her.

What would Gregory Bateson have said? 1963
COINED WORDS

Bateson and I talked about words: I think we talked about the famous phrase Bateson had coined, "double bind". He told me his father had also coined an interesting word: "metamerism", meaning the biological multiplication of successful units, such as the segments of a millipede or centipede, or the scales of a fish. (Bateson did not mention that his father also coined the word "genetics".)

I wanted to talk to Bateson about my interest in social strategics, and I spoke very carefully because I venerated him so. 'It seems to me,' I said, 'that greeting behavior is essentially a gateway procedure that changes the context of an encounter into a different social state.'

"Of course," said Gregory Bateson.

I think he left CRI shortly after that, and I had no further chance to talk to him, which I greatly regretted.*

> *There is a footnote. The famous phrase "A woman without a man is like a fish without a bicycle" originated with my great friend Charlie Harris. It started as "a man without faith is like a fish without a bicycle", and I put it in one of my musicals at Swarthmore. Charlie has traced the history of the phrase after that; apparently the line went from Bateson to Herb Caen to Gloria Steinem, who switched it to "a woman without a man."
>
> I think it will have been I that passed the phrase to Bateson, as a link in that immortal chain.

=== Fall 1963 (I was 26)

~ MAKING MOVIES ~
movie editing
The Dolphin Sex Movie, 1963

Partly to test my movie-making ability, Lilly asked me to edit some amusing footage for a conference. It showed our two adolescent dolphins in sex play: Elvar splashing around in the tank with an erection and Cheechee putting up with it, possibly teasing him. Actual intercourse did not happen in the footage. Elvar was also a showoff, rolling his eyes at the camera throughout.

I edited it down to about a minute and a half. It took a long time. Lilly said to call it "Mating Behavior of Tursiops Truncatus," which was a rather grand title for such sparse action, but I edited the film and put the title on.

Because of the conference deadline, I worked on it for something like thirty-six hours straight. (For me, the art of film editing consists of trying to get the transitions really smooth, and it takes a lot of time.)

I ran it for Lilly. "Where's your name?" he asked. He said to give myself an editing credit, which in this setting was hardly important but I think part of his wanting me to motivate me to make the feature. I shot the title and spliced it in. Getting the title developed and spliced in took several more days.

Public Events

Living in Miami, I experienced the Cuban missile crisis at first hand (seeing missiles on trucks and feeling the fear all around). Later, Debbie was with me when Kennedy was shot. Not to mention these events out would be absurd, but there's no room to discuss them further.

~ MAKING MOVIES ~
DEFINING MOMENTS
The End of the "Man and Dolphin" Movie, 1963

I think it was Saturday afternoon that I took the finished dolphin sex movie to the office and went straight to bed. But the phone rang almost at once. It was the nasty lady who ran the office. 'Dr. Lilly wants you to take your name off the film,' she said. 'You put it on without authorization.' I told her that Lilly had explicitly told me to put it on; she said I was lying.

I got out of bed, went and did as I was told, and handed in my resignation at 8 am the following Monday.

In the exit interview, Lilly asked me, "What about 'Man and Dolphin'?" I just shrugged.

This was the first of the times I was too angry to negotiate. I am sure that if I had told Lilly what had happened he would have tried to make the movie happen, and get the nasty lady to lay off me. But I so hated the woman in the office that I figured it was impossible, and I just wanted out of there.

It was a huge mistake. Out of rage, hatred and impatience, I threw away a really clean career shot. It might not have been a feature, maybe just a half-hour TV item, but it would have been the start I wanted in movies.

Transition

I married Debbie, a lovely and warm young woman I had known at Harvard, and moved back north.

The Turnip Shop

By now I had a van, a Ford Econoline. (I have never understood why people want conventional cars rather than vans.) We packed in all our stuff—including my heavy books and notes—and headed North for Christmas. The cartons reached within four inches of the ceiling.

Bad luck: we drove too long and too late. We almost stayed at the "South of the Border" motel between the Carolinas, but because the price was high we kept going. The price was going to be much greater.

Debbie was driving when the van hit ice on a bridge and began turning sideways. "Just steer!" I shouted. We slide sideways into the center strip and flipped over—Kabump. Kabump.

We were hanging upside down from our seat belts.

A cop came and called a tow-truck; we watched our heavy-laden beast being pulled away. That night we slept in the jail with the door open, with very dirty pillows.

The next night, Saturday, we stayed at a motel, but no one warned us that there was no place to eat on Christmas eve in St. Paul's, North Carolina. All we had were candy from vending machines and some grapefruit we'd bought as we drove through Indian River, Florida. However, that grapefruit was delicious.

The van was resting at a place called the Tune Up Shop. On Monday a nice man came from Allied Van and we made the arrangements with him.

He was to pick up our stuff at the Tune Up Shop, but for some reason he wrote on his form as the starting point, "The Turnip Shop". This was charming.

Debbie and I took the bus north and joined Jean and Pop at the farm. The Allied Van came later with our stuff.

Not understanding the ways of insurance, I chose to "total" the van I loved—meaning they would supposedly pay what it was worth– instead of having it repaired, which they would have done. Huge mistake. I got back a measly sum, much less than the vehicle had cost, and was stuck with awful cars for the next five years.

~ MAKING MOVIES ~
Ralph's Breakthrough Movie

I had not expected it. Ralph was always tightlipped. You never knew what he was planning or thinking (except I learned to see it coming when he was going to attack).

I had him pegged as a *television* director, more of a military role, as in the extraordinary night where I had seen him talk the cameras through. I thought *I* was going to be the movie-maker, working in a different medium where you built piecemeal, taking shots over and over one at a time. But then, in the fall of 1963, he unexpectedly broke through into the movie business with a hit feature, which he had not told us he was going to do.

"Lilies of the Field" was heartwarming and a bit silly, but everyone likes it. It was a huge hit partly because it broke taboos, showing a black hero among white women, involved charming people, and had singing without quite being a musical. It was a feelgood movie with an interracial subtext, which was very clever of him. The movie made a lot of money, and suddenly Ralph was a Hollywood director.

········ A Note from the Present
In the ensuing 25 years Ralph Nelson would make some twenty features. But that is another story.

Chapter 9.
POUGHKEEPSIE ERA, 1964-8

Debbie and I moved in with her father, who lived in a big house on the edge of the Vassar campus. She had a wonderful family. When her two sisters came there was constant merriment. Her father, L. Joseph Stone, was an eminent child psychologist and the nicest possible man. He was also a film-maker, creating a wonderful series of movies on child development.

I taught sociology briefly at local colleges. Then, of all things, a job opened up at Vassar, teaching sociology.

The little Nelson family, sweet while it lasted, Christmas 1965.

=== Fall 1964 (I was 27)

The Hall of Euthenics

My office was in a building called Blodgett—officially, according to a plaque, the Minnie Cumnock Blodgett Hall of Euthenics.

Coined Words

The plaque further explained that Ms. Blodgett, the donor, foresaw Euthenics as the science of right behavior, just as eugenics was the science of right reproduction (or so they thought in the 1930s). Since "eugenics" was by now a discredited point of view, I found this a doubly silly and doubly amusing word.

The Vassar girls were painfully attractive but fun to teach. I worked hard to prepare my courses and the students enjoyed them.

Now, it is traditional among sociologists that the fun of teaching the introductory is in shaking up impressionable young minds and making them question all that is shallow, conventional, pompous and smug. I did that.

Especially the cynics among them, some of whom went on to major in Sociology.

------- A Note from the Present

I was told later that while I was there the number of students planning a major in sociology went up (I think by 50%); after I left it fell back to the previous level.

Tall Dogs

My first conference was at Watson research labs, in 1964. Watson labs were south of Poughkeepsie, not too far, and I guess I got the invitation from some IBMer I had met.

I think the conference was called 'Linguistic Data Processing,' or the like. It was my first chance to meet computer people on a collegial level.

AI Bullshit I

It was at this conference that I first became aware of AI bullshit, that is, the exaggerated claims that Artificial Intelligence people have always been making. Let me make it clear that I have the highest regard for the achievements of Artificial Intelligence;[*] it is the false claims and naïve wild extrapolations that have always pissed me off.

[*] E.g. heuristic search, neural networks, genetic programming. The greatest simple demonstration of AI in action is Karl Sims' little film "Evolved Virtual Creatures," on the net.

I was not about to be intimidated by these guys.

When somebody said to that voice-recognition was right around the corner, I was dubious. I had heard the songs of a vocalist named Little Richard, who supposedly sang in English, my native tongue, and I could not decipher a single syllable. I had no doubt that voice recognition would someday be practical, but I did not know when and was not about to hold my breath.

I made one friend at that conference, a linguist named Martin Kay, who was at the Rand Corporation. We talked about the problem of character-sets for different languages. (Eventually I sent Martin Kay a full photocopy of Dr. Seuss' book *On Beyond Zebra*, wherein the good doctor proposed such new alphabetical characters as Yuzz, Fuddle and Quan.)

FANTASM STORY Sherry Amott's puppets (~1964)

I had a student at Vassar named Sherry Amott. In one of my classes I must have mentioned my Fantasm system, with my optimistic hope that it would be ready in a few years, and how realistic such puppets would become, actors in the films of the future. Sherry came up to me and said she loved puppets and would like to design puppets for the system. I said that was great, I would love her help, but I couldn't say when.

-------- A Note from the Present

Sherry Amott, after graduating from Vassar, went on to a distinguished puppet-designing career that included designing Muppets for Jim Henson.

Sketches showing conjectured inputs to Fantasm for 3D image synthesis. Both methods are now employed throughout the industry (although puppeteering has become 'body suits'. (Slides from author's talk at Union Theological Seminar, 1968.)

 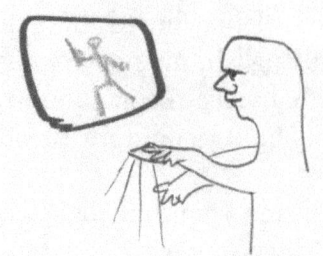

I took to visiting the local IBM rep in Poughkeepsie from time to time. When I told him I had been to a conference at Watson Lab, his eyes widened. "They've got some tall dogs down there," he said.

I marvelled at this example of corporatespeak.

DESIGN INFLUENCES: Paolo Soleri, when I was maybe twenty-seven

Paolo Soleri was like Frank Lloyd Wright and Corbusier and Bucky Fuller -- all wanting to improve our lives with new structures and ways of being. But unlike those others, whose constructions were stark and cold, Soleri's, designs, like those of Dalí, looked organic. He wanted them somehow to *be* organic, but had to guess imaginatively at what organic forms of architecture should be.

His experimental communities of Cosanti and Arcosanti, in Arizona, looked beautiful, and I heard that Soleri had no shortage of female volunteers. Perhaps that was the business to get into.

CINENYM STORY
movie editing

EDITING MOVIES BY COMPUTER, 1961~4

I don't remember when this occurred to me, it might have been as late as 1964: it was now time to edit movies by computer!

Videotape machines were now controllable electronically; but editing had to be by footage numbers. People were still punching in numbers, this was ridiculous. Why not link it to the script and to the logging—the written lists of what's in each shot?

My approach was simple: TAKE THE TEXT SYSTEM AND LINK IT TO THE VIDEOTAPE. This was fairly trivial. Choosing among multiple takes, and fine-adjusting, would be done by light-pen.

I worked out the details.

=== 1965 (I was 27)

-------- A Note from the Present

WHERE TEXT SYSTEMS WERE THEN

The reader may have a hard time imagining how it was in that distant past.

In 1965, five years since my epiphanies, I had still heard no one else speak of reading documents on computer screens. (Actually, this was an arcane field being funded by the Department of Defense; I would soon find out two labs that were doing it.)

Almost nobody then—and I talked to hundreds of people-- could imagine what interactive computer screens would be like. Almost nobody now can imagine what the world could have been like without them.

DEFINING MOMENTS
Philosopher's Holiday

At Vassar, the word had gotten around that I was doing something with computers that was innovative, exciting and radical, and everyone was interested. In early 1965 I was asked to speak in a lecture series called "Philosopher's Holiday," which was held once or twice a year. Apparently this name meant it was a lecture setting where a philosopher could let her or his hair down.*

> *Cf. the etymology of "Plato's Retreat," later.

The talk was advertised by a remarkably portentous handout signed by three Vassar faculty members, indicating that it was going to be very important. I have never seen such a notice before or since, at any college or university, anywhere.

On the day, Blodgett Auditorium was packed. Hundreds came. Everybody on campus wanted to hear my radical new ideas, or at least say they had been there. I believe it was standing room only.*

> *A review of this talk, by my student of that time Lauren Wedeles, is on the web. I even have a tape of the talk somewhere.

I simply said what I always tried to tell everybody, except that they gave me 45 minutes, so I could say it much better.

I told them that the future of humanity was at the interactive computer screen—that everyone would have computer screens, so that meant we would be reading and writing on computer screens.

Unfortunately I'd discovered that nobody could imagine what a "computer screen" might be, let alone a *responding* computer screen, no matter how I explained it.* To help them visualize the concept I showed the Sketchpad film from Lincoln Lab. Then I explained that we would be able to access documents interactively across the world by digital transmission, and that I was designing a system for non-sequential reading and writing.*

> *Because of my background I had instantly gotten the concept from a picture or two, and for years could not get over the idea that it should be a snap concept for anybody. But by 1965 I had learned that most people needed far more help. The Sketchpad film, narrated by Larry Roberts, was the best thing I could find.

The people filed out very quietly.

Vassar's remarkable invitation to the author's first talk on his software designs, written by the author but framed by august endorsements of the Science Club's faculty members. Note that the word "systems" was put in quotes by them.

Note also that the contents of the talk, as described, still represent the author's views quite exactly.

VASSAR COLLEGE

January 5, 1965

```
TO:       Members of the College Community
FROM:     Faculty Science Club
SUBJECT:  Lecture on Computers by Theodor Nelson,
          Instructor in Sociology
          8:00 p.m. Wednesday, January 27 - The Aula
```

The Faculty Science Club is pleased to sponsor the talk described below for the benefit of all members of the College community interested in learning more about uses of the computer in the academic environment.

COMPUTERS, CREATIVITY, AND THE NATURE OF THE WRITTEN WORD

No special background is necessary to understand this; indeed, "special" background may well be detrimental.

Everybody's misimpression of electronic computers -- a misimpression peculiarly acute among "computer people" -- continues to restrict the general use of computers to essentially numerical tasks. Inherently these machines have far broader capacities; the limits are not of technology, but of imagination.

This talk will first describe the structure and generality of the stored-program digital computer. The computer is NOT mathematical: if it is the most perfect adding machine, it is also the most perfect typewriter, electric train control, filing cabinet, movie projector, and musical instrument. But whole new attitudes will be needed, and liberal-arts personages will have to learn to program, before computers can make their real contribution to civilization.

The speaker will describe his own experiments in this direction -- trying to build "systems" for the handling of creative (and academic) materials -- ideas, words, and other things. A succession of approaches, and their increasing generality, will be explained.

The philosophic consequences of all this are very grave. Our concepts of "reading", "writing", and "book" fall apart, and we are challenged to design "hyperfiles" and write "hypertexts" that may have more teaching power than anything that could ever be printed on paper.

Please feel free to invite any interested students.

Sue Lumb, President
Robert Rehwold, Vice-President
Stanley Novak, Secretary

No one on the Vassar faculty ever spoke to me again.*

    * Except my father-in-law, Joe Stone, who could not avoid speaking to me, and who I think was terribly

embarrassed by this public exposition of what he considered to be my delusions. 'He thought you were crazy, Ted,' says my former brother-in-law, Maurice Eldridge.

COINED WORDS

This was the first time I publicly used the word *hypertext*.

What would Vernon Venable have said? 1965

Just recently (2009) I ran into Jeanie Venable, who in 1965 was the teenage daughter of Vernon Venable, head of Vassar's philosophy department. She remembers what he said when he came home from my big "Philosopher's Holiday" talk—the first talk I ever gave on my ideas. Vernon Venable said of me that day:

"He is brilliant.

"He is a madman.

"He is way ahead of his time."

But like everyone else on the Vassar faculty, he did not talk to me about it.

What the hell, I had been used to ostracism since boyhood. At least the ideas were now on record, as well as the word 'hypertext'; some day they would all know. Those who were still alive by the time it all caught on.

Articles Accepted

I had heard academic publishing was hard. No such thing! I submitted papers to several conferences and they were all accepted, only one requesting modifications ("peer review"). I talked to my two reviewers on the phone—one had an Indian accent, as I recall— and they requested some changes, calling my paper "very exciting".

That was the big paper, to the ACM 20th National Conference, the top of the field. I made the changes.

The most important acceptance was for the ACM National Conference, in Cleveland. As I was writing the paper, I kept making changes in my design.

Monday, Monday

I was revising my submission to the ACM, with the noodles of text all over the diningroom table at Joe's, on a Monday, and, as it happened, listening to the Mamas and the Papas singing "Monday, Monday" when the call came.

CUT -- AND -- PASTE -- -- -- -- -- -- -- -- --

> The user must be able to maintain different drafts of the same work.
> The system would provide spin-off ~~facilities over time~~ *facilities*, allowing a draft to be preserved while its successor was created. Moreover, these alternate drafts would remain indexed to one another, so that the user could compare their different parts, ~~regardless of how~~ *however* he might have changed their sequences.
>
> Three particular features, then, would be specially adapted to useful change. The system would be able to sustain changes in the bulk and block arrangements of its contents. It would permit dynamic outlining. And it would permit the spin-off of many different drafts, either successors or variants, all to remain within the file for comparison or use as long as needed. These features, taken together, we may call evolutionary.
>
> The last specification, of course, was that it should not be complicated.

Excerpt fom the noodle draft of the author's big 1965 ACM paper. At the time he was apparently using fully-clinched staples, a mistake.

As I was rewriting the draft, news came to me that Edmund had died. He was 92 and had been an inspiration to many and everyone loved him.

It was a punch in the gut but I had to keep on.

(The design of the software I proposed– zipper lists– confused people, and now I see why. It combined a number of my concerns into a clumsy structure.)

•XANADU TECH
My 1965 Design, Quite Bad

I realize now that my design of 1965, the ELF or Evolutionary List File, was strange and hard to understand. In fact, it was quite bad.

I was trying to reconcile two things:
- units of text
- correspondence and side-by-side comparison between documents

Indeed, it was very like my first thinking of 1960, where the idea was for one file card (a unit of text) to be in two different places.

It was still my 1961 design, not well thought out. It was just text units on chains, with sideways links or transclusions between the units.

------- A Note from the Present

The ELF design was fairly useless and incomprehensible. I can say now with embarrassment that it was a very bad design, perhaps my worst ever, but at least it got me prestigiously published.

And yet it led in two directions—
- to the proper Xanadu designs (it had transclusion, though my other defining paper of the time did not)
- to multidimensional irregular list structures (hyperthogonal structure, or ZigZag).

In other words, somehow it represented different structural concepts deep inside me that were later clarified separately. This is one of the Mysteries of Life.

READER CAN CHASE FOOTNOTE TO ITS SOURCE CONTEXT

TRANSCLUSION IMPLIED. Slide from my oral presentation to the ACM, Cleveland, 1965 (not in the paper as published).

=== Summer 1965 (I turned 28)

DEFINING MOMENTS
Real Downtowners, August 1965

My big talk in Cleveland, presenting before the ACM, was the biggest moment in my career.*

> * This is sometimes called "starting at the top." The problem is that it can be downhill from there.

The ACM 20th National Conference was held in Cleveland, a place considered a hick town by New Yorkers like me. The hotel in Cleveland had a sign in the elevator advertising their restaurant: 'Real downtowners eat at the Clevelander Grill,' or whatever it was. The notion of being a Real Downtowner, the Cleveland ideal of a sophisticate, was most amusing to a New Yorker.

But the people who came to my talk were indeed real sophisticates. I believe that most of the computer scientists in the world were there that day (scarcely possible now). In the air, we all felt the importance and primacy of what we were doing. I counted the seats in the auditorium before it spoke—I think there were three hundred, and they all seemed to be filled when my talk began.

In the oral presentation I did not read the paper or give technical details. I showed colorful sketches with captions and changed the slides quickly. My slides were punchy. The last three slides showed the word CHANGE, getting bigger and bigger.

There was enormous applause.

(For years, people would occasionally tell me they had been impressed or inspired by my presentation.)

What would Bob Taylor have said? (1) 1965
DOUG AND ME ———————→

Right after a big conference talk there is usually a break, and people come up to talk to the speaker.

I had just given my big talk at the 1965 ACM conference; I believe most of the computer scientists in the world in the room, and many have told me since that it influenced them strongly. The last slides said CHANGE, CHANGE, CHANGE—to indicate that users would have ever-changing projects that needed deep support software.

Bob Taylor came up and introduced himself. He was a little older than I, with a crew haircut and dark suit; he said he was with ARPA. (I knew that ARPA was funding a lot of basic stuff.)

Taylor asked me if I'd heard of Douglas Engelbart. Engelbart, he said, was also working on interactive text systems with screens. (I had thought I was the first; only now did I know there were two of us.) Taylor did not tell me that he himself was Engelbart's principal sponsor.

What would Steven Furth have said? 1965
What would Bob Taylor have said? (2) 1965

That night, after my big talk, there was a gathering with drinks, and I happened to be with Steven Furth of IBM and Bob Taylor. We talked on various subjects. Then Furth asked me, "How come you know so much?"

I didn't know how to answer; Bob Taylor answered for me. "He reads," said Taylor laconically.

(The Actual First Hypertext Paper)

While the ACM paper of August 1965 was my really major paper, I had already published a definition of hypertext elsewhere, in D.C., at a conference of the International Documentation Federation (FID, I believe, at that time).

"The Hypertext." (In full.)

Proceedings of the World Documentation Federation, 1965.

> THE HYPERTEXT. Theodor H. Nelson, Vassar College, Poughkeepsie, N.Y., U.S.A.
>
> We are at an historic divide like that created by movable type. To supplement movable type came such further inventions as the footnote, preface, magazine, bookshelf and editor. The technology of automatic display, stored-program computers and bulk information storage call now for a like range of inventions and conventions: display modes, organizing arrangements, and academic and professional roles and practices that will give us the most from these new devices.
>
> This paper proposes a new medium, the hypertext. This is a generic term for texts (and combinations of texts with other materials) which, because of their structure, require automatic handling and display devices. The hypertext will typically be non-linear, branching, and large, with various options to the user.
>
> The idea of the hypertext is distinct from Information Retrieval (specialist dissemination and query search), Information Display (presentation of data desired in a known context) and Programmed Education (restricted-sequence presentation and drill.) None of these fits the general case. The hypertext is suited not just to specialty materials (which fit on paper nicely), but to give general reference and instruction. It may contain a corpus of general and special materials, with their many interconnections indexed. Arbitrary boundaries of subject matter can be ignored. Hypertext may be built out of existing writings, not mechanically heaped but personally assembled, according to considerations of showmanship and pedagogy. Like any anthology, the hypertext may contain interrelated texts and information from diverse original sources. It may also contain summaries and abstracts written at different levels, permitting separate entry to users of different backgrounds, competences and interests, allowing them to pursue such details or overview as they desire. A hypertext system could provide instant lookup of definitions, biographies, or explanations. It could have new types of graphic material (moving or mnemonic), ways to show relations (indexes, footnotes, marginalia), even of browsing or reading (e.g., stroboscopic). Discursive, conceptual and general-purpose, it will permit self-education according to interest and motivation, even exploiting natural curiosity and intellectual gumption, which so often hinder conventional instruction.

The FID didn't typeset-- they photographed what I sent in-- so I crammed in extra text with narrow line spacing.

My Box of Crayons, 1965

My slides were not tekkie-looking, with neatly ruled squarish boxes and arrows and neat stenciled letters. They were free-form, done in crayon and black marker, in my swash hand-lettering, and shot with my Exakta.

I tried to convey, in these slides, how computer screens would look—where you would put messages, how users would respond, what would twinkle.

Slides from my first ACM presentation, surprising to many, obvious now.

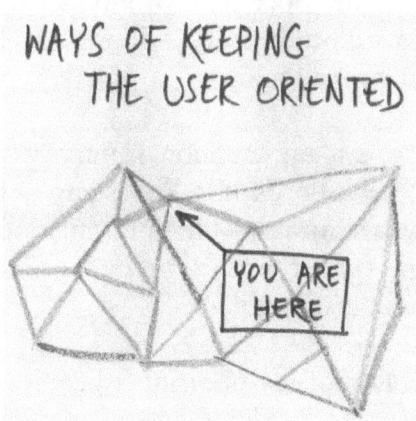
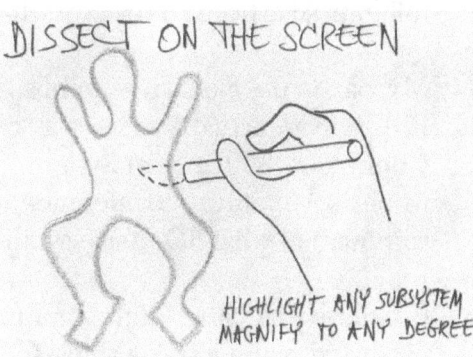

People had not imagined what I predicted on the screen and told me, at various times, that they had found my slides very inspiring.

I just thought I was saying the obvious, but it meant a lot to others.

One slide in particular from my ACM presentation was darkly accurate, predicting the cacophony of today's jangling, competitive web pages. I think it was the first illustration that showed a profusion of competing, colorful choices on a computer screen.

I believe no one else had imagined in those days that we would be doing more than one thing on a screen, or that people would intentionally distract us.

Unfortunately, because all my papers were accepted immediately, I got overstretched in writing them and preparing them for printing.

FANTASM STORY Space-ships, dinosaurs and SMPTE (1965)

Among the flight of papers I published in 1965 were two "preprints" for the top movie technical society (SMPTE, the Society of Motion Picture and Television Engineers). They were supposed to be followed on by full journal articles. However, that went wrong (below).

My paper on Fantasm— published just as a presentation summary, an IOU for an actual paper— was called 'Realistic Pseudo-Photography by Computer: the Fantasm System.' It was a summary of the presentation I would give at the conference. However, it was a pretty accurate summary of what 3D image synthesis has become today.

(I believe that either in the oral presentation or the preprint I specifically predicted realistic space-ships and dinosaurs.)

However, the presentation was not very good. I don't think I managed to make slides for that one. I got a volunteer from the audience, and simulated ray-tracing to the tip of his nose with a string. It didn't go over well.*

> **2:45**   **#28**
> **Realistic Pseudo-Photography by Computer: The Fantasm System**
> THEODOR H. NELSON, The Nelson Organization, Inc., New York
>
> The Fantasm system is a new alternative for motion-picture and video-tape production. Instead of using the customary scenery and actors, imaginary animated scenes are created with a computer system and photographic film or video tape. This system's output is indistinguishable from ordinary photographs of real people and settings. Scenery, props and actors are created as required. Since the system can produce its own traveling mattes, its contributions may be used to supplement conventional production in foreground, background or both. Sculpture and puppet theaters are used for easy modeling and smooth manipulation. In the production system, "roughs" will probably be made on video tape before going to more expensive high resolution on film. Cost parameters for everything can be completely controllable through the choice of resolution or deletion of material. The objects are stored in the computer only as coordinates of surfaces, color descriptions and other parameters. By appropriate manipulations and calculations, however, the system will handle curves, shadows and specular reflections. All systematic departures from realism can be eliminated.

The author's summary of his plans for a 3D imaging system, to be called Fantasm, from the 1965 SMPTE preprint. (The actual paper was not published, partly due to the death of the SMPTE editor.)

───── COINED WORDS ─────
* The term 'ray-tracing' did not yet exist, at least publicly; I don't know what I called it.

BIZ STORY --

Despite my cynicism, in those days I still expected some kind of Horatio Alger backer to come to technical talks and spread his checkbooks. The Fantasm presentation got, instead, a grumpy reception.

However, Victor Allen, the editor of the SMPTE Journal, was eager for me to publish full papers of both. This would have been a very good thing. Unfortunately, Allen died before I could write the paper. Not only did I lose a friend, but a great opportunity.

The Vasty Deep

> *Glendower.* I can call spirits from the vasty deep.
> *Hotspur.* Why, so can I, or so can any man;
> But will they come when you do call for them?
>   Shakespeare, *Henry IV Part I*

Here is what I wrote in my big ACM paper:

> "The ELF* could help us understand the interrelations of possibilities, consequences, and strategic options. In a logically similar case, evaluating espionage, it might help trace consistencies and contradictions among reports from different spies."
>
>   * Evolutionary List File, my name for the Xanadu design of that time.
>
> -- Theodor H. Nelson, "A File Structure for the Complex, the Changing and the Indeterminate." *Proc. ACM 20th National Conference*, 1965. (Refereed.)

This was not a random musing. I was jiggling bait where I knew fish lurked. The intelligence agencies had money and flexibility of operation; it might be a low-red-tape way of getting backed.

Just a couple of weeks after my big Cleveland presentation, I got a call from a guy identifying himself as head of information processing research for the Central Intelligence Agency, and would I like to talk about working with them?

This was the approach that I had invited and trolled for. What a frisson, what sense of power in the world, it gave me. I could indeed call spirits from the Vasty Deep.

He suggested we talk about working together.

Soon, weeks or days later, he came to our house in Pougheepsie! It took me thirty seconds to reach the door, but already he was turning away. Stern, these fellows.

He came in and we chatted at length.

He said his organization could sponsor me through a university, or, if I wanted, through a corporation. This was my preference. I had always wanted my own setup, and I hated university red tape. We chatted about their setting me up with my own corporation for hypertext research; I was willing and eager. This was what I wanted: to bypass university politics and hassling within conventional corporations; to go straight to a company of my own!

Now, many readers will wonder why I, as a certifiable (but not recognizable) idealist, would consider working with the Central Intelligence Agency, an organization with certain dark doings in its past.

The answer was simple. Why not turn some of their money to good deeds? And I liked to play with fire.

He said he would put someone in touch with me.

=== Fall 1965 (I was 28)
To the Real Work

From then on I let Vassar slide. I had knocked myself out with course prep and done a good job, but obviously it was time to get to my principal endeavor, which Sociology was not. I taught my courses from the previous notes and got to work on patents and trying to raise money.

CINENYM STORY

THE PROPOSAL TO LESSARD, 1965~6

I had given a paper about video editing with computer controls at SMPTE, but no one in the industry had responded.

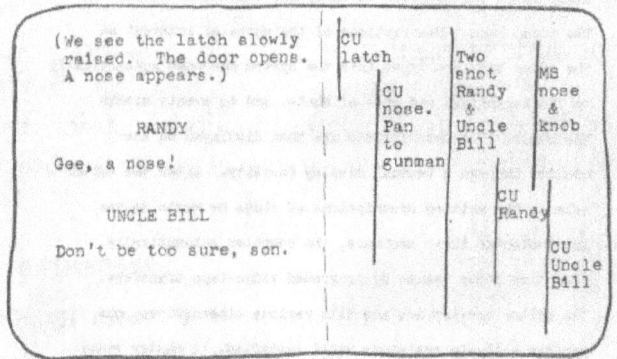
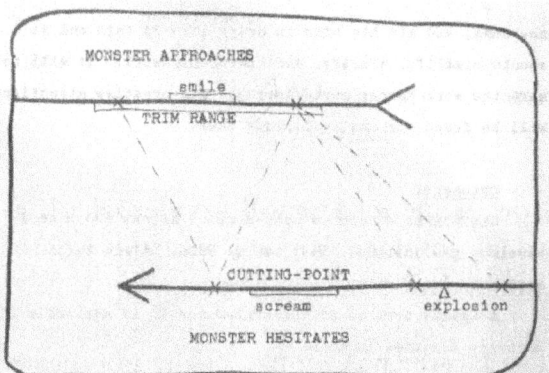

Visualizations of the Cinenym interface. (From "A Complete Computer-Based Editing System," preprint of the SMPTE national conference, 1965.

I asked around. Who in the video industry might be interested in developing my computer-based video editing system?

I was told that a fellow named Lou Lessard, at a company called Teletape, was the most forward-thinking guy in the industry. I called him up. He was friendly, said to send a proposal. I sent it and heard nothing.

After a couple of months I called Lessard and asked what had happened.

He said, 'I read the first two pages and went cold all over. Then I put it in my drawer for a month.'

By and by he showed it to his company; they looked at it and decided it was impossible. The "Engelbird Mouse" in my proposal (that's what they called it) was one of the things that sounded too wild to them.

FANTASM TECH ca. 1965: My god, mantles exist in *Nature!* [edge of Vassar campus]

I was thinking about a combination of ray-tracing and list management for managing complex scenes and lights.

In my notes, I used the term "mantle" for the illumination from a given light in a scene. The light struck the nearer surfaces, and would drop off from edges of the earlier surfaces to other surfaces further on. (Keeping track of these dropoffs with list-processing software was part of my design at the time.)

Note that since lights and cameras are geometrically the same, you could have a mantle for the surfaces facing a light and a mantle for the surfaces facing the camera.

Anyway, one night I was walking home. Walking along the edge of Vassar campus, I looked at the shadows of the trees in the hazy night. The edges of the shadows were visible as they dropped from one illuminated surface to the next.

'My god, *mantles exist in nature!* I thought.

'Mantle' was my private term for the surfaces facing a camera, then the dropoff from edges to the next visible surfaces. I was planning to manage this by a list-processing method, keeping track of where surfaces led to other surfaces.

=== 1966 (I was 28)

Crying on the Right
DEFINING MOMENTS
INTERACTION STORY

Now that I was published, a few computer people took an interest in me. I think I went to both Lincoln Lab and Mitre Corporation. Both of these were shadowy semi-secret outfits— buildings with very public exteriors, but just what they *did* was secret. A lot of what they did had to do with Command and Control, i.e. missiles and warheads.

However, I knew that much defense R&D had more benefit to the public as to defense—for example, Sketchpad, Ivan Sutherland's great prototype graphics system, the granddaddy of all sketch systems today, was paid for by ARPA just as if it were a missile system.

I believe Larry Roberts showed me Sketchpad at Lincoln Lab, though I've seen his little Sketchpad movie so often I may be confusing that with the experience itself.

Then I visited Mitre Corporation.

Don Walker, at Mitre, was a kindly older man (like maybe 50). He was warm and avuncular. I think he understood my position and my feelings— I was not like the people he worked with, in defense research or engineering; I was a young idealist excited for the future and its possibilities and eager to get something going.

We sat down at his screen system, which he'd worked on for several years. It was not a secret system and he had published papers on it. (I vaguely recall that it was driven by a Stretch, the biggest computer at that time, but that could be an incorrect memory.)

This was the first time I had ever sat at a computer screen. I had gone afire in 1960 when I saw pictures of computer screens– a few pictures of SAGE and air traffic control systems and the PDP-1. The only text screen I had seen live was a text console at the Tall Dogs conference at IBM Watson lab (IBM had bought it from a company named Straza), but that was all. I had not sat at a computer screen or touched one with a pointer. (It may have been a day or so previous that I had seen Sketchpad, but I had not actually touched it.)

I sat down beside Don Walker at his system.

The system had two parts, called OakTree and Oak-Treet; I have no recollection of what those parts were. It was a system for exploring documents organized as tree structures. I didn't argue.

It was a line-drawing system, showing simple diagrams of lines and text pieces (which I think it drew as individual lines). They trembled because each part was being refreshed by the CPU on a low-resolution screen, and it was a big system only by standards of that time.

He let me hold the light pen.

And I started dragging the images on the screen—scraggly lines and paragraphs, as I recall.

It was a moment I had anticipated for six years. I was manipulating text and graphics on a screen!

And it was *JUST THE WAY I'D IMAGINED!* Rougher and shakier, because of the refreshment method in the systems of that day, but I had been right.

I had known all along how it would feel.

I had been right all this time.

A tear came to my eye. The years had not been wasted. Or so I thought.

But because I did not want Don Walker to see me cry, somehow I manage to control it so the tear came only from the eye on the right, the one he couldn't see.

What would J.C.R. Licklider have said?   ca. 1966

I went to see J.C.R. Licklider, whom everyone called Lick. He was extremely warm.

"Will there be one hypertext, or many?" he asked.

That stopped me. I had to think. I think I said both.

The answer, of course, is that we can think of a given hypertext (created by an individual or team) as one hypertext, but then all the hypertexts unite, conceptually, into one grand hypertext, comparable to 'the whole of literature'.

Crossing the Eagle, ca. 1966
BIZ STORY --
CIA STORY --

Sure enough, the CIA sent me a handler* named Bob. (Of course, I was never shown credentials. Anyone could do a scam claiming to represent the CIA. You could base a comedy-thriller on this.)

Bob was a jolly fellow. Bob called me and said I should come to CIA headquarters in McLean for a visit.

> *Joke. A handler is someone who deals with a field agent, not a potential contractor, which I was.

I drove down to D.C. in our VW bus. I don't recall where I stayed. But the next morning I went to the big building in McLean. Yes, I walked across that great eagle's head inlaid in the entrance floor, and what a frisson it gives.

Mainly it was an office building. Bob introduced me to some researchers in one of the offices. The atmosphere was pleasant in the room. They had a remarkable way of carrying coffee-cups: on a disk-coaster that had three strings going up to a handle. Surprisingly, the coffee did not spill, even if you swung the cup. (I do not know who discovered this or on what research contract. I'm surprised it hasn't shown up in the novelty/airmall catalogs.)

But the guys in the room were AI guys, and I sensed again the competition between AI and hypertext. (To me they always seemed unrelated, but that's competition for you.)

We took an elevator down to lunch. Everyone wore badges that had a number and their picture but no name; the men had their badges on clips in their shirt or jacket pockets, the women had them on chains around their necks. The cafeteria was a huge room holding many people with many badges, many Special Forces guys, many dirty looks for me (my hair was long then, and long hair meant a lot ideologically in those days).

Bob and his friends asked me for a proposal. I departed with handshakes all around.

=== Summer 1966 (I turned 29)

CINENYM STORY
movie editing

CINENYM PATENT APPLICATION, ca. 1966

It was my first patent application. My friend Robert Fiddler, a patent attorney, advised me on the disclosure and claims.

I described how the editor of movies (or videotape) would use text to select shots, according to shooting record and loggings of the footage. This would of course be followed up by detailed back-and-forthing, as with ordinary movie editing.

I had expected to be able to follow through on the office actions, but I had no money to do so, and let the patent application lapse. This was not the last time this would happen.

-------- A Note from the Present

As far as I know, nobody has yet arranged the retrieval of shots by text description. A mystery to me.

BIZ STORY --
Just One More Proposal (1966~72)
CIA STORY --

I had sent a first proposal to Bob at the CIA, in 1966. (Actually, to his home; that was they way they did things, I was told.)

Then Bob asked me for another proposal, and then another. $10,000, or $50,000, or whatever, was just around the corner, he would say. He kept calling me and kept asking for just one more proposal (at one point he said there was $50,000 just waiting for me). On one infuriating occasion he said that a criticism of my last proposal had been 'Wherever you say hypertext, you might as well say gobbledygook.' This pissed me off but I kept sending in that one more proposal, one more proposal, till I think around 1972.

-------- **A Note from the Present**
* When the CIA finally commissioned a hypertext system, over a decade later, it was simplistic and one-way. I believe I would have given them— and the world— a much better one.

The Rattling Teacup

William Jovanovich, the president of Harcourt, Brace & World Publishers, was a king. He was regal in manner. He conducted his business like a king. His office was a throne room.

It wasn't a corner office, but it had a lot of window area and Vasarely paintings (I later learned) on the wall.

I told him some of my computer and hypertext ideas. He asked me if I would be interested in working with Harcourt, and the teacup, in its saucer, chattered in my hand. (So corny! Couldn't put that in a movie.)

Suddenly I was a commuter.

=== Fall 1966 (I was 29)

DOUG AND ME ⟶

Doug Senses My Hope: Mouse and Skateboard at SRI, 1966

Jovanovich and I flew out separately to California. He wanted to meet someone at Stanford about computer-assisted instruction. I wanted to meet Douglas Engelbart and see a real screen-based text system, which I had so far only imagined.

I think I went out a day early, giving me a free day to see Engelbart before the Stanford meeting. I had been in the Bay area once before, but never before with a car, and it was an amazing experience. I think I stayed in Palo Alto, at a wacky motel shaped like a castle. Next day I went to Doug's Lab at Stanford Research Institute.

The atmosphere there was very happy. Doug's warmth was obviously a major factor in what held the lab together.

They showed me editing and linking. His system, NLS, was controlled with a little alphabetical language, and was hierarchical. This was the opposite of the swooping kind of interface and non-hierarchical structures I favored, but I was there to learn.

Doug showed me his new pointing device, the mouse. Until that minute I had assumed we would be using light-pens, or putting a pistol-grip on a light pen for comfort and machismo. But Doug and Bill English (who had built the thing) showed me their little box on two knife-like wheels, and how easy it was to use, and I was at once persuaded. Okay, it'll be the mouse, I figured.

The mouse was for one hand. For the other, Doug had a little one-handed keyboard with which he typed straight ASCII—exactly what I'd planned to build with Richard DeVore in Miami three years before!-- except this one wouldn't work surreptitiously in your pocket. This made me more determined to get my portable unit.

Someone else in Engelbart's group* showed me another new invention—the modern skateboard. It was not like the skateboards I'd seen in New York as a boy, which were the front and back of a metal-wheeled rollerskate nailed to a board with a wooden vegetable-box as a sort of handlebar. That one didn't steer, and it had all the skidding problems of the metal wheels.*

> * Doug tells me lately that the skateboard enthusiast was a guy named Smokey Wallace.

But this skateboard was a something new. They had taken soft high-traction rubber wheels out of a Xerox copier—wheels whose friction pulled the paper along—and put them onto a skateboard board, with mountings that steered by tilting. (The New York skateboard didn't steer, except by pushing it sideways.) This skateboard was entirely new.

I was convinced. I had always wanted a portable vehicle. I had tried spring-shoes as a boy and a unicycle in graduate school, in hopes that it would be convenient. It was not. Now, Smoky assured me, the skateboard would be everything I wanted in a portable vehicle.

I believed him.*

> * Later, at the age of forty, I took up skateboarding and found that it was not practical, any more than the spring-shoes and unicyling which I had tried with similarly high hopes. What is really needed was a bicycle that folded into a dispatch case. That was a spec I had come up with in high school.

I asked Doug about a possible job. Doug said what he needed right then was a programmer. Probably I should have bluffed my way into the job and tried to learn it as I went, but I didn't.

Also I did not like the fundamentally hierarchical structure they had at Doug's lab. I hoped to do something entirely different, with Jovanovich's sponsorship. It seemed within my grasp.

'Doug senses my hope,' I wrote that day on a diary card I found recently.

DEFINING MOMENTS
Stripes in the Universe

The next day after I first saw Doug, I think, Jovanovich and I went to Stanford to visit Richard Atkinson.

Atkinson was a professor of psychology, collaborating with Patrick Suppes on Computer-Assisted Instruction. They had a whole scheme for how computers would teach kids. Indeed, they had had a cover article in the *Scientific American*. Here was their scale of "education"—
- "drill and practice" (rote drill, which was important and reasonable)
- "computer-assisted instruction" (telling and testing, telling and testing— requiring large-scale flowcharting of instructional plans)

- "Socratic instruction." This was thought to be the ultimate in quality education, where the student would type questions as whole sentences and get back answers as whole sentences.

I had no objection to the first two, but I always considered conversational interaction with the computer to be an absurd objective– what a waste of time and programming effort! Wasting time and effort to give the computer a pretend-personality is a misleading and annoying intrusion, particularly since the user then has to try to figure out what is *really* going on.

What would Richard Atkinson have said? (1966)

In his Stanford office, with Jovanovich, I tried to tell Atkinson about hypertext. "We don't know how to do that yet!" was his reply.

Richard Atkinson was the most pig-headed man I have ever met. It was utterly impossible to get through to him. I tried to tell him about hypertext, but he kept shouting me down.

"We don't know how to do that yet!" he would roar. I tried to tell him how to do it, but he wouldn't let me say a word.

Presumably he thought I was talking about Socratic systems for CAI— systems that would dialogue with you, answering specific questions. So here was a man ostensibly trying to create dialog systems for teaching-- dialog, simulating mutual communication, right? Yet it was utterly impossible to get through to him.

I tried repeatedly to get through to Atkinson with the hypertext concept, but he would not hear of it. Atkinson's agenda was to make a pitch to Jovanovich, and I was a young staffer getting in the way of his pitch, to be kicked aside.

Then Atkinson said, "Of course, I get all my ideas from Jack Parcheesi". And he named my nemesis at Swarthmore, the guy who wanted to impose his ideas without discussion.

OF COURSE!

The "Of course" which I think Atkinson put at the beginning of this sentence, was the maraschino cherry on top. OF COURSE!!! Of COURSE you get all your ideas from Parcheesi! YES! THERE ARE STRIPES IN THE UNIVERSE!*

> * I believe the phrase "stripes in the universe" came to me at this moment, referring to hidden commonalities, like the connection between

Atkinson and Parcheesi, that only show under accidental polarized light.

If anything validated my ability to find connections, this was it! I had found a connection no one else could know-- this made me a true nexialist! I had uncovered a brotherhood of aggressive don't-listen academic jerks! If I had had the slightest doubt of my ideas and intellectual directions, this moment of truth vindicated them all. I had won my stripes. In the universe.

-------- A Note from the Present

It is interesting to note that Richard Atkinson has only recently retired as president of the University of California. His impenetrable, single-minded belligerence must have served him well, taking him to the top of that vast educational nation of grantsmanship, politics, hundreds of thousands of students and thousands of faculty.

BIZ STORY ---
The Personal Software Industry, 1966-70

I had met only one person who also imagined a personal software industry. He was Calvin Mooers, a mild-mannered man who had also presented at the ACM 20th national conference. He had a language called TRAC(R), which he rigorously trademarked. He expected everyone to learn to program in TRAC.

I did not think most users would program, but TRAC was potentially more accessible than most computer languages for the kinds of personal software I wanted to create-- it did not require compilers or development environments, just a small interpreter, and its structure was simple.

-------- A Note from the Present
I would have later adventures with TRAC, which was well-suited to text terminals.

I was not aware for several years that TRAC was isomorphic to LISP. However, the LISP manual, which I'd bought, was absolutely opaque, and LISP was cultish and closed, being the property of the AI guys on their mountaintops.

Mooers and I spent many hours on the phone discussing the future software industry. I believe that in the nineteen-sixties, we were it.

Both of us were strong believers in copyright as the principal means of support for creative people. He also instructed me in the use of trademark as an inexpensive and powerful tool available to the low-budget developer.

We talked about issues of software sale and possible software piracy, and how to prevent copying. (I believe we came up with several of the schemes that eventually came into use, including tweaked disk drives and the dongle, though not under that name.)

However, at this time neither Mooers nor I had any access to a computer, let alone a functioning language processor. (That access would come later through a surprising route, a kids' club.)

But we were preparing for the new world.

=== Summer 1967 (I turned 30)

Power Lunch with Leverage, ca 1966
BIZ STORY --
Creative Control -------------------------
DEFINING MOMENTS

Some business guy took me to lunch in Manhattan. I took along my annotated copy of "As We May Think." I had found it only in 1964 or 1965, and realized it was the closest thing to my ideas. I had covered it with notes.*

> * I do suspect my family read it out loud from the *Atlantic* when I was eight, and that I saw the reprint in LIFE a few months later, so it may have implanted itself in my psyche those decades before. But there is no way to be sure.

I learned a lot of things from that Businessman. I heard for the first time the slogans "A rising tide raises all boats'" and "Good ideas are a dime a dozen"—a statement with which I heartily disagree.

He talked a lot about Leverage (which he couldn't define). I learned about going public, and buying public shells, and making a bigger and bigger company by acquisitions. It sounded very heady.

I asked him about creative control. He said the secret was to own 51% of your company.*

> * I later learned this was very, very simplistic.

I showed him the Bush paper. He asked to take it with him to show to his technical guy, an Israeli, and said he would return it. Reluctantly I parted with it. 'We'll let you know you if it's valid,' he said. In a pig's eye, how would you or your guy know? I thought.

Of course he never returned it. I wish I knew what I wrote on that paper, since it probably expressed the core of my ideas at that time.

So that day I learned a lot of business fundamentals.

I learned a different perspective: that backers have their own agenda, and someone with a project is merely an accessory to that agenda, a temporary insect on a tangent, to be used, discarded, squashed– or worse, redirected– at whim.

But my most important lesson of the day was this: many businessmen don't just want money or advantage. **THEY WANT TO TAKE AWAY WHAT IS MOST IMPORTANT TO YOU.** The guy didn't want my annotated paper because of what was on it. He wanted it because it was important to me, and taking it away gave him pleasure. It was a hard lesson but a very important one.

XANADU STORY
The Xanadu Name at Harcourt (October 1966)

On the thirteenth of October, Jovanovich okayed the name 'Xanadu.' Tears came to my eyes. He also approved the drum for the 338 and a second console.

We were going through the budget for my project, which would be DEC-based. It would be a honking big PDP-8 with a 338 graphical system, which was the hottest graphical computer at the time.

However, I underestimated the forces that were gathering against me.

The guy who headed the computer department at Harcourt did not want any computer in the company that was not under his control: it was a serious threat. And his friendly IBM salesman was very much on his side, not wanting a DEC machine in the building.

I had been far too open about my plans.

The Dark Brown Project (1960s)

Note:

I have written to the presidents of Brown University and the Association for Computing Machinery, requesting an ethics hearing on how I was treated at Brown University in the 1960s.

Predictably, both parties declined. However, the story in this book is complex enough already, and I will let that chapter wait for a future edition, if any.

ORIGIN OF THE BACK BUTTON, 1967-8 The author's only widely-deployed software
design is the BACK button, now on every web browser.

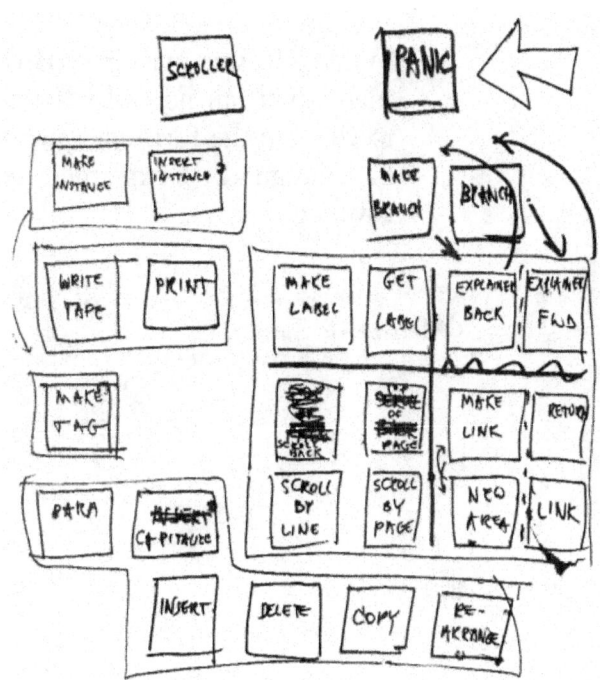

The author persuaded the HES group at Brown, with some difficulty, that a series of addresses on a stack, plus a BACK (and FORWARD) button, would be help hypertext users travel around (such traveling was not yet idiotically called by the nautical term 'navigation'). Multiple windows on a screen were not possible at that time-- -- indeed there were only a few hundred interactive screens in the country; the BACK and FORWARD buttons were a simple way to jump around. They still are. (This was not a screen menu but a proposed layout for the button-box of the IBM display.)

This illustration by the author somehow made the concept more plausible to the team. (Note that "LINK", on the right, means "jump on link", and "RETURN" is now called BACK. There is no FORWARD button here.

This illustration includes certain ideas by others which I disagreed with and hoped would go away, such as "Branch" and "Explainer", but it was a game attempt to unify them. I also wanted to represent forward and back by screen controls, and keep them off this menu, but that was rejected.

(The illustration could also be called "controls for the first hypertext browser," except that "browser" meant something entirely different at that time.)

=== Fall 1967 (I was 30)

FANTASM TECH ca 1967   Fairing-function from Strauss

While I was visiting Brown University, I met a mathematician named Charles Strauss. I persuaded him to give me the formula I needed for the fairing-function I had designed. I explained exactly what I wanted and he gave it to me.

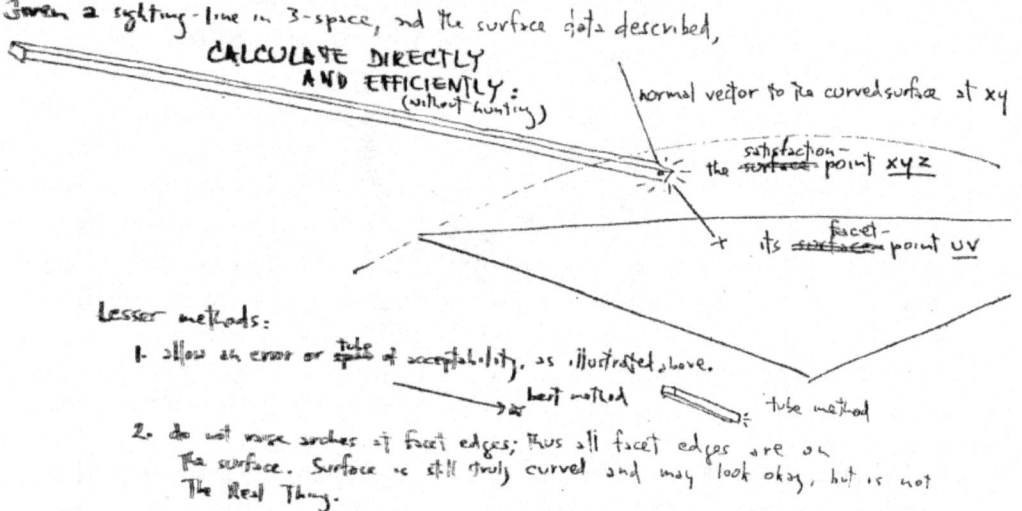

Fantasm fairing process (ray-tracing on bubbles automatically generated over triangles). I worked it out as the spatial mechanism shown; Strauss set up the formula for this process in algebraic form for the patent application.

My Box of Crayons, 1967

YOU WANT METAPHORS? While the author dislikes 'metaphor' thinking in software, he proposed it in this 1967 slide.

Chapter 10.
CONSULTING ERA, 1968-72
=== 1968 (I was 30)

Debbie, my son and I moved to New York City-- a little apartment on West 20th St. at Tenth Avenue. I think the rent was $150 a month. (Nothing like the long palatial apartment Jean and Pop had gotten for that amount 25 years earlier.)

Learning that I had fallen behind on the Fantasm project, I went berserk.

FANTASM STORY 1968: The Utah pix

I think the first work I saw on 3D images by anyone else was in 1968. It was some pictures by guys at the University of Utah.

I had a huge sense of loss and falling behind. I think I threw a chair.

This would be only the first of many such experiences.

Work and Family

I could not manage being with a family and moving forward in my work.

She, reasonably, wanted a Nice Life; women want that sort of thing. Whereas my life was all about my ambitions, and trying to get leverage and my own setup for the work I wanted to do. I realized I was desperately losing ground.

We agreed to part.

They moved out. It was an incredibly sad moment, taking them on the bus to Grand Central.

(I went to see my son whenever I could, and Debbie has been a friend and great support all these years. She did not understand the ideas in detail, but all these years she believed in me.)

"Soon we'll be reading and writing on computer screens," late 1960s

In the early sixties I tried to tell everybody my vision--
    'Soon we'll be reading and writing on computer screens.
    'And there'll be new forms of publication for the screen.
    'And you'll be able to call up any document out of millions.
    'And everyone will be able to publish in this new medium.
    'And there'll be many new kinds of connection among them.
    'And you'll be able to see every quotation in its original context.
    'And you'll be able to quote without limit without permission.
    'And there'll be an automatic royalty to each author for the part they wrote.'

In the late 1960s, people would frequently reply--
"Is it like a tape?"

I had no idea how to reply. I should have just said, Yes.

FANTASM STORY ca.1968: MAGI visit

I was visited in my apartment on 20th street by a guy from MAGI (Mathematical Applications Group, Inc.) They were doing computer movies with 3D synthesis. He showed me their technical papers, which looked fascinating.

He said he was going to leave me the papers but he did some sleight-of-hand at the end; the papers he left had no technical content. I don't blame him. He saw me as a rival, and, at the time, so did I.

FANTASM TECH 1968 MAGI's system

The MAGI system was based on constructive solid geometry— that is, they represented basic shapes (like spheres and boxes) and added and subtracted them. This supposedly made the ray-tracing of the scene more efficient.

Because their system had begun with the intention of modeling nuclear radiation and its hazards, their method of scene representation was quite special. Their system is of lasting theoretical interest because it combined geometrical construction with ray-tracing.

My Box of Crayons, ca. 1968

I made a slide representing 'the computer of tomorrow'—a sort of smiling octopus attached to CRT, keyboard, mouse and loudspeakers. (At that time the tekkies imagined the computer future as structured database queries.)

As I recall, people thought this sketch was incredibly radical, but just possibly an imaginable wild future.

It was, I believe, the first depiction of what the personal computer turned out to be.

1968 sketch by the author, conjecturing multifunction personal computer. Box in center is the computer. Clockwise from top: screen, speaker, pushbuttons, input dial, postal scale, piano keyboard, input tablet (mouse would have been too hard to explain), more pushbuttons. The usual text keyboard is omitted for emphasis. Postal scale and piano keyboard meant to stand in for arbitrary

hardware that would become available. (Slide from author's talk at Union Theological Seminary.)

About six years later they started building computers like this at Xerox PARC.

The Iphone? (Slide from author's talk at Union Theological Seminary, 1968.) Keyboard and microphone are shown attached to camera.

What would Vannevar Bush have said? ca. 1968

I believe I read Bush's "As We May Think" when it came out in 1945-- twice, indeed; first in The Atlantic, which I think was read aloud around the Saturday lunch table at our farm; and then when it was reprinted in LIFE. (Since I was eight when it came out, there is no knowing, but my family subscribed to both magazines and the article was certainly on my wavelength.)

In the Vassar days of the mid-sixties, as I stepped up my computer reading, I found the article cited repeatedly in the artificial-intelligence literature, to which it was supremely irrelevant. But I cited it in my foundational hypertext articles, and it became the semi-official Beginning of the Hypertext Field.

In 1968, I think it was, I was at the Spring Joint Computer Conference in Boston. I got a handful of change and picked up the payphone and simply called information. Vannevar Bush was listed in some Boston suburb. He himself answered the phone.

I told him I was working on ideas similar to his memex and would like to get together with him to discuss it on some later trip.

He wanted very much to discuss it with me, he said.

But I hated him instantly. He sounded like a sports coach. I knew I would not follow up, even if I managed to get to Boston again.

I am very sorry now, of course.

=== Summer 1970 (I was 33)
The End of Art

I met with the curator of the show. He grandly that the show would be The End of Art. I am still not sure what he meant. I think it had to do with the Art World, which is a dense community of strange art endeavors and back-biting. I met a number of these people and still don't understand their thoughts or the world they live in.

The show was called "Software." It was supposed to chart the impact of computers and "software" (in some grand new metaphysical definition) on the art world. Centerpiece was to be a PDP-8 computer, donated by Digital Equipment Corporation. I believe it was going to have an 8k memory and a 640k disk, something like that; it was the lab workhorse of its day. To the best of my recollection it had a list price of $64,000.

Unfortunately the PDP-8 delivered by Digital was a lemon and nobody could get it working in time for the show. It was the end of art in a way that had not been intended.

What would Nicholas Negroponte have said? (1970)

Nicholas Negroponte and I were both preppies and liked to wear blue shirts with a white collar and a necktie. There the resemblance ended. In 1970 we worked together on the "Software" show at the Jewish Museum in New York City.

"You shouldn't design your house, you should have the computer design your house," he said, in some conversation.

This pissed me off. It went against my religion (human creativity, among other things) and I took him for a con-man, since there existed no such system, nor would there for the foreseeable future. Since then we have had a somewhat abrasive relationship.

At that time Negroponte was in architecture. However, I wrote a piece called "The Crafting of Media," which was in the catalog of that art show.* I think it may have switched his line of endeavor from architecture to media, and thus indirectly created the Media Lab.

* A scan of the article is an appendix of this book.

=== Fall 1970 (I was 33)

What would Thomas Kuhn have said? ca. 1970

I met Tom Kuhn under very unusual circumstances. I was getting advice from an extremely bright group of computer-savvy kids, who unlike stuffy adult computer scientists would listen and consider what I said, and they were very smart. One, John Levine, was a particularly good adviser; at sixteen, he were near professionals, working on Princeton's PDP-6 on their own processor for the TRAC language.*

> *John and Peter are successful professionals now; John and his sister Margy and Carol Baroudi wrote *The Internet for Dummies*, and Peter has a company offering circuit-simulation software. Lauren has had a number of professional positions, especially as a communicator, in the computer field. Nat, the black sheep, got a PhD in mathematics and then became a psychiatrist.

Nat, the most amusing member of the group, was twelve, but a very bright twelve, and we exchanged a lot of banter. I told my girlfriend of the time about him. "What did you say his father does?" she asked. "He's an historian of science," I said. "You know that book on your bed-table that I lent you?" she said. It was indeed The Structure of Scientific Revolutions, Tom Kuhn's central book.

The Kuhns had me to dinner.

Thomas Kuhn had been a Junior Fellow at Harvard, an honor I had yearned for. Junior Fellows get a full stipend and Harvard privileges for three years, with two requirements: they join the group for lunch once a week, and they not work toward a degree.

I said, 'You know, it has seemed to me that the careers of former Junior Fellows could be summarized in one sentence.' I reeled off names-- I think Skinner, Chomsky, Birkhoff, William Foote Whyte, and others I was able to remember at that time.

Tom Kuhn put down his knife and fork and stared at the GOD BLESS OUR PARADIGM sampler on the opposite wall for what seemed like several minutes. It was an intense moment. None of us spoke.

"I can't think of a single counterexample," said Thomas Kuhn.

That gave me comfort for not having been a Junior Fellow. I did not intend to be a person whose career could be summed up in one sentence.*

> * However, a couple of years later there would be a stunning counterexample, a former Junior

Fellow, economist and Marine who risked his freedom to expose the truth and end the Vietnam war, one of the greatest men of our time-- Daniel Ellsberg. That's still one sentence, but he deserves far more.

XANADU STORY
Xu70: COMPARING TWO VERSIONS

In New York alone, I worked out a full Xanadu design. Let us call it the multistream design, though it also goes by the name xu70.

It was a software design, I think rather elegant, for comparing two versions on screen.

It used parallel streams of data.

XANADU TECH

xu70, STREAM-BASED—
with two versions side by side

In working out the details of 1970 Xanadu, I came up with two ideas---
• Streams pointing at each other (zip structure)— with content in one stream, pointers in the other
• Ways of moving streams through memory compactly.

But this multistream design wouldn't generalize. I saw it as a dead end for what I really wanted Xanadu to do. (However, it was better than conventional methods, for text, and Zip design would be used several times more.)

I called this method Zips because it was an adaptation of the zippered list method from my 1965 ACM paper.

Xu70 used the Zip method, I think for the first time— with streams of pointers pointing at streams of text.

~~XANADU~~ ~~TECH~~
BABBLING IN BEDS:
Content Rolling through Ring Buffers

My multistream design was based on refreshing the screen out of the original content (I had argued for this at Brown.). Now, however, it was at one level of indirection-- transferred to ring buffers (given the problems of Direct Memory Access and memory allocation).

RING BUFFERS
I was obsessed with ring buffers at the time. There were several parallel streams in the design, and they would roll through the ring buffers without jarring displacements in core (we didn't say "RAM" in those days). When you allocated a ring buffer to a stream of text, it would stay in that particular closed location; there would be no surprises about memory allocation.

Since we were dealing with text streams, I called the buffers "beds" and the process of moving the stream through the bed "babbling". In the countryside, streams babble through beds, right? And of course the individual portions of content in the stream were called "meanders"—that's what a portion of a river or stream is called, right?

I was enamored of this method. I had gotten excited about the idea and realized it could be applied to streams in several dimensions.

Babbling in Beds

In 1970, as I worked on my xu70 design, I was fascinated by moving streams of data in and out of the computer. I called this "babbling" (because streams babble). Real-world streams babble through beds, so wouldn't a data stream babble through a bed (my playful word for a ring buffer) as well? And why would these terms not apply to the multidimensional streams I'd worked out?

I thought this terminology was very funny—as funny as the ideas they described were exciting.

One night I explained this to my date, an intelligent and lovely ex-nun. The next morning she left me a sweet note:

> *May you babble in bed in all dimensions.*

Had I talked in my sleep?

=== 1971 (I was 33)

XANADU STORY
JOT story
INTERACTION STORY

THE FIRST WORD PROCESSOR?
(The Jot Box™, 1971-2)

In 1971, I think, a friend introduced me to a young man who said he was interested in backing me. I shall refer to him as M.T. Flagon. He said he was interested in helping me because the project sounded good for humanity.

He was unctuous in a way I did not like, and our relationship was strained, but I think he was sincere, at least up to a point.

My plan was this: to create a text system for authors that could be built up to the larger Xanadu system. We would add the hypertext connections later.

I proposed to create a stand-alone text-editing system, the Jot Box, that would allow you to edit a big document on the cassette tape.

The term 'word processing' did not exist at the time, but that is what this system was going to be.

XANADU STORY
Actually the point was to move ahead with a Xanadu implementation, but the way to do this was to create a saleable product that would actually have the Xanadu internals.

I persuaded Flagon that we needed to buy a machine we could develop on. Then, having the machine, we could give demonstrations on it and sell our software package.

I believe our Jot Box would have been one of the first stand-alone word processors to get to market. (Wang Labs did not deliver their first successful stand-alone word processor until 1976.) But this is a conjecture.

JOT would have been easy for authors. Underneath, we would be building the Xanadu system.

What made it possible: MASS MEMORY ON A SMALL MACHINE, AT LAST!

At last you could get a small computer with big storage! A little company was packaging a storage system that would hold millions of bytes—this had never been possible. The whole package was just $10,000, payable to the company that hooked them together (call them Cass-O-Matic, I forget the name).

That was the first mass memory under a hundred thousand dollars, as I recall. Or maybe twenty thousand. These year-to-year differences grow dim.

•XANADU TECH

Cass-O-Matic offered a Nova computer hooked to a Sykes digital cassette drive, with their own cassette operating system.* It came with the Algol language, which was small enough to work on this setup.

* 16 bits and 16k of memory, as I recall. Small, huh?

To be a saleable product, though, it would have to be a text system for authors, which I called JOT (Juggler of Text). I intended that the system would work smoothly and feel comfortable to use.*

* See 1978 endorsements by Mark Miller and Jonathan Post of the smoothness of the JOT interface.

And an author would be able to work on a very big document. My ringing challenge was: 'Edit *War and Peace* on a cassette! This was of course impossible in everybody else's mind, because of the way that text was conventionally edited* (and is still). But with great care I knew it could be done, and that was my intent.

> *Bring it all in, swap it around, then read it out again. See Bill Duvall's vindication of the method, 1978.

This required completely different approaches to text handling from what was conventional. Others told me this was crazy, "That's not the way you edit text internally." I was used to hearing this sort of thing and paid no attention.

~~XANADU TECH~~ A Note from the Present

The standard approach to text editing was, and is, to bring the whole document into fast memory—in 1971 that was still called core, not RAM—and allow the author to rework the order of its bytes.

Then the document is written back out to storage.

In the Xanadu approach, used by JOT, newly-typed material is permanently stored in mass memory, and the document is edited as pointers to the stored material.

(See Bill Duvall's validation and endorsement of this internal method, 1978.)

CAL DANIELS

Working for Cass-O-Matic was a swell fellow named Cal Daniels, who knew the system well. He was a soft-spoken, warmhearted programmer– 29 (as I recall), tall, black. We got together and he agreed to moonlight on the Jot Box project with me. To avoid conflict of interest, and possible loss of rights, I asked him not to work on machines belonging to Cass-O-Matic.*

> * I have since conjectured that he probably did try it on their machines, and perhaps the software actually worked, but we will probably not know.

The language that was supplied with the Cass-O-Matic was Algol, which was an unusual choice, but certainly doable.

I would drive to Cal's place in Queens and we would go over the algorithms and improve them. In answer to his questions I kept making adjustments.

JOT story / INTERACTION STORY / XANADU STORY

THE JOT INTERFACE

Unfortunately the computer setup from Cass-O-Matic came with an all-caps teletype, a big clunky thing; to put a proper Selectric typewriter would have raised the price, perhaps another thousand.

But I figured I could design a smooth interface that writers would want to use, EVEN ON THE TELETYPE. Then we could worry about better peripherals, as the price went down.

If I were to prove myself as a software designer, this was where I had to really deliver—to make this system smooth and easy to use.

The problem had several levels--
- what would be the simplest and cleanest functions?
- how would these feel easy to the user?
- how would we show it?

I worked many hours on the design, making diagrams, thinking, imagining. I often wiggling my fingers with my eyes closed, testing how the system would *feel*. (Many say this is impossible.)

JOT TECH

THE PRINCIPLES OF THE JOT INTERFACE

The JOT interface design had a few basic ideas:
- the system would use as few control keys as possible
- the user would step through text using the space bar—a word at a time, a sentence at a time or a paragraph at a time
- there would be no input command; you would just type a word wherever you were (this is now standard, but wasn't then)
- capitalization would be automatic at the beginning of a sentence; the user would only have to capitalize names (permacaps)

- the system would be optimized for constant rearrangement, which authors need

I worked many hours on the design.

JOT TECH - - - - - - - - - - - - - - - - -
HOW CAPITALIZE AUTOMATICALLY?

Obviously this would not work on ordinary textfiles. The system would store all text as lower case except the permacaps, and a sentence division would be recognized by two spaces. This was the typist's convention of those days, so it made perfect sense.

JOT TECH - - - - - - - - - - - - - - - - -

LOLLIPOP NOTATION

I had never heard of state diagrams, but I figured them out. I flowcharted the entire system as a state diagram in a notation of my own, which I called Lollipop notation.

For every possible keystroke there I drew a lollipop (a circle with a vertical line below it).

The circle at the top held character received from the user (but not yet echoed). To the left of the lollipop stick you listed a set of conditions which would have an exact consequence. To the right of the lollipop stick you said what to do in each case. (Sometimes this included an echo of the character typed, sometimes it did not.)

It worked very nicely both for organizing the design and for communicating with Cal.

Lollipop notation might work interesting for object-oriented programming, but I'm not going there.

JOT story ---------------
INTERACTION STORY ─────────

THE FINAL JOT INTERFACE DESIGN: CREAMY SMOOTH?

I won't get into details here, but I was certain, as I finalized the design, that it would feel creamy-smooth to the user.

Alas, I would not be able to prove this until ca. 1977-8. (See testimonial by Mark Miller and Jonathan Post, 1978.)

=== 1971 (I was 33)

What would Laurens Hammond have said? ca. 1971

In 1970 and 1971 I drove a cab part time in New York City, a part-time occupation many artists have taken.* I thought I would enjoy it because I love driving in Manhattan, but the hard part was finding fares, and that was not fun.

> *On BBC, I think, I heard this anecdote: composer Philip Glass, well known but not yet prosperous, was driving a cab in New York to make ends meet. One customer said to him, "Do you know you have the same name as a famous composer?" He played dumb.

One sunny afternoon I pulled up at the Plaza Hotel and an amiable old man got in. He just wanted to go three blocks east to third avenue for a doctor's appointment, he said. Fortunately it was around five and traffic was slow, so there was time to talk.

"You look like an interesting young man," he said. (I had my Page Boy haircut, down to the collar.) "What do you do when you're not driving a cab?"

"I'm an inventor," I said.

"I used to call myself that," he said genially. "Have you heard of the Hammond Organ?"

I couldn't remember his first name. "Are you... Mr. Hammond?" I asked.

'Why yes,' he said.

The Hammond Organ had been explained in my highschool physics text—simply polygonal wheels spinning past induction coils, yet making a lovely sound. I told him how much I admired the design—the beauty that came out of such a minimalist structure.

He was pleased that I knew. 'But I didn't start out to invent an organ,' he said. 'I used to make clocks. They were synchronized with the line current by polygonal wheels, and I had a patent to show I had invented it. Then someone infringed, and I sued, and it turned out that had been invented in Germany the year I was born.

'So there I was, stuck with a lot of little flat-sided wheels.'

His warmth, and his shining example, left me glowing after he had left the cab. What a wonderful example of the Lemonade principle—If you're stuck with lemons, make lemonade; and if you're stuck with polygonal wheels, build a glorious musical instrument.

(At the time of this cab ride I didn't even remember the clock that had to be started by turning a flywheel. I had rented a room off campus in 1956, just go get my paper written in the quiet, and it had this unusual clock. Just plugging it in would not start it, you had to turn a wheel. So as not to keep looking at the clock I set it to running backward. It had said HAMMOND.)

FANTASM STORY 1970-1   *The Fantasm patent application*

Staying at the farm with Jean and Pop, I wrote an application for my Fantasm system.

By this time I knew there was a lot of competition and that my chances in the area were growing slim.

I no longer remember what my reasoning was for pursuing the patent application. There was actually no longer much point in continuing, since I had little chance against the others who were doing similar work with backing and equipment.

However, I wanted to at least try for the patent—
- having a patent application in the pipe might get me last-ditch backing for the system.
- possibly to get some rights to my invention of the surface-function that had no spline vectors

- possibly I might sell the patent to someone conglomerating in the area
- because, like any project, it had momentum of its own, I couldn't just put it down. I was proud of what I had figured out.
- to reach a respectable closure and finishing-point
- Also, the machine design I'd come up with was really humorous. But that is another story.

But the point had really been to patent the operations.

Note that a patent application does not have to describe a real object or system, only a plausible object or system— enough to support the claims. The actual payload of a patent is the claims which the patent office finally grants, and the charade of the patent application is describing an object or system about which the patent claims can be made.

Let us say you apply for a patent on a paper-mache camel-- not because you want a camel, but because you actually want the rights to the camel-saddle on top. It's an arcane literary form.

So the machine I was designing was zany. It had two levels and a peculiar set of operations to be performed. (Continued shortly.)

Proofing with Pop

I asked Pop to help me proofread the Fantasm patent application, as a way of including him and being with him. He would read aloud from the typed version and I would check it against my noodle draft (cut and pasted like Tolstoy's).

Amusingly, he could never pronounce the word "format" (– not in the usual way, to rhyme with doormat). He kept saying *for maht*, the Norwegian ending to thanking someone for a meal.

(As before, I did not have the funds to pursue the office actions, and so the patent application died.)

FANTASM TECH The Fantasm Scene Machine

The Fantasm Scene Machine (that is, the never-to-be-built wacky design) had two modules. The lower-level module was a hexagonal unit which would hold (digitally) the spatial coordinates of the triangles of a curved shape. Onto these hexagons fit bow-tie units. Along the way the digital coordinates were to be transformed to analog, for analog calculations. It was not intentionally silly, but I was thinking out the mechanisms of searching for a 2d point (on the surface) with a specific 3D result (in space).

The intended claims actually had to do with the mechanism of defining a surface by points alone, and various operations to take place upon that data.

The processes were certainly valid, though not the fictitious machine. Whether the patent could have gone through or had business value is now unknowable.

=== 1972 (I was 33)

A Long Goodbye, 1971-2

My grandparents had become edgy about wanting me to leave. There were many factors. Though they loved me, they couldn't be sure that what I was doing made any sense whatever.

It was also plain that Jean was coming to the end. She was ninety-one and seemed to be made of matchsticks. I could hardly bear to leave.

However, I had a job offer from the University of Illinois, and they were anxious for me to go. I had to wind things up quickly.

I was juggling my patent applications and the work with Cal Daniels on the Jot Box, as well as work with other youngsters (John Ridgway and Harry Mendell). I put in a lot of mileage.

Priority went to Cal Daniels, as we fought the clock to get the Xanadu internals working for the Jot Box before I had to move to Illinois.

XANADU STORY •————————
JOT story - - - - - - - - - - - - - - -

DATA INTERNALS OF THE JOT BOX

The JOT Box had two parts, tightly coupled but completely separate logically—

- the text interface, JOT, of which I am very proud
- the data system for editing by pointers, of which I am also very proud.

They were my two most complete achievements in computerdom to that time. Each of them reached a complete and final design, and was implemented. (They may also have been operational, if Cal tried running them.)

For the first time I worked out the actual mechanisms of write-once editing on a massive scale. In the course of this I discovered a very powerful class of data structure, the enfilade.

JOT TECH — — — — — — — — — — — — — —
~~XANADU TECH~~

JOT BOX INTERNALS:
Text on a Cassette, Never Moving

Few computer people would want to edit text on a cassette—let alone answer my ringing challenge, 'Edit *War and Peace* on a cassette—but it's what I set out to do.

In 1972, we were hampered by a very small computer (I think 16K of 16-bit memory), a 33 ASR Teletype, and a cassette drive. (Disks then cost many thousands of dollars; mass storage, through the cassette drive, had only just become available.)

No one else would have tried to do this, but it was doable.

To work in that tiny machine, obviously we had to have a clean and simple algorithm and data structure. It could not have exceptions or loose ends. It had to be one method that kept on working as the content grew indefinitely (one cassette could probably have held the works of Tolstoy, and we wanted this to be something Tolstoy would have used).

The cassette drive fit with the Xanadu model. From 1960, the Xanadu idea was always to have permanized content, cumulative and read-only, and revise that into documents by pointer methods.

Here is how it would work on a cassette drive.

An author's new text would continually be added at the end of the tape. None of the content on the tape would ever be moved. The evolving document would be virtual, revised by changing pointers to the original and appending any new text to the growing body of content.

As the author writes, the text is constantly rearranged and inserted into. This process has to be supported by the data structure, as follows--
- The text, arriving in pieces, must be stored permanently and maintained by pointers.
- As the user rearranges, inserts and deletes, the pointer structure changes.
- Only the text being viewed at a given time would need to be actually brought from the cassette. The rest would be handled internally.

I mulled and mulled over the question of how to manipulate pointers to the cassette in a clean, exceptionless fashion. How could we cleanly handle the pointers to this ever-expanding and ever-fragmenting body of content, regardless of how big it got and how chewed up?

This was the thinking that led to the discovery of the enfilade—that is, the first one.

But first, let's consider how text had to be rearranged in such a system.

Splitting and Rearranging Pointers
Here was the basic design:
- Each individual segment that the author typed in would be stored as it arrived; this would be called a *meander* .* If the first draft of the document arrived all at once, then that whole draft would be a meander. We would create a single pointer (start,length) to the meander when it arrived, stating its position on the tape.

> *Many streams and rivers are divided into meanders, that is, serpentine loops, lovely to look at from the air.
> • When the meander got divided—whether by insertion, deletion or rearrangement-- the pointer would be split in two. (Or sometimes more.)
> • The corresponding portions could then be separately rearranged in the overall (virtual) text, simply by rearranging the pointers.
> • As the document was successively rearranged and divided up with insertions, the pointers would be split and rearranged. The rearranged pointers at any given instant then represented the current (virtual) sequence of the text.

But in order for this to work cleanly in a small machine, it would have to work as a small unified algorithm.

•XANADU TECH
The First Enfilade

Somewhere in 1971 or 1972, I think, I discovered the enfilade, or rearrangeable indexed tree.*

> *I worked out a lot of the details in dialog with Cal Daniels (and to an extent with John Ridgway), but I believe the original idea was entirely mine, and it was I who insisted on pushing it to make it do what I wanted.
>
> It may be thought that I am trying to steal credit from a dead man, but once again, all the thinking that took place, and when and by whom, should be in my notes of that time.

I discovered that a tree of pointers could be used to edit the content very efficiently. The system would only have to actually fetch content that was shown on the screen; manipulation of addresses would do the rest of the work.

The trick was this: each pointer had a count of the number of characters below--
- the bottom-level pointer contained the number of characters in the meander itself.
- the bottom-level pointers were assembled into blocks. The next-level pointer pointed at the block of pointers, and this pointer had the sum of all the characters below it.
- this was repeated on upward. As the text got bigger and more and more split up, more levels would have to be added.

This was a clean algorithm. I called this pointer design a *crum* (Code, Recursive and Universal, for Meanders).*

> *This is, of course, a joking reference to the 'trail of crumbs' in the Hansel-and-Gretel story.

------- A Note from the Present

These data structures, enfilades, continued to be the heart of Xanadu implementations from 1972 to 1992. In the recent simplified Xanadu versions (XanaduSpace and other new designs) they have been set aside as a needless optimization.

Enfilades would be later generalized by my 1979 colleagues into General Enfilade Theory—the principles of editable trees with upwardly propagating metrics and downwardly imposable arrangements. Unfortunately this has never been written up by those who understand it fully.

FANTASM STORY 1970-2 I let the Fantasm patent application go

I couldn't afford to pursue the Fantasm patent application (the second time I couldn't afford it, as with Cinenym).

I let it go.

That was the end of the Fantasm project, but I continued to imagine a role for myself in the industry that would come .

XANADU STORY
JOT story

How the Jot Box Went Down—
Flagon Pulls the Plug

Unfortunately, the backing was kicked out from us.

Flagon declined to buy the machine; his father said it would make much more sense to rent one. I said that made sense in fields where objects had stable valuation, but not in the computer field, where objects lost their value so fast. To rent it for six months would cost more than half the $10,000 price! And we'd then own no machine to use or demonstrate.

We rented it, and the work went very well but too slowly, and so the computer had to go back before the algorithms could even be tried. It had been a great waste, but Flagon somehow thought he'd been astute. (I think he threw away a great fortune.)

That was the fate of xu72—man-years wasted, and a product within our grasp that would have been first or second to the market— and priced way under the competition.

I apologized to Cal and the project went on ice. There was no other way I could find ten grand.

(My grandfather was very supportive, but not when it came to putting money down. He did not trust my judgment in financial matters, and of course this plan looked to him like a wastrel get-rich-quick deal, but it might well have worked.)

End of the Goodbye

As 1972 drew to a close, it was plain that Jean would not live much longer. She was gaunt, practically a skeleton; but she and Pop were adamant that I should move to my new job in Chicago. It was with heavy heart I loaded my car, knowing I would not see her again.

Chapter 11.
SLABS: CIRCLE CAMPUS ERA, 1973-6

The name of the university was "University of Illinois at Chicago Circle", which was confusing because the traffic circle referred to had been demolished. But everybody still called it, informally, Circle Campus.

Circle Campus was an offshoot; the main campus of the University of Illinois was downstate, at Champaign-Urbana. That one was a traditional campus; Circle was an urban version, a brave new campus; a rather unpleasant campus of forbidding and unpleasant slabs. Did the architect provide tunnels between the buildings against the Chicago blizzards and ice? No. Could you find your way around? No; indeed, the administration building seemed a deliberate maze. But the architecture of Circle Campus had won prizes. Who could argue?

The Essence of PLATO

I had been invited by vice chancellor Joe Lipson to come and work with Project PLATO. Lipson was an enthusiast and an idealist and he appreciated my publications. The question was what I could do with PLATO.

Professor Donald Bitzer at the main campus, who created PLATO, claimed that it was "all you needed for education".

PLATO was a terminal, with an orange screen, that connected to a mainframe computer in Champaign-Urbana. It was ideal for drill and practice, but not much else.

Now, drilling and practicing is very good for arithmetic and memorization tasks, but real education is a much larger arena, and "all you need for education" was a silly claim. But Bitzer's determination, and the plasma screen it was built around, made PLATO impressive.

However, after looking at PLATO for a couple of days, I could see that PLATO had nothing to do with what I believed in. There was no way for students to create or store content; it was merely a way of inflicting programs on users. This could be useful, but not for me.

I told Joe Lipson PLATO wasn't anything I could use for my ideas.

'Well, you've got a year here, what are you going to do?' he asked.

I said I thought I would write a book.

DEFINING MOMENTS
The Title Says It All, 1973

I had a year to write a book, courtesy of Joe Lipson and the University of Illinois. But wasn't sure *which* book I would write—what it would be about, or what would be its slant, or how I would publish it, except of course I very much preferred to self-publish.

I thought perhaps it should be an introduction to computers. No, an *exposé* of computers, revealing all the things they've been hiding from the public. I toyed with titles like *The Counterculture Computer Handbook*. But that had no ring.

On the 28th of February, 1973, I received word that Jean, my grandmother who had raised me, had died.

I was strangely numb. I went out for Chinese dinner with my new girlfriend, Sheila.

Sometime during dinner, I think she said something about Women's Lib", still a hot topic in those days, and the name of my book came to me:

Computer Lib.

That said it all. That gave the book its slant, its direction, its tone, its agenda.

It would be a book of liberation. The reader and I would be setting the computer free— and ourselves.

And I began to weep and weep.

That title had set *me* free. Free to weep for Jean, the grandmother— the mother in all but the technical sense—that I had just lost forever.

Computer Lib in the Living Room

I spread the layout all over the living room. It took much longer to write because I had so much to say, and I felt I had to be very careful, especially on such things as the IBM chapter. It took longer than the expected year, but friends found me additional precarious employment at Circle Campus, even though I didn't fit into the agendas of any of the standard departments.

What would Jean Piaget have said? ca. 1974

(At Harvard I had dated a Canadian gal named Eleanor Duckworth. She was a fellow grad student in the Soc Rel department and I considered her a friend. She told me she wanted to go to Geneva to work with Jean Piaget, who was famous for what were considered his radical views on education. I was cynical about Piaget. I told her I thought Piaget was another fascist fart who just wanted to substitute one set of teaching sequences for another; his cognitive stages were based on his own children and therefore on Swiss culture. Nevertheless, Ellie headed off, and I heard no more of her for years.)

While I was working on Computer Lib, I was also a photographer for the media department at Circle Campus (it was called the Office of Instructional Resources Development). They had me writing and shooting a slide-show to advertise the campus; I went around with a big Nikon, accumulating pictures for it.

On short notice, the campus was informed that Jean Piaget would be speaking, and that faculty were to come in academic gowns.

I was not faculty, I was staff. I was told to be there and take pictures of Piaget and the doings for the Office of the Chancellor.

It was quite an occasion. It was in a big room, full I think with some five hundred people (and empty seats reserved in front). At the appointed hour, in trudged twenty or thirty faculty members in full academic drag, with the colorful ones (from the oldest universities) in the front.

I believe first to come was the Chancellor, and behind him Piaget, and at his side was Ellie Duckworth!

We signalled helloes as they walked down the aisle and I snapped away.

After the introduction, Piaget began to speak in French, and Ellie translated. He went on and on, and I did my job, which was taking pictures. Then Piaget said something she did not translate, and there was a silence, and everyone looked at me.

Someone tugged at my sleeve and told me what Piaget had just said. 'He says that if you don't stop taking pictures he will have you thrown out.'

So that was the next cognitive stage imposed by Piaget: to sit down and hear it all again. However, Ellie's translation and mellifluous voice made it less irritating.

------- A Note from the Present
COINED WORDS

New words that I put into *Computer Lib* included "intertwingularity" and "dildonics." I didn't expect them to catch on, but they did take off, about twenty-five years later. (The more common form of the latter is now *teledildonics*, someone else's extension.)

Computer Lib Delayed

I was hoping *Computer Lib* would be out in time for the computer graphics conference in the fall of 1974—the first SIGGRAPH*— but it wasn't ready; so I had the printers print eight of its pages as a poster, which I took along. Three of us drove to Colorado from Chicago, with cartons of my posters.

> * I co-authored the second paper at the first SIGGRAPH conference, but didn't think much of it at the time.

SIGGRAPH was a funny conference—about a hundred guys in T-shirts and lumberjack shirts, I think, all surprised that so many other people were interested in computer graphics.

I handed out the *Computer* Lib posters, thinking there'd be one-by-one orders. Then I was astounded when Ken Knowlton, a hero of mine from a decade before, ordered *twenty*! Things were looking up, I hoped.

BIZ STORY ----------
The Joy of Publishing, Fall 1974

I published *Computer Lib* myself, laying it out on the kitchen table, taking it to the printer, and paying the printer for the boxes of books.

I thought the book would take three months to put together. It took much longer.

No matter what I told people, nobody could imagine the book till they saw the final version. (Except I, of course, who had planned its tricks of layout gleefully.)

The joy and exhilaration of publishing my own book filled my soul—laying it out, explaining it to the printer, loading the boxes in the car, selling it to stores. For weeks I was uplifted and able to enjoy life, as I rarely can.

My friend Hugo McCauley, who had a book distribution service, agreed to handle the distribution at first. I myself took it to downtown bookstores, and was delighted when I personally took an order from Marshall Field's, where Jean had taken me as a boy.

BIZ STORY
What I Hoped Computer Lib Would Bring

With the book *Computer Lib*, I had a two-pronged agenda:

First, to make enough money to support myself and get free of the pestilential jobs I had to take.

Second, perhaps, to find an idealistic backer who would support my designs.

But I made some fundamental mistakes:

- Too few pages, too small type. I was pushing forty years of age, but I could still read the finest possible print, and (like so many computer kids today) was not interested in accommodating those too old to read fine print.

- Too much content. I should have saved the second side, *Dream Machines*, for a sequel.

- Much too low a price (seven dollars). That was absurd. I could have charged twenty—but it would have been *immoral*, it seemed to me, to charge too much. There was a lot I did not yet understand about business.

- I got involved with the wrong distributors; I didn't like the guys in suits, so I trusted hippies instead, and they turned out to be swindlers, as far as I can tell. I never saw my share for the 50,000 copies they said they sold.

Computer Lib did bring some great moments of encouragement, like an order from the White House.   A whole seven bucks.

> THE WHITE HOUSE
> WASHINGTON D.C.
> 20500
>
> [rec'd. ca. 4 Jul, '76]
>
> Gentlemen:
> Please send me one copy of "Computer Lib" by Ted Nelson.
>
> Thank you,
> Dr. Gus Weiss

"Soon we'll be reading and writing on computer screens,' mid-1970s
   (after the Altair and personal computing had begun)

In the early sixties I tried to tell everybody my vision--
> 'Soon we'll be reading and writing on computer screens.
> 'And there'll be new forms of publication for the screen.
> 'And you'll be able to call up any document out of millions.
> 'And everyone will be able to publish in this new medium.
> 'And there'll be many new kinds of connection among them.
> 'And you'll be able to see every quotation in its original context.
> 'And you'll be able to quote without limit without permission.
> 'And there'll be an automatic royalty to each author for the part they wrote.'

And in the early 1970s, after the Altair and personal computing had begun, people I'd talked to earlier would say--

'Oh, I get it, *that's* what you were talking about!'

And I would say,
"That's part of it."

BIZ STORY
The Itty Bitty Machine Company, 1975-7

The name was a real inspiration (I had to fight for it, persuading the partners, but it really paid off). It got a lot of attention, since "Itty Bitty Machine Company" had been a traditional joking reference to IBM.

How did IBM like it? They actually steered customers to us! On several occasions, people called IBM saying they'd heard of computers under a thousand dollars. The person answering for IBM would say, 'Oh, you want the Itty Bitty Machine Company, in Evanston!' It was an incredible boost.

BIZ STORY
Xanadu Stands (1974+)

Computer Lib and The Itty Bitty Machine Company were sideshows, I was always thinking about the main thing: Xanadu. I did not intend to go to the capital markets to get Xanadu going. What's the secret for expanding a business on low capital? Why, start a franchise! It's worked for a lot of people. That was exactly my plan.

I was very impressed by McDonald's. I believe this shows a certain astuteness: these were my thoughts in the late sixties, when McDonald's was far smaller and many people, especially non-drivers, did not notice it (I think a franchise at that time cost only $10,000!) But the model was simple: the franchisor creates the business system, the franchisee puts up the money and operates the facilities.

My plan was to create a turnkey Xanadu operation. The franchisee would buy (or lease) computers and a building I would design, and put up the money for the operation. The Xanadu company would supply the software, accounting system, networking connections and so on. (Note that at this time there was no Internet; I assumed that leased lines would be required.) A customer would rent a screen, and, if wanting to save content, would set up an account. The contents stored by the customer would of course be available world-wide by modem or at other Xanadu stands.

Because Silver was the color of the future (since my childhood), the color of Art Deco and Buck Rogers interiors and the 1939 World's Fair, silver was also the official color of Xanadu. The Xanadu stands would be called Silverstands.

Just as McDonald's has a character, Ronald McDonald, I planned on several trademarked characters to amuse the children and literati, like —
- the Colonel of Truth™

- the Person from Porlock™
- the Hobgoblin of Little Minds™ (this guy would have several small heads)

... and maybe others I've forgotten.

——— A Note from the Present

Gory Jackal, the Xanadu-hating journalist, claims that "The Xanadu franchises were silly." Let's see, which part was silly? Here are some aspects of the Xanadu stands I was planning. These were unique services that no one else had thought of yet. Which aspect was silly, was it—

- Public hypertext service? Gee, that's sure caught on.
- A company that would broker computer services to individuals? That's now called an ISP, and very popular world-wide.
- A place where a customer could rent a computer by the hour? That's now called an "Internet café."
- Selling digital storage services to consumers? That's also an industry.

I believe I was the first to propose any of these.

I guess we have to conclude that Mr. Jackal's malice has gotten in the way of his objectivity.

BIZ STORY ————————————————————
Hobbiests
The Problems at Itty Bitty

There were about five partners at the Itty Bitty Machine Company, depending on the week.

I have dealt with many people I have disliked or considered wrongheaded, but often I have respected them as intelligent adversaries. However, I lost nearly all such respect for my partners at The Itty Bitty Machine Co. I thought one or two of them had brains, but I won't say which, so each can think it was he. One was a professor of engineering from another country. He was thoroughly out of touch with American culture. I shall refer to him as Professor Pudditat. The other guys held him in undeserved esteem.

I kept telling my partners at Itty Bitty that the real market was the home. However, Professor Pudditat was sure that the market for little computers was an abstract individual he called "The Hobbiest" (this is how the Itty Bitty guys wrote it in memos, as a superlative—as in *hobby, hobbier, hobbiest*).

Now, it is true that there were computer hobbyists in those days, and they were the backbone of the first computer stores. There might even have been a hundred or so computer hobbyists in the Chicago area. But these were guys who would only buy something every other weekend, and worked on long-term projects, thinking they were building the future.

The real market, I insisted to my Itty Bitty partners, was the private consumer. I said people would be leading a new kind of life around the computer screen, and that is why I wanted to create my suite of software.

They wouldn't hear of it. The Hobbiest, they insisted, was the market, and so they would need to have racks and racks of printed spec sheets for various technical objects.

Meanwhile, the store was not being run well. None of us had time to work in the store, and whoever was in charge there didn't seem to do too great a job of it. However, there were several highschool students of considerable talent—Dave Levine* among them.

------- A Note from the Present
*Dave Levine went on to a distinguished career as a programmer. Among other things, he created the *Ballblazer* game, which was exceptionally clever, subtle and original, despite its fast pace. He designed it backward from the idea that a clumsy beginner's strategy—pushing the stick forward—should be a viable move. The interior logic was quite tricky but the performance and design were elegant.

BIZ STORY
The Discussion of the Pies

I have been in many discussions about founding a business, and most of them always get around to the Discussion of the Pies. Any third-grader should be able to understand it perfectly. The Discussion of the Pies is an agonizing bore, especially because participants often pretend not to understand what is being said as they try to jockey for a bigger share.

It goes like this:
    Let's say this pie is the whole company.
    It's divided up into smaller pies, which are the shares of different individuals/coalitions.
    Now we have to decide who is entitled to what blah blah blah ...

with insufferable repetition and pretense of incomprehension.

I recall the Pie Discussion at Itty Bitty more agonizing than most of them, possibly because some of the participants may actually have been intellectually challenged by it, or may have thought we were talking about actual pies we were eating.

BIZ STORY
Not Predigal

The general level of misunderstanding at Itty Bitty was considerable. Professor Pudditat would keep using the phrase "not predigal". I thought for months that this was some unusual term having to do with predication. Only later did I find out that it was how he pronounced "Not practical."

I mentioned to Professor Pudditat that his name might be considered as referring humorously to a domestic animal. He didn't care.

What would they have said at Xerox PARC? (1)   1975

After *Computer Lib* came out, Dick Shoup got me an invitation to speak at PARC. For no money, of course.

I found the atmosphere at PARC to be intense and harsh, but in a pretend-friendly way. Xerox public relations has made all the journalists believe PARC in its glory days was a happy playpen. It sure didn't look that way to me.

Development of Smalltalk was already underway. (Smalltalk was to be an object-oriented programming language for the public, and supposedly for children.)

Before my talk, Alan Kay showed me his version of Smalltalk of the time, telling me how children would be able to program it easily. (That version had distributed parsing of commands, which I liked a lot, but it was dropped from later versions.

Then I gave my talk. A number of guys lounged on beanbags. I talked about interactive software and my ideals about interactive software design, and about the Xanadu design.

At the end someone said, "We're with you, Ted.' I believed it, then.

Already I didn't like the atmosphere very much, but they encouraged me to apply to work there. I planned to send an application when I got home.

What would they have said at Xerox PARC? (2) 1975

Right after I had spoken in the Beanbag Room at PARC, I started picking up my notes, slides, etc.

Only one guy stayed around. He was very nasty. He kept saying "I pity you, Nelson!" I think he followed me from room to room, saying "I pity you, Nelson!"

He was pretty unpleasant. (I think I know who it was but won't guess.)

That decided me not to apply. This confirmed my impression of the place as abrasive and unpleasant.

That became another reason for my dislike of Xerox PARC—not just for the things they have done, which I believe had malign consequences for the world, but for the "I pity you!" interchange that I kept remembering for years.*

> * I believe that I have been able to keep this persoonal dislike separate from my criticisms of paper simulation, the PUI and the evil "clipboard".

BIZ STORY —————————————————————————
Altair Egoes

With my Itty Bitty partners, I flew to the First World Altair Computer Conference in Albuquerque. (It proved to be the *only* World Altair Computer Conference.)

The Altair was the first personal computer kit, appearing in early 1975, and it had an enormous impact. Now their head of marketing, David Bunnell, was calling together everybody who was interested. It was a zoo of eccentrics and fatties, about eighty of us as I recall, but in retrospect a comparatively far-seeing bunch. (Naturally the snobs from Xerox PARC did not come—they were happy on their high-salaried mountaintop.)

Diary cards recounting the author's first meeting with Bill Gates at the World Altair Computer Conference. The [epithet redacted] individual was probably Altair founder Ed Roberts.

Saying that Gates "stood by him" does not refer to placement in the room, but means that Gates supported Roberts' position that Basic was "the final language" [author's wording in these notes], "though surely he knew better." However, by supporting this position publicly Gates was both proving himself a company man and acting in his own interest.

A version of the Basic language was being offered by Altair. This was a big deal at the time; I don't think there were any other languages (beside assembler) available for the Altair. A longhaired Harvard student told us about the language and how great it was. This was Bill Gates, whom all would get to know.

Some people didn't want to reveal their true motivations, sensing competition everywhere. A fat old guy wore a name tag that identified him as HOW DEE. Later I found out he planned to make computer furniture, but didn't want it known.

The whole thing was exhilarating. Though the group was disparate and mutually suspicious, we knew we were at the cutting edge.

BIZ STORY
Computers Arise!

For Itty Bitty, I did a big poster with my own airbrush painting, "Computers Arise!" It showed a computer with big eyes, on two cartoon legs, shaking off its chains of slavery.

I tried putting a mouth on the character but it came out wrong— finally I gave him no mouth, and it worked. (This is rather like what Disney did with Dumbo—after various tries at making him talk, they finally made him silent.)

The poster was also a brochure, which I'd also illustrated by airbrush. It had eight pages of catalog items for what we were selling at the time. It also introduced characters we might use in advertising, especially Captain Computer™ and Itty and Bitty, the Computer Clowns™.

I gave the poster to a friend of Sheila's who was in advertising. He thought it was terrific. "You've given them a hundred thousand dollars worth of publicity!" he said.

Unfortunately my partners didn't think so. They didn't think the poster/catalog appealed to the Hobbiest.

BIZ STORY
Personal Systems
Ted Nelson's Softworld™: We Break with Itty Bitty (1975)

The Itty Bitty operation was going in a very different direction, if any. I wanted to get loose.

One of my hopes for Itty Bitty was to create a suite of personal software.

──── A Note from the Present
At that time there was nothing that I would call "personal software." There were word processors and databases— my favorite was called *Whatzit?*—but nothing like an organized suite. And there was as yet no spreadsheet.

William Barus and had agreed to program my suite of personal software. (It would be my designs and his very thorough implementations, using our own version of TRAC.*)

* IMPLEMENTED, and very well too, by William.

Here was the software package I was planning.

- **JOT**™ was my creamy-smooth editing system, optimized for multiple rearranges while writing. (I still hadn't felt it but knew it would feel creamy-smooth, which was confirmed later.*) Mind you, this was before there was spreadsheet or word processing. (Electric Pencil, the first word processor for personal computers, would appear a year later.)

  * IMPLEMENTED, around 1977-8, by Mark Miller and Jonathan Post in our TRAC (Superlanguage).

- **Planorama**™. This would be a very simple scheduling system with unobtrusive PERT capabililties, based on the SKED system I'd designed as an exercise for Mark Miller, and visually based on the Planalog system designed by my friend Stanley Mendell.

- **ThingEez**™. This was to be a simple database for possessions, purchase records, refill designations, warranties, etc.

- **FlapDoodle**™, also called **Pictrola**™). [IMPLEMENTED] This was a drawing program with animation capabilities. You could make individual pictures (lo-res, blocky) by positioning the cursor and typing a letter into the selected space; you could also *move back and forth in time* through the series of frames, reviewing the movement between frames. It was very simple but very smooth.

- **LedgerDomain™**. This was to be a very simple program for tracking money, like Quicken but simpler. However, it generalized in different directions—you would be able to keep track of other exchanges, including gifts, Christmas cards, invitations, favors and grudges.

I planned to integrate these programs in amusing new ways, but that is another story.

Professor Pudditat (Itty Bitty's out-of-touch guru) said it would take an organization the size of IBM to program what was listed in my design. The designs were actually very simple (we actually did the graphics program), but he had little comprehension.

This indicated that Itty Bitty didn't need me and I didn't need them.

We agreed to split up. They would give us the right to the software we had done so far, and William and I would go our way with it. And they promised to send me a computer in time for my upcoming classes at Swarthmore.

⸺ A Note from the Present

(Remember, in those days the number of personal computers was only in the hundreds.)

Chapter 12.
THE TRI-STATE ERA, 1977-81

During the years 1977-81 I rushed around amongst Pennsylvania, New York and New Jersey. I call this the Tri-State Era because of the following story:

> At one point I rented a car in Pennsylvania, and the guy warned me, "Now, you know you can only use this car in the Tri-State Area."
>
> "*Which* Tri-State Area?" I asked. *
>
> *What an amusing example of naïve nominalist philosophy. How could one speak of *the* Tri-State area, when of course Pennsylvania can be thought of as being in at least fifteen different tri-state areas, counting Pennsylvania plus only two of its contiguous states?
>
> "New York, New Jersey, Pennsylvania and Connecticut," he said.
>
> Oh, *that* Tri-State Area.
>
> How silly of me.

Those were terrible years. I was driving around crazily trying to be with my son, with Pop, and with my collaborators, trying to accomplish something with Xanadu and make money with less ambitious software.

The first four months of 1977 I had a teaching gig at Swarthmore, with two courses on computers. The guys at Itty Bitty had promised to send a machine immediately, but they welshed, and I was stuck just arm-waving.

I was immensely depressed.

Swarthmore: You Can't Go Home Again

Amazingly, the college had given me (for the semester) the very apartment that had been Mr. March's, where he held the course on Dostoevsky Mann and Proust. I had powerful memories of those very rooms from that wonderful course.

My own courses, however, were punk. Between having no computer and my paralytic depression, it was talk and hand-waving.

The students were great, though. One in particular, Stuart Greene, was especially remarkable. He had been a holography instructor at fourteen, a Buddhist monk and a film-maker, and he was unbelievably smart in very strange ways. For instance, he had once flunked a physics test by giving a correct but extremely bizarre and wonderful answer—

> Question. Why do objects farther away look smaller?
>
> Expected answer: equations of perspective.
>
> Stuart's answer: *because the diameter of the iris is finite.*
>
> (Not exactly wrong, but highly unexpected.)

Another student dropped in from Yale. Mark Miller had read *Computer Lib* and it set him on fire; he came to lecture us on his way to do a versioning tree (a topic in the book*).

> * I have recently learned that Danny Bobrow, at Stanford, was working on revision trees at that time. Did he get that from me, or was it independent?

The reaction of the students to Mark's lecture, I later heard, was: *O no, not another one!*

######## A Note from the Present
XANADU STORY

> Both Stuart and Mark would figure importantly in my life and work for decades to come.

Calls from Tesler

Meanwhile Larry Tesler, who had left PARC for Apple, kept calling me asking for interface ideas.* I was honored but there was no mention of money, and I had barely enough energy to do what I had to do without consulting for free as well.

######## A Note from the Present

> *Larry does not remember this (2010).

Personal Systems
BIZ STORY --

Softworld Moves Forward: Flapdoodle and JOT ~1976-7

William Barus' Superlanguage—our name for TRAC – took longer to get going than we thought, but it worked excellently by May 1977.

Flapdoodle*

                                * also called *Pictrola*™.

William implemented Flapdoodle in our TRAC (er, Superlanguage). This ran on an 8080 machine, the SOL. In my design I used the number pad for arrow keys, and allowed the user to position a character anywhere on the screen. (The 'blank' character, in reverse video, turned out to be the most powerful, as you could do great lo-res graphics with it.

Personal Systems
INTERACTION STORY ────────────────

FLAPDOODLE'S ANIMATION

The best feature of Flapdoodle was the animation. The system had three dimensions: the X and Y of the screen, and T for Time. You could work on one particular frame, flip through the other frames to watch the animation, then continue to work on the particular frame. It worked very nicely.

Kenneth Iverson, great inventor of the great APL language, saw Flapdoodle at a fair (actually, on Swarthmore's Parrish porch). He couldn't understand it. He was mystified by the use of the number keys for arrows (a practice which became common later, though I think I came up with it independently). He kept trying to parse the numbers as an input string, rather than seeing that they were merely being used as arrows. This is a nice example of a brilliant person's mind-set getting in the way.

Snubbing Apple, ca. 1977

I went to some early personal computer conference—I think it was Philadelphia— with the Itty Bitty guys. I believe there was a huge display of my book *Computer Lib* at the entrance to the conference.

I kept hearing from the Itty Bitty guys that 'those guys at Apple want you to come and talk.'

I asked, 'Does their computer have lower case?'

No, said my partners.

> * It was a couple of years later that someone named Paymar brought out the "Paymar adapter" that allowed you to get lower case on the Apple II. After which Apple made up for lost time.

I said, 'Then it's not worth discussing. Text is going to be the center of everything; the Apple guys must be really out of it,' and so I didn't bother to talk to the Apple guys.* Definitely a tactical mistake. I was right about text being the center of everything, but stupid not to talk to them.

> *At least, not until a decade later, when Apple president Sculley summoned me to an audience—at my own expense.

"Soon we'll be reading and writing on computer screens,' late 1970s
 (after the Apple II came out)

In the early sixties I tried to tell everybody my vision--
    'Soon we'll be reading and writing on computer screens.
    'And there'll be new forms of publication for the screen.
    'And you'll be able to call up any document out of millions.
    'And everyone will be able to publish in this new medium.
    'And there'll be many new kinds of connection among them.
    'And you'll be able to see every quotation in its original context.
    'And you'll be able to quote without limit without permission.
    'And there'll be an automatic royalty to each author for the part they wrote.'

And in the late 1970s, after the Apple II came out, people I'd talked to earlier would say--

'Oh, I get it, *that's* what you were talking about!'

**And I would say,
"That's part of it."**

Sex Generalized

I had long wanted a *real* sexual revolution—not just gay or straight, one-on-one. It had been years since the Supreme Court's 'consenting adult' ruling, and yet things had moved very slowly, although the book *The Velvet Underground* had documented scattered group-sex initiatives.

Finally things seemed to be getting underway toward a more open and interesting sexual world. My new gal and I went to Plato's Retreat, I believe the week it opened in 1977.

Contrary to what Wikipedia says, the first location of Plato's Retreat was not the former Continental Baths—they moved there later— but I believe it was in an industrial loft on the east side of lower Fifth Avenue, around 13th Street. In those days, starting up, they even had an open bar—a bartender with a cart (I think) parked among the mattresses.

We had a swell time. (It was the Swinging Seventies. Briefly, anything went, when The Pill reigned and we all thought there were only two venereal diseases, both curable.)

Why in the world did they give an orgy club the name "Plato's Retreat"? This was explained in an interview I saw or heard with founder Larry Levenson. He said that Plato was a philosopher, and philosophy was very difficult!—so this would be a place where Plato could get away from philosophy!!!

This is hilarious. Where is there more philosophy than at an orgy, where there are so many interpenetrating principles?

**What would they have said at Plato's Retreat?
1977/1980**

When *Playboy* finally got around to reviewing Plato's Retreat, the reviewer— I think it was Buck Henry—signed in with his gal as "Scott and Zelda." The receptionist looked up brightly and said, 'Oh, Scott and Zelda—you've been here before!'

How many Scotts and Zeldas cavorted at Plato's Retreat during its brief heyday I do not know, but I am certain that I and my date were the first.

The Ad

After the fun at Plato's, my gal and I placed an ad in a local sex tabloid. It was simple, something like 'Bi couple seeks same.' We put in my actual phone number. Unfortunately we did not know the mechanics of such things.

It seems that very few advertisers put in real telephone numbers, and this was a boon to the publishers. They had lots of box-number ads, but few with phone numbers. Most of the ads required sending letters; an ad with a working phone number was more enticing! It also legitimized the less plausible ads.

Our ad apparently reverberated through the swinger publications, and started *growing*. Additional lurid offers of every kind of sex were added to the ad.

Long after that girlfriend had gone, the ad kept growing and spreading, with more and more lurid offerings, enumerating orifices, lubricants, manipulations, whatever.

I never actually saw the ad in any of its forms, but callers would read it to me over the phone as it grew. (Usually a guy would hesitate and say hoarsely, "I'm calling about the ad." Usually I would just swear and hang up on them, but it depended on my mood.)

I should of course have changed my phone number immediately, but it was a great phone number (543-2111) and I wanted to keep it. I wasn't in denial, I was in ignoral, thinking it would eventually die down. I kept the phone number for years, but the thing apparently kept expanding and lavishly offering more.

Of course some people thought (and probably still think) this bloated nonsense was intentional on my part. People will believe what they will believe. (I did have a couple of amusing times from the ad, but not worth the overall mess.)

This has probably gotten me a reputation as a sex crazy. But putting it in context, it was another experiment. I have always lived a much more experimental life than most people. That is what they call crazy.

What would Frederick Pohl have said?   spring 1977

I had bought the first issue of Galaxy when it came out in 1950 (I was thirteen), and I believe I still have the first three years of it somewhere. It was in those pages that I read *The Space Merchants* by Pohl and Kornbluth (when it first came out, under the name *Gravy Planet*). I believe it is just as important as *Nineteen Eighty-Four*. Where Orwell was predicting a future based on Soviet Communism, Pohl and Kornbluth were writing about a future based on advertising, consumerism and government by lobbyists—perfectly predicting the world of today. So I admired Pohl enormously.

We were both speakers at the West Coast Computer Faire in 1977. I believe my talk, "Those Unforgettable Next Two Years," quite exactly predicted what was coming.

Pohl gave a luncheon talk, but in the introduction I was astonished to hear that he was the adviser to the Encyclopedia Britannica on the subject of the Emperor Tiberius.

This was a coincidence of cosmic proportions, because that was exactly the subject I had looked up when I sought to judge the Adler Britannica in a bookstore.

Now, the Encyclopedia Britannica used to be a standard encyclopedia with alphabetic reference. But Mortimer Adler, a dictatorial academic politico (he had already decided what the 100 Great Books of the world were) had persuaded the *Britannica* to let him redo the whole thing. This was the 15th edition of 1974. (Many editors quit the Britannica in protest over Adler's high-handedness in personally deciding every academic controversy. Somewhere I have clippings on this, but I can find nothing about it on the web.)

Adler addled the *Britannica* completely. He created a three-level hypertext: summary, mid-level, depth (with silly Latin names).

Standing in a bookstore, I did a quick evaluation of the 15th. I looked up the emperor Tiberius to see what Adler said about the conspiracy of Sejanus, the culminating event of Tiberius' reign.

I could find nothing about it. So much for the *Britannica* 15th, I thought.

So, in 1977, after Pohl's talk, I asked the obvious question: 'Why is it that the article on the emperor Tiberius in the current Britannica has nothing about the conspiracy of Sejanus?'

There was a bit of a rumble. Some people probably thought I was just faking and showing off.

Pohl blanched. 'It was there when I sent it in,' he said.

Afterward he came over to speak to me. 'Was the conspiracy of Sejanus really not there?' he asked.

'Well, I couldn't find it when I looked,' I said.

Maybe it is there (I should check). But the point is that if I couldn't find it easily, there is something fundamentally wrong with Adler's format. No surprise.

The Burning Scroll (1978)

At Thanksgiving in 1977, Pop had changed. He was suddenly weak and sickly. It was clear he was near the end.

The diagnosis was leukemia. The doctors said they could keep him going with weekly transfusions, but after a few of the transfusions he said no more, and lay down to die. I stayed with him as much as I could at the apartment on Central Park West. He hung on for six months.

He began having hallucinations. Once he thought we were underground together, and he shouted to an imaginary person: "You there! This is my grandson, Ted Nelson! You'll be hearing more of him!" Another time he read strange poetry, apparently from a burning scroll that he saw in front of him.

And soon after he was gone.

JOT story - - - - - - - - - - - - - - - - - - -
JOT Lives (ca. 1978)

At last my beloved JOT was implemented, also in TRAC, by Mark Miller and Jonathan Post. And my claim that it would feel creamy-smooth was tested.

JOT story - - - - - - - - - - - - - - - - - - -
INTERACTION STORY

PROVEN CREAMY-SMOOTH

JOT was now at last demonstrable, at least in part. Had I been right about its feeling creamy-smooth?

You betcha.

What would Mark Miller have said about JOT? (ca.1978)

Mark Miller says this about the feel of JOT:

"The result worked amazingly well. Ted's model of how people form models, and of what models they form, is somehow more accurate than I can understand.

...

"Ted successfully designed a system that leveraged these intuitions to give the users more power, more quickly, and more intuitively, and through a thinner interface, than I would have thought possible. Even I, when I went to use JOT, found that it would effortless [sic] do what I expected it to do, and what I wanted it to do. So long as I could make myself forget what I actually knew about the underlying formal complexity, JOT always seemed simple."

-- Email from Mark Miller to the author, 2005.08.11.

What would Jon Post have said about JOT? (ca.1978)

Jonathan vos Post worked with Mark Miller on a version of JOT for the Z-80, as I recall.

As they worked, Jon said to Mark, 'Ted's got some good ideas, but I think we should fix them.'

Mark replied, 'I know Ted better than you do. Let's try it his way first.'

Both were surprised by the result. Here is Jon's reply when I recently asked him to summarize:

"… your genius was not just in that JOT worked as you said it would, albeit with 100 times more lines of code than you predicted, but that it FELT the way you said it would. You are the greatest genius of software design in the world because, among other things, how astonishingly well you intuit … Virtuality."*

* "Virtuality" meaning the seeming of a system—look, feel and conceptual structure, a usage that I would argue goes back hundreds of years. (Others use it simply to mean 3D.)

IBM Comes Sniffing

After the success of the Apple II, IBM was finally considering putting out a personal computer. But this was a secret.

-------- A Note from the Present

> This brave inquiry of IBM's represented an immense corporate policy change that would eventually destroy the company. Once the 'IBM clones' got a foothold, the whole company was doomed.

I was contacted by a consulting organization. They told me that a mysterious major client was considering putting out a computer, and would I please come to a seminar to discuss this idea in general terms, for several thousand dollars? Yes, I would.

I was the only member of the seminar who actually brought a computer. (It was my Sol, from Processor Technology, which I had unwisely chosen as the machine to back, over the Apple, since it had lower case.)

Partway through the seminar, the consulting folks told me confidentially that the client was IBM.

Then it happened *again*. I was contacted by a second consulting organization, who said that a mysterious major client was considering putting out a computer, and would I please come to a seminar to discuss this idea in general terms, for several thousand dollars?

And once again, partway through the seminar, the consulting folks told me confidentially that the client was IBM.

What would they have said at IBM?

The following are extremely complimentary remarks by Bill Lowe about a presentation I gave in 1978; yet they show how far perceptions can differ from an intended message. Lowe was deeply inspired in a direction I had not intended, and he in turn inspired IBM to build the PC-- based on this insight that was not my intended message.

> "An important meeting that took place three years prior to the launch of the PC would be a harbinger of the future for me. In 1977, I had the pleasure of meeting Ted Nelson. I was so impressed with him that I invited him to speak at an IBM executive team meeting where I was hoping to garner support for the development of microcomputer-based products within the company. The meeting was ultimately held in Atlanta in 1978.
>
> ...

"When I engaged Ted Holm [Nelson] to speak at this IBM management group meeting, he was a young guy, and he didn't wear a tie-- this was almost anathema to the buttoned-up IBM managers who were attending this meeting. He had put a two-hour presentation together for this dinner meeting. I have to say, it was very amateurish compared to what we were used to, but the message was powerful. He had created images which he projected onto the wall with a slide projector. They showed him accessing information from the middle of the jungle,[1] on a sandy beach,[2] and from other remote locations. He called this process "XANADU."[3] His whole message that evening was that communication and computer technology was moving in the direction of "*making all information available to all people, no matter who they were, or when, where and how they wanted it.*"[4] This is a concept that seems fairly simplistic in today's world of wireless communications and the Web, with Blackberrys and iPhones everywhere. But thirty years ago, it was revolutionary thinking. Not only was I intrigued with this message and with the vision of where it could take us, but it was a defining moment for me. It helped shape a new perspective about a new information age, and I began to be able to communicate its power to those at IBM who had remained thus far unconvinced and resistant to change.

[1] I don't believe I ever had any such slide.

[2] I don't believe I ever had any such slide.

[3] "Xanadu" was of course my intended hypertext system, not at all the general process he enthusiastically heard. I was (as usual) hoping to get backing for my own system.

[4] That sure isn't what I thought I was saying. I was talking about a proprietary document system, not 'information' in this general sense.

"Based in part on this early, innovative vision from Ted Holm [Nelson], together with my subsequent experiences in launching new technology, I have become a firm believer that the best way to judge the viability of new ventures in the technology industry is to determine whether they are truly making progress in the direction that Ted outlined thirty years ago-- a direction that has proven itself to be even more viable today than it was then, in its infancy."

-- Bill Lowe with Cary Sherburne, *No-Nonsense Innovation*. Morgan James, New York, 2008, page 18. [Note: this is from a near-final version provided by Cary Sherburne.]

Nobody, Nobody Understood
XANADU STORY

Hardly anyone at all could imagine what I was talking about, though I talked and talked and talked.

I was astounded when a lady I had been with a long time denounced my work as creating a system for 'passive viewing'—totally the opposite of what Xanadu was about.

Personal Systems
BIZ STORY
Ted Nelson's Softworld™:
The Story Ends (~1978)

William had done an excellent version of TRAC. I was going to call our version SuperLanguage™.

> **Personal Systems TECH**
> In 1978, TRAC was a good choice for a language. It was compact and simple. It wasn't efficient or good for graphics, but those were the days of text terminals and undemanding users.
>
> Bill and I decided to create a TRAC processor as the kernel of my Softworld package. Bill got to work programming it in 8080 assembler, and did an extremely fine job. We had already delivered a system based on it to one customer (it even had typeahead, which I think I thought of independently and William implemented in machine language.)

Now, I had considered Calvin Mooers my good friend and ally. He was right on some things, especially the value of trademark. But he was way wrong on other things. Mooers had the extremely unlikely notion that developers would not only buy the TRAC language processor but also that *developers would pay a royalty for every program they distributed that was written in TRAC.** I told him that would kill the language, no one would submit to it.

*This deal has been tried by others, but I don't know if has succeeded anywhere.

GETTING PERMISSION FROM MOOERS

I called Mooers to ask Mooers to waive, for William and me, his crazy requirement for royalties on TRAC programs written by customers. We had to have a viable product, and no one would use a language with that requirement.

Mooers had the extremely unlikely notion that people would pay him a royalty for every program they wrote in the TRAC language. I convinced him, I thought, that that was impossible and he'd have to be satisfied with royalties on the language processor. We made that agreement over the phone. Orally he agreed to waive this inane demand for the our version of TRAC. (He believed that trademark protected the design, which I doubted, but I was not going to fight with him about it.)

When SuperLanguage (our version of TRAC) was all ready for market I called Mooers to finalize the deal. I should not have waited so long. (If we had been only halfway done—or if I had *told* Mooers we were only halfway done—he would have had incentive to go along with our plan. I played the hand badly.)

'I don't remember giving any such permission,' he said.

I was furious. I hung up on Mooers and never spoke to him again.

This was stupid on my part. It was one of the times I was too angry to negotiate. William Barus and I had a great deal of effort wrapped up in that product, and it might have been rescued somehow.

That then was the end of the Softworld project.

It had been a great implementation, and I had already familiarized myself with it, writing a lot of small programs in TRAC (with the help of my young son). But there was no point in continuing with it if Mooers was going to stand in the way.

FANTASM STORY ca. 1978: I take Ralph to the Academy

Amazingly, I had somehow gotten an invitation to an event to be held at the Academy of Motion Picture Arts and Sciences, discussing image synthesis systems. I happened to be in L.A. at the time, and I took Ralph, my father, to the event.

He was in an unusually bad temper. I don't know if it was because he thought I was trespassing in his industry, or because he didn't like the idea of computers involved with movies, or the talk of synthesized actors, or didn't like discussions he couldn't understand; probably all of the above. We sat together for perhaps twenty minutes and he left.

What would Marvin Minsky have said? (ca.1979)

Marvin kindly hosted the 1979 Hypercon (Hypercons were big Xanadu parties) at the AI Lab. We stayed up late and played audio episodes from "Hitchhiker's Guide to the Galaxy."

When I said I wanted to smash the educational system, Marvin said, 'You can't eliminate the schools, what else is going to keep them out of the churches?

What would Marshall McLuhan have said? ca. spring 1979

It's now a standard rhetorical question posed to students: "What would Marshall McLuhan have thought about hypertext?"

Only I (and Ron Baecker) know.

I had followed Marshall McLuhan since 1957, when I first heard about him from my professor Zellig Harris, when I took a reading course with him at the University of Pennsylvania. Harris had recommended McLuhan's magazine *Explorations*, which I read at the U.Pa library and found very inspiring. I cited McLuhan's books in my first published papers of 1965.

Then, around 1979, Ron Baecker invited me to speak at the University of Toronto, and Ron actually set up a lunch with McLuhan. (McLuhan was by now a full media celebrity-- a term derived from his own popularization of the term "media"-- the pinnacle of which was his wacky cameo appearance in "Annie Hall" in 1977.)

I had hated Vannevar Bush immediately on the phone, but in the same way I loved McLuhan immediately. He was very grand and dignified-- a vanishing Canadian type I had met before as a boy. He was pompous, but with a remarkable warmth. (I believe he had a mustache on that occasion, though he is usually depicted without one.)

I started to tell McLuhan about hypertext, and he intoned something like, 'The computer cannot alter its plan of action in any way!' He went on for some sentences more about the inexorability and invariability of computer behavior, possibly distinguishing between computers and humans in this regard.

In other words, he didn't get it at all. He didn't understand that the possible variations of computer behavior are what make the computer so powerful, nor could I explain to him the computer's media potential, or about hypertext.

So it was a frustrating but fascinating conversation. Here was a very intelligent, influential, famous and charming man completely cut off from understanding something very important. But I was very glad to have met him—partly just for the chance to bask in his warmth.

"Soon we'll be reading and writing on computer screens,' late 1970s
 (after Bulletin Boards started up)

In the early sixties I tried to tell everybody my vision--
       'Soon we'll be reading and writing on computer screens.
       'And there'll be new forms of publication for the screen.
       'And you'll be able to call up any document out of millions.
       'And everyone will be able to publish in this new medium.
       'And there'll be many new kinds of connection among them.
       'And you'll be able to see every quotation in its original context.
       'And you'll be able to quote without limit without permission.
       'And there'll be an automatic royalty to each author for the part they wrote.'

And in the late 1970s, after Bulletin Boards started up, people I'd talked to earlier would say--

'Oh, I get it, *that's* what you were talking about!'

**And I would say,
"That's part of it."**

DOING IT RIGHT (Summer '79)
XANADU STORY

Many would have thought us crazy. Indeed, many did. Few knew what we were doing, though we told everybody all the time, but our words seemed meaningless to people in those days.

We all convened: Roger Gregory the irascible, who had signed a non-disclosure agreement on the engine of my van as we hurtled through the midwest night; Stuart Greene, the mystic who'd taught holography at 14; and Mark Miller, who as a college sophomore had come to lecture my class at Swarthmore on versioning trees. We determined to sit down as a team and design Xanadu right.

We came together in Swarthmore, on the third-floor screened porch of my apartment, for much of the summer of 1979.

(This is written up in my book *Literary Machines*.)

Roger, Mark, Stuart and I were joined by Roland King, a linguist (who like me had been influenced by Pike's tagmemics) and Eric Hill, then I believe 15 and already an indicted felon (brought up before a judge for computer cracking, he had been dismissed by the judge with admiration; those were the days).

The Bad Guys Are Coming

We had a great sense of history and of hurry. Hypertext had to be done right.

We all were deeply concerned about the Bad Guys, who we saw as a combination of IBM and the government. (The others were all Libertarians, I still called myself a Cynical Socialist.) The Bad Guys would spy on people, withhold and block information, and give us inferior hypertext. We had to Do It Right, to help prevent this.

This meant using the standard business defenses—especially non-disclosure agreements (I made all of them sign) and secret proprietary algorithms.

Above all we had to hide the enfilade, we thought. But Roger thought my joking pretense that our secrets involved trigonometry calculations for disk drive optimization was lame.

LET'S IMPLEMENT! Roger and Mark were hot to get the system working. But we're going to do it *right*, we said, with a clean generalized design, rather than a compromise mess that can't be properly extended, like almost everything else in the computer world.

With My Artists

We were starting over. I had to persuade them about everything. (That's always how it is when you take a new programmer on— and this was not just one but five.)

I expatiated, I cajoled, I pleaded, I tried to inspire them. I worked and worked to explain and persuade— persuade them the design had to be deep and general.

Creative Control

At last I felt things were right, I had my team; I felt like Disney with his animators. In a way, this was what I always wanted—a warm working relationship with brilliant people who would accept the framework I was laying out, and with whom I would negotiate the details.

Except it would have been nice to have more money and prestige. They felt this more keenly than I.

XANADU STORY

THE PREMISES AT THE OUTSET

I laid down the specs. Here were the premises I had to sell the guys on, as best I recall:

A Note from the Present
At this time there was no Internet, and we were thinking about leased lines.

- We were going to build a world-wide publishing system where anyone could publish hypertext.

A Note from the Present
This was going to be OUR kind of hypertext, as described below. Do NOT confuse this system with the World Wide Web, which

appeared over a decade later, and which implemented a few of these ideas and prevented the rest.

• We would have to design the system for hundreds of millions of users.

• The delivery network would be built on small computers—what were at that time, inanely, called *microcomputers*. Many people had told me you had to have a vast network of mainframes. I said no, the problems were disk and bandwidth, since these machines are not calculating, just shovelling, and not much has to go on inside them.

──── A Note from the Present
This is precisely what the World Wide Web did—use small computers for a system of servers, as I predicted. Yet I had gotten a lot of sneers for that idea.

·XANADU TECH
THE SPECS WE WENT OVER, 1979

Here were the specs we went over. The Xanadu issues were always the same.

1. Content would be permanized, stored with a permanent address on every byte (or video frame or audio sample).

2. A document would be maintained as a list of pointers to that permanized content.

3. A document would not necessarily look like paper; there would be multiple views. A view that looked like paper would be only one option. Another view would show documents side by side, with their connections. New views could be programmed by users.

4. Overlaid on these documents would be links and other markers and relations connecting to other documents.

──── A Note from the Present

Links in Xanadu are NOT EMBEDDED—they are overlays, utterly different from those of HTML (but like those of the little-known Microcosm system, which did work and went through various generations.)

These overlays—call them xanalinks-- could be of many types, including markers, relations and templates of many types. They could not be embedded because that would pollute the content for other uses.*

    * See my peer-reviewed article, "Embedded Markup Considered Harmful," on line.

Links would be separately published and could be re-used on the same content elsewhere.

5. We would want to be able to see all the re-uses of the same content everywhere.

In hindsight, this last requirement was insane. Everything else on the list was simple, and still is. The last one killed us. (But not for a long time.) It is amazing how well we did it.

    Be careful what you ask for.
        Folk Saying

BIZ STORY
Sheldon Liederkranz, 1979

At our get-togethers and parties, I would give an imitation of a fictitious venture capitalist named A. Sheldon Liederkranz– "You can call me A." Shelley, as we called him, was domineering, sly and ignorant.

Shelley was a hit with the lads.

His were the clutches we sought to avoid.

Hunkerdown

We hunkered down. We wrangled the whole summer.

THEY ACCEPTED MY SPECS.

THEY LIKED ENFILADE STRUCTURE. (Later, they extended it brilliantly.)

Afternoon after afternoon we sat on the porch, the six of us, wrangling over points and possibilities. We had no whiteboard; we made our diagrams on an oval of opaque white glass.

my clipboard was where we made our diagrams. Sometimes we would cook and party together. Girlfriends were found but the work was the main thing.

At the end of the summer we were all agreed in general on the design, though a lot of specifics had not been worked out.

"We'll do it," they said. And I believed them.

They went elsewhere to work without me.

They moved to another Philadelphia suburb. Roger, Mark and Stuart rented a house and continued the design work. I would visit from time to time and hear the latest ideas and terminology.

XANADU STORY
The Tumbler Design of 1979-80

They called that Xanadu design xu88 because 1988 is when they expected to deploy it. I'm not sure when the design itself was completed—sometime in 1980, I think.

I am calling it here the Tumbler design because they created a unique new system of numbers, later called tumblers, for managing the entire system.

That resulting design`is a masterpiece of originality. (Note that I am complimenting *their* design; I was just the instigator, they were the architects.)

XANADU TECH

I had been puzzled about how to do links, on top of editing by pointer, for years. Here was their solution –

> • as always in my Xanadu designs, represent the text by a list of content addresses to be fulfilled when the document is shown. (The result of editing by pointer.)
>
> • make the links *another, separate* list, to be applied to the content brought in by the first list.

(See illustration, Appendix 0.)

------- A Note from the Present

Actually I am explaining their design in terms of the simpler design I have cooked it down to today. I explain it here as two lists, which is my present method. The guys combined both lists. Ingeniously, as I have said.

The only problem was, this simple design was essentially incomprehensible, because of the upper layer of brilliant optimization (tumblers—two-part numbers based on transfinite arithmetic; permutation matrices, and three enfilades all built on tumbler mathematics).

------- A Note from the Present

It would take me until 1985 to begin to understand their design and write them up (as *Literary Machines,* the technical edition), and until 2000 to find its simple essence—that is, reduce it to the two lists shown.

XANADU STORY
Let's Implement!

Roger ordered a Sun Workstation with his own money. (It was the first Sun an individual had ever bought, and Andy Bechtolsheim at Sun, who had to do the transaction, had no idea how to handle a customer's personal check.)

So Roger, Mark and Stuart started programming in C on a Sun. The code was designed to be simple and small.

The program was, however, not simple, and every part had to work.

Work began to flag. Stuart and Mark got offers elsewhere, and Roger was left programming alone.

Somewhat Creative Computing

For a time I was the editor of a national magazine.

By 1980, there was a big market in personal computers, and all the software was being made by garage and garret operators, which I was still trying to be. A prominent magazine was *Creative Computing*, which ran a lot of programs you could type into the computer in Basic. At that time many people believed that was what personal computers were for.

I got a call from Dave Ahl, the publisher of *Creative*. 'Some people think I'm crazy,' he said, 'but I'd like to offer you the job of editor.'

Thus I became the editor of a national magazine. A small and tacky one, but good-hearted and influential.

I did a good job as editor. I relaxed and didn't get caught up in trying to do wonderful things, which is my weakness. I just approved articles and vetoed them, and did small fixes. (An exception was an astronomy program sent in by an 11-year-old; I worked hard on that one, because being in a national magazine would be so important to him.)

The Publisher, Dave Ahl, was a very conventional fellow posing as a Wild and Crazy Guy. But I hand it to him: he dared to hire me, and benefited.

Circulation went up under my editorship. However, the company was not doing well overall and the job disappeared as *Creative Computing* began to sink.

JOT, THE STORY CONTINUES

I had not given up on JOT. The text interface was still very special and I was sure it would be creamy smooth to use.

(At this time lower case had just gotten to the Apple II—you had to buy a little circuit called a Paymar Adapter—but it meant that the Apple could now be used for text.)

I worked with a wonderful woman, Laura McLaughlin, who started implementing JOT for the Apple in Applesoft Basic.

JOT TECH - - - - - - - - - - - - - - - - -
Unfortunately there were undocumented problems in Applesoft Basic, making JOT impossible, so if it was going onto the Apple II it would have to be by other means.

Chapter 13.
TEXILE, 1981-88

My friend Steve Witham, who was working with me on a new version of JOT for the Apple II, agreed to come down to Texas with me. I would pay his expenses and he'd finish the software.

The move to Texas was saddened by many things—especially having to move my archives off the farm. This was another time I was too angry to negotiate.

Steve and I drove south in Bessie, my red van, which was loaded to the top. There was room only for the driver and for the other person either to sit, or to lie in the very back within two feet of the top. The rule was that the passenger had to sleep with feet forward, so his neck would not be broken in case of a collision or sudden stop.

I was not happy to be in Texas, but I was getting twice what Dave Ahl had given me at *Creative Computing*, so that was some compensation. But I was too depressed to stay in touch with anybody, except to call my son every week. The two women I had been seeing undoubtedly considered me a deserting heel, but I was simply too depressed at being in Texas to talk to anyone.

JOT TECH -----------------
Doing JOT in FORTH

Steve and I were still trying to put JOT on the Apple II as a stand-alone word processor. Since Applesoft Basic wouldn't work, we had switched to the FORTH language, which had recently become available.

Steve had gotten things working very nicely by the time we went to San Antonio, but there were finishing touches needed to productize it.

I'll Clean His Clock

Datapoint was for me a culture shock, with a jungle machismo I had never seen. In the company's sudden rise to success, many departments were created—I have heard the company had twenty-four vice presidents, but I do not state this as a fact—and the competition between the departments was atavistic. Important men in the company were referred to as "big swinging dicks." When one guy was offended by another, he would say, "I'll clean his clock!" Heaven knows where that expression came from, but the meaning was clear.

Thunder Hop'n'Pop

My message—of interactive vividness and clarity—was hard to get across in the Datapoint environment. My immediate boss, Klavs (pronounced "Klaus"), was from Denmark, and quite aggressive and hostile to me. HIS boss, head of advanced research, was Victor Poor. Victor Poor looked and acted like a grouchy old man, though we were nearly the same age.

I took both Klavs and Vic, separately, to video-game parlors. I had to get across to them that software needed to be vivid and clear. Vic accepted this idea rather grudgingly; he was an engineer, and had thought that software was a branch of engineering. Klavs referred to my ideas scoffingly as "operator entertainment"—but showed his fundamental understanding with an excellent phrase. He said software should be *self-revealing*, which I think says it best. I think that term may have originated with Klavs Landberg.

To show how even our character-based screens could be made exciting, I directed three little demos—

These were all combined into one fancy demo, which we called "Thunder Hop'n'Pop." Considering that it ran on character-based equipment, it was fairly special.

And I believe it convinced Vic Poor that we were right. Or he used it politically in some way. He was very sly.

Back to the Future

Datapoint wanted a snazzy new software suite and I intended to oblige them.

I worked from the inside out. Getting the data structure right was vital, and nothing could be done about the screens till later.

Out of the past I gave them my Xanadu design from 1970, eleven years before. (Talk about Back to the Future.)

I called the text system Vortext.*

  * This is now someone else's trademark.

~~XANADU~~ ~~TECH~~ VORTEXT

The snazzy text system I designed for Datapoint would support links and transclusions. It was based on parallel streams with pointers between them, a continuation of my 1970 parallel-stream design.

Vortext was bundled in a big package with a number of other things the department had been working on, especially a graphics console and various inner technicalities that Mark and others did. It was packaged to management as Datapoint's future direction.

Too Futuristic

Word came down from the president: our design was 'too futuristic,' their current offerings were just fine.

Spun Down

"Spun up" was a Datapoint term for ready and eager, as when a disk drive has reached speed.

After the collapse of the Vortext project, I was spun down. I was paralyzed with depression for months.

In a move visibly contemptuous toward the president of Datapoint, Vic Poor—the head of Datapoint R&D—said he was taking a year off. This was as much as saying, the ship is sinking.

I went and withdrew my meager savings from the Datapoint Credit Union, not knowing that credit unions are insulated from the companies they are attached to and that even if Datapoint crashed, savings there were safe.

But I knew Datapoint would crash. Just not immediately.

Vic found me other work to do.

JOT story — INTERACTION STORY

STEVE RUNS OUT OF STEAM ON JOT

Meanwhile, my pal Steve Witham had run out of steam on JOT. He didn't like it. He didn't like that he had to ask me how to do each feature; he wanted a system of premises he could naturally extend himself.

That's not how it works in this system, I said. It's too idiosyncratic.

Also, within my cinematic view of software, of *course* you act the director about each proposed element.

But Steve didn't see it that way, and he quit working on JOT. He stayed on in San Antonio as a friend.

ZIGZAG STORY
The Ultimate Structure, Unifire*

*Note that "Unifire" is now someone else's trademark.

If I had a new idea Datapoint would own it, unless they specifically released it to me; that was in the contract. (I had specifically gotten exceptions for Xanadu when I signed.) When I got my revolutionary idea, as I recall, I went in to tell my boss, Klavs Landberg, about it.

I believe he said "Get out of here with your crazy ideas."

I took that for an official release of the idea by Datapoint.

The idea was simple, and I consider it the ultimate data structure.

ZIGZAG TECH
HYPERTHOGONAL STRUCTURE, or ZIGZAG

I now use the trademark "ZigZag" for hyperthogonal structure. Hyperthogonal structure is a system of irregular multidimensional tables.

All other data structures can be built from hyperthogonal structure. In addition, ZigZag offers many different possible views, which other general data structures do not. While we now have excellent videos (available on the net), the power of the concept has not yet reached most people.

At first I called it Unifire (planning to claim it as a trademark), on the hope that it could be a unifying structure for all software.

I thought to put it on the Commodore 64, which was the hot cheap computer at the time.

The problem was: how represent the ever-changing multidimensional connections? This held up the project for over a decade.

Mark Miller and his partner, Terry Stanley, actually worked on a storage manager for ZigZag. However, turned out not to be an appropriate direction for development.

DEFINING MOMENTS
XANADU STORY

1983: THE SILVER AGREEMENT

I believe it was around October 5, 1983, but that is a wild recollective guess. (Though perhaps a dozen came, no one who was there can find their signed copy.)

Roger Gregory had been fuming over the fact that I was keeping all the Xanadu rights in my hat. I was hesitating till I saw a clear path to do the right thing. I had two principal concerns.

- Making sure the development went in the right directions and didn't cut corners or betray the central ideals. That can happen easily.
- Creating a publishing system where everything would be available for interconnection, annotation and quotation.

Roger brought down a very fine guy, Phil Salin, who was a brilliant negotiator.

Phil proposed that we divide Xanadu into two companies—
- one company to own the technical rights, do the development and find backing (this would be Roger's);
- one company to own the publishing system and develop the service to the public (which was what I wanted to do).

We went around and around discussing this for hours.

Phil was very convincing. His deal gave everybody what they wanted. Roger got to raise money and develop the system. I got to control the publishing system, and assure the universal connectivity I so believed in.

It was also a very clean division. This was extremely important.

This was all about making me agree. I agreed. We all signed. We signed it with big silver brush-pens, since silver was the color of the future, the color of Xanadu.

Thus our signed paper came to be called the Silver Agreement.

Roger was freed to look for backing in his own way. And I trusted him to develop the incredible system he had designed.

And I continued to make my plans for the world publishing system.

I didn't think I would need backing. Once it worked, we could just start deploying; and I could franchise the stands soon after.

"Soon we'll be reading and writing on computer screens," early 1980s (after the IBM PC came out)

In the early sixties I tried to tell everybody my vision--
'Soon we'll be reading and writing on computer screens.

'And there'll be new forms of publication for the screen.
'And you'll be able to call up any document out of millions.
'And everyone will be able to publish in this new medium.
'And there'll be many new kinds of connection among them.
 'And you'll be able to see every quotation in its original context.
'And you'll be able to quote without limit without permission.
'And there'll be an automatic royalty to each author for the part they wrote.'

And in the late 1970s, after the IBM PC came out, people I'd talked to earlier would say--

'Oh, I get it, *that's* what you were talking about!'

**And I would say,
"That's part of it."**

What would Robert Heinlein have said? ca. 1983

It was at some sci-fi convention in Houston.

Roger Gregory marched me up to Robert A. Heinlein. He was a short man with a mustache.

'I'd like you to meet Ted Nelson,' said Roger. 'He wants to create a world-wide network of connected documents people can access from computer screens.'

Heinlein looked at me with interest.

"How is it different from The Source?" he asked.

Now, a number of people had asked me that, and I had thought it was a very stupid question. But if Heinlein asked it, it was obviously NOT a stupid question, since Heinlein was very very smart. (I've often said there is no such thing as a stupid question, but emotionally I don't always feel that way.)

I don't remember my answer.

=== Fall 1984 (I was 47)

The Arrival of the Macintosh

With hoopla, the Macintosh came out from Apple. (I had supported Apple's windowing effort—the first big effort being the Lisa— with my paper "Hiroshima, Sputnik, Lisa." But the Lisa, at ten grand, had been a flop.)

Now in 1984 came the Macintosh, with the famous commercial by Ridley Scott. I got one. The fonts were fun, but it stopped there.

You couldn't program it. You couldn't rethink the windowing system. It was a locked environment. There were separate environments called "applications", each controlled by a different company, but Apple controlled the whole thing.

AND YOU COULDN'T HAVE YOUR OWN INTERFACES!

Worst was something called "the clipboard". But there was something else called "the scrapbook", which I found incomprehensible, especially in its interactions with "the clipboard". (It turned out that both these beastly mechanisms were much simpler and stupider than I realized. I was trying to make deeper sense out of them.)

"Soon we'll be reading and writing on computer screens,' mid-1980s (after the Macintosh came out)

In the early sixties I tried to tell everybody my vision--
    'Soon we'll be reading and writing on computer screens.
    'And there'll be new forms of publication for the screen.
    'And you'll be able to call up any document out of millions.
    'And everyone will be able to publish in this new medium.
    'And there'll be many new kinds of connection among them.
    'And you'll be able to see every quotation in its original context.
    'And you'll be able to quote without limit without permission.
    'And there'll be an automatic royalty to each author for the part they wrote.'

And in the mid-1980s, after the Macintosh came out, people I'd talked to earlier would say--

'Oh, I get it, *that's* what you were talking about!'
And I would say,

"That's part of it."

CUT -- AND -- PASTE ------------
THE HIDEY-HOLE

The Macintosh had two operations for moving content around.

One operation made something disappear and hid it. This operation was called "cut."

The other operation made the content chunk reappear. It was called "paste."

I was outraged. This was a total change in what those terms always meant. It misled users into thinking this was a decent way of editing text, somehow related to the Cut and Paste of old—that I knew from my grandmother's Tolstoy story, from my highschool writing endeavors, and from my experience as a copyboy at *The New York Times*.

They called this abominable hidey-hole "the clipboard". This to me is the worst of many computer evils today. Calling it a "clipboard" seems somehow reassuring, except that it does not resemble a real clipboard in any way—you can't see it, it only holds one object, and if you put a second object on it destroys the first. In every other respect it resembles a real clipboard, but *there aren't any other respects*. This is called a "metaphor", and to me symbolizes everything else that is wrong with the computer world today.

-------- A Note from the Present

There still exists no decent system for deep rearrangement— true cut-and-paste, before those terms were redefined by the Macintosh.

It is vital for people to understand the importance of these functions that have been taken away from us by today's software.

- The French national library (BnF) mounted a marvelous exhibit showing the different rearrangement systems of different authors. The exhibit was called *Brouillons d'écrivains*; there is a marvelous catalog, and it may be perused on line at http://expositions.bnf.fr/brouillons/index.htm.

- This just in: I have heard lately that Balzac wore a knife around his neck for the very purpose of cutting and rearranging his manuscripts.

- The Xanadu system was always designed around these functions.

However, the Macintosh, with simplifications of everything and especially the fonts everyone loved to play with, redefined the computer world.

The Macintosh was of course the popularization of the PARC User Interface, or PUI. It dumbed down the computer.*

*There is no space here to discuss the windowing system I had proposed in 1972, which explicitly shows connections between things inside the different windows. These are now called "transpointing windows", and you can read about them on line.

Waiting for His Time to Come

A friend of mine reported to me an interesting conversation. Someone asked a woman, 'What's Ted Nelson doing in San Antonio?'

She answered knowingly, "Waiting for his time to come." I wish I knew who she was.

Datapoint kept me on for a couple of years. I stayed in San Antonio not knowing what else to do, and hoping that Roger would finish programming the Xanadu code.

It turned out that San Antonio was a livable, pleasant and boring place—nothing like my stereotype of Texas. However, I found very few people I could talk to.

I will not discuss here various writing projects I got into, or the wonderful help I got from Lauren Sarno, the former Resistor, who came and stayed with me awhile. (We were briefly engaged.)

"Soon we'll be reading and writing on computer screens,' late 1980s (after HyperCard came out)

In the early sixties I tried to tell everybody my vision--
 'Soon we'll be reading and writing on computer screens.
 'And there'll be new forms of publication for the screen.
 'And you'll be able to call up any document out of millions.
 'And everyone will be able to publish in this new medium.
 'And there'll be many new kinds of connection among them.

'And you'll be able to see every quotation in its original context.
'And you'll be able to quote without limit without permission.
'And there'll be an automatic royalty to each author for the part they wrote.'

And in the late 1980s, after HyperCard came out, people I'd talked to earlier would say--

'**Oh, I get it, *that's* what you were talking about!**'

**And I would say,
"That's part of it."**

=== Fall 1985 (I was 48)

Making Movies

Ralph's Best Movie

Ralph by now was retired in Santa Barbara. (His third wife, Barbara, had died after a long sad illness) Ralph and I were speaking again, but it was hard., especially since he rarely spoke. I visited him with my French girlfriend Catherine.

He brought out a videocassette he said he wanted me to see, and left us watching the TV.

It was 'The Man in the Funny Suit,' which he made in 1960.

It was wonderful. I am sure it was the best thing he ever did. It is heartwarming, powerful and a true story.

'The Man in the Funny Suit' is a complex, self-referential movie. It's about making the original 'Requiem for a Heavyweight', which Ralph had directed four years before.

In the original 'Requiem', Kennan Wynn was to play a boxer's manager, and due to an accident his father, the comedian Ed Wynn, was asked to play the boxer's trainer.

Here was the problem: Ed Wynn had been on stage all is life, but he didn't know how to act! All he knew was how to say stupid lines in goofball intonations. This talent (suited to the 1920s) had gotten him fame and fortune, but now, cast in a drama, he was out of his depth. Yet the rehearsals went on. An expensive show, and the careers of Rod Serling and Ralph Nelson, hung in the balance. This was live television (before videotape) and no chance to do it over.

Compounding the problem was the embarrassment Ed's son Keenan felt when Ed couldn't read his lines. Keenan wanted his father out of the show to keep him from being hurt when it all failed.

Somehow overnight, just before the final show, Ed Wynn suddenly understood how to act, and turned in a magnificent performance. This actually happened.

And at the end of the show, Keenan is proud of his father.

That's the true story told in 'The Man in the Funny Suit"—written, produced and directed by Ralph Nelson, with the roles of Keenan Wynn, Ed Wynn, Rod Serling and Ralph Nelson played by themselves.

It is a beautiful show, beautifully done.

But Ralph's showing it to me was more than that. It was about forgiveness, and reconciliation and understanding at the end between father and son.

Showing us that movie was the closest Ralph ever came to saying he was sorry and he loved me, but I received those messages and accept them.

And I was deeply moved and happy to know that he'd made a film so wonderful.

Oops! He'd apparently worked on film before me. Here I had thought I had made my first film before his, in 1959 when he was still working with live TV cameras, but "The Man in the Funny Suit" was dated 1960, so he was likely working on it film as I was making Slocum Furlow. Ah well.

What would Bill Gates have said? (March 1986)

Bill Gates was actually a supporter of mine for a time, a patron. When Microsoft published an edition of my book *Computer Lib* he personally signed the contract. He had me do a track keynote speech at the first Microsoft CD-ROM conference.

Gates somehow thought, I realize now, that I was going to become a tame Microsoft member and spokesman. I suppose he was proud of what he'd accomplished and thought anyone else would be proud to join such an organization. He could not have had the faintest idea how awful I thought his company was, and that I would have considered it *immoral* to work for Microsoft, given my strict sense of morality of that time. (While I had recently been living with a prostitute, that I did not consider immoral.)

In my keynote I did the wrong thing, very rude. It was a conference on the wonders of the CD-ROM. In my keynote talk I spoke slightingly of CD-ROM and talked about Xanadu instead.

Afterward I dined privately with Gates, Alan Kay, Chuck Simonyi (creator of Microsoft Word) and Dave Cutler (creator of NTFS, the improved file system for Windows). Gates said nothing, but seemed to be studying me intently. He just didn't understand my world-view or motivation.

Ecstasy Trip by Water

The last day that the drug Ecstasy was legal, I gave an Ecstasy party. (Mind you, it was all legal, for the party ended well before midnight.) A number of us floated down the river on inner tubes. It was quite lovely.

What would Bob Abel have said? ca. 1986

NO RUNNING TIME!

I got a surprise call from Bob Abel, the filmmaker who had used computers so innovatively. He wanted me to come to California to talk to him at his own expense.

I thought this might lead to something. I was excited. He was a filmmaker, the profession I thought was really my own. He had his own studio, which was what I wanted. And he was amazingly successful at doing complicated new things.

Abel talk to me for an hour. He was warm and friendly. It seemed he wanted to get into interactive production. I don't recall the details of the conversation.

I don't remember what he asked me to describe, but I laid out some interactive plan. then Abel asked, 'And what would be the running time of this sequence?'

'No running time," I said. 'It depends on what the user chooses.'

"NO RUNNING TIME!" he exclaimed, astounded.

He left me with the impression that we would be doing something together. He indicated that he would pay me $50,000 for a treatment. Wow!

I was hugely exhilarated by our talk, and full of ideas when I got back to San Antonio. But when I called Abel back on the phone, he was harsh and dismissive, and I realized I had been had. The dangled offer of $50,000 was just a mean trick; he knew I badly needed the money.

(In the high that followed my Abel visit, I had an inspiration for a possible interactive machine— one that would have proper graphics and sound—and I thought of a great name for it. I thought I would call it the PlayStation. But unlike a number of other good product names I thought of, I did not try to trademark this one-- even though trademarking a name was so simple to do: you merely publish the name with a TM on it. But in this case I did not, unfortunately. I'm sure Sony, or somebody, would have paid me a good chunk for the name.)

BIZ STORY
Not Selling Out to Bill, 1983-7

Bill Gates was for a time my patron (I didn't quite realize that; I simply thought his solicitude was my due) and I wasn't responding appropriately.

It would *never* have occurred to me to sell out to Microsoft. I wanted my *own* company, not to be a captive in such a place.

"Selling out" had always been at the top of my list of Evils, worse than kicking puppies, almost as bad as murder. And I was outraged by Microsoft's software, not to mention their image (shallow, conventional, pompous and smug).

If I had had my wits about me I would have sold out *for a little while*, gone to Microsoft for a year or so, bitten my tongue and been polite, made a lot of money and left, like my friend Bob Wallace, creator of PC-Write (And perhaps I could have found a way to rationalize it to my readers, if not my conscience.) No one in the world would have reproached me.

But politeness and toadying and accommodation with awfulness are not my thing. I am a truth-teller and that's that.

What would Murray Gell-Mann have said? ca. 1986

Friends often tell me, "Oh, you should get a MacArthur Genius Grant!" Yeah, sure. Unfortunately the MacArthur is something you cannot apply for; you have to be noticed and recognized. (Also, you have to be doing something everybody understands.) The MacArthurs go to people who look good on paper, with polished and well-understood achievements already behind them. Since I have achieved little and my ideas are not generally understood, I don't profile for it.

Nevertheless, in the 1980s I had a friend who thought she could get me a MacArthur grant. She actually managed to get to the man in charge behind the scenes. It was none other than Murray Gell-Mann, the physicist who discovered the quark; he was running the MacArthur selection as a pro bono operation, or so she told me.

She had in her hand a paper on Korzybski that I had written. (On someone's request, I had written a long paper on how Korzybski related to my schematics work-- not because I was a Korzybski fan, but because someone had asked for it with the hint that it would bring money. It didn't. But it was a good paper.) Now my friend profferred my Korzybski paper to Murray Gell-Mann, the Nobel physicist.

Gell-Mann looked down at the paper.

"Korzybski?" he expostulated. 'Never mention this man Nelson to me again!'

What would Robin Williams have said? ca. 1986

It had been a wonderful afternoon. Tim Leary and I had met Robin Williams and his wife for lunch in San Francisco. Robin is not only an incredible comedian but perhaps the fastest mind in the universe. After lunch Tim and Robin and I went through computer exhibits at the Civic Center (I forget what Conference).

Robin went through the exhibits like a tornado, wisecracking his way across the computer world, making incredibly relevant cracks in exhibit after exhibit. He would pick up diskette-boxes and use them as hand-puppets, he would remark about strange features and complications that no one wanted to see or acknowledge, about the styles and colors and dorkiness of the equipment. The salesmen were all dumfounded with laughter. (I hope I got some of it on video.)

Somehow we ended up at a wine-and-cheese reception at the Vorpal Gallery. I think I was sitting on a hassock balancing a glass of wine and a plate of cheese.

Robin Williams squatted down beside me. He said something like:

'I think it's wonderful what you've done for the world.'

I have no idea what he thought I had accomplished, or what Tim had told him. But here was one of the people I admired most in the world, second only to Daniel Ellsberg, saying he admired *me*. It has given me strength in the hard times since.

What would Thomas Schelling have said? (3) 1987

On a trip to Cambridge Mass, I think in 1987, I visited Schelling (he was still at Harvard).

He didn't remember me, or that he'd once called me his favorite student. Sigh.

I asked what he was doing. He said he was no longer working on nuclear war. Instead he was working on issues of "self-command," like how to stop smoking. He had himself stopped smoking only with the greatest difficulty, and he was lecturing on this topic at high schools.

To quit smoking had been terribly difficult for me too, I said, but I had worked out a system exactly based on his approach to the Hot Line. As I explained it his jaw dropped. Schelling was astounded, because he was hearing a perfect Schelling example that he himself had not thought of, on a subject that mattered to him.*

> * No time to include this, but it's on YouTube in my '70th birthday lecture' at the University of Southampton.

What would Thomas Schelling have said? (4) 1987

Schelling strongly agreed with my proposed system for AIDS reporting, but wouldn't endorse it. 'I don't do endorsements or reviews', he said. This was a clue that he was going for the Nobel, which he later got.

What would Thomas Kuhn have said? (2) 1987

In Cambridge I saw Tom Kuhn and asked him how he felt about my extensions to his terminology, like "paradigm lock" and "paradigm warp."

'Do what you like,' he said, 'I've run it into the ground already.'

What would Stewart Brand have said? ca. 1987

When Microsoft published a revised *Computer Lib*—an edition that still makes me deeply unhappy—they solicited comments from various people. Stewart Brand said:

'Ted Nelson is the Thomas Paine of the computer revolution.'

I kind of liked that; I had admired Paine since highschool. But the remark makes me just a writer, not a designer, which is where a lot of people want to pigeonhole me.

Chapter 14.
AUTODAZE, 1988-92

=== 1988 (I was 50)

THE AUTODESK DEAL

The deal with Autodesk didn't take long to set up, it turned out. They, and Roger, wanted it a lot more than I did. I had a terrible impression of the lawyer, and no clear impression of the company.

However, as I got to know Autodesk and my new masters, I like it fine.

The founder, John Walker, was an amazing man. His previous venture had been a failure, though he had done is superbly: he had built the computer (engineering it upward from the chip); he had written the compilers; he had run the office and answered the phone. His computer was superb and the company failed.

Next time, Walker resolved, would be different. So he gathered together some programmers he knew in Marin County, and said "let's go after money like a hungry rat."

They decided the IBM PC was going to be a big success, and their agenda was to be a key software maker for that machine.

They created five programs for the PC. One of them was called "Autodesk", and that is what they named the company. However, the program that brought them success was a different one they hadn't even programmed– someone had brought in the door and they added it to their catalog of offerings.

This was the first program that put computer-aided design onto an IBM PC. They called it AutoCAD. It was a runaway success, so they throw away the other five programs and concentrated on that.

By 1988, AutoCAD had made millions for Autodesk, which they were prepared to invest in my Xanadu project.

Except it was no longer my Xanadu project. By the terms of the Silver Agreement, Roger was free to decide all the technical details, in return for which I would have the right to control the publishing system.

Creative Control -------------------------

My insistence on control of the publishing system wasn't about greed, of course. My central concern was to create a publishing system with universal quotability by transclusion, a concept I saw as vital, in the face of a great deal of shallow and dimwitted incomprehension. This seemed to me as vital for civilization as anything possibly could be.

Roger, on the other hand, wanted creative control of the development. He was angry at my "interference" (tactical maneuvering around the politics of the system, and concern to understand and approve the technicalities). I was doing my best.

Roger wanted control of the "technical" side, but no issues are purely technical. All technical decisions are political. As we found out in spades.

In this new company, Roger would have that free hand with Xanadu that he wanted. I wanted him to have it too, since the technicalities were decided. But the resulting schism put me disastrously far away from the project.

California At Last

Ralph's death was like being set free. I would not have expected it—I loved him after all, though painfully—but it was as though the dark clouds over California parted. Now California opened up for me.

What would Jack Lemmon have said? 1988

I should not have gone to The Gathering after Ralph's death. My father had told me he wanted a party after he died, like the one Bob Fosse (the dancer-director) had planned; however, Fosse bequeathed money for his memorial party (I've heard ten thousand dollars), and Ralph made no such mandate or provision. When a relative started sending out notes saying there would a Gathering— the word 'party' was not used— I should have seen what was coming and I should simply not have gone.

I think I met with Ralph's other kids the night before; we were all staying at that circular hotel above Sunset. We got together and had drinks or dinner.

It felt wonderful suddenly to have two Nelson brothers and a sister; I had been separated from them by the bitterness with Ralph.

But the next day was The Gathering.

The Gathering was at the home of Frank Schaffner, Ralph's good friend, I forget where in L.A. Ralph and Schaffner had parallel careers-- army veterans who first directed at CBS-TV and won Emmies, then moved on to directing films in Hollywood.*

> *Schaffner is best known for directing "Planet of the Apes", "Patton", "Boys from Brazil" and "Papillon".

Several actors came that I knew, including Dick van Patten, but he was the only member of the old "Mama" cast who was in L.A. Sidney Poitier came and shook hands all around-- he was incredibly charismatic in person-- but he didn't stay.

Then The Gathering began, and it became a series of testimonials to Ralph Nelson. They were lugubrious and one-sided and I got edgier and edgier.

I have always considered myself a truth-teller, the person who has to say what nobody else dares to say. So I said a few negative words about Ralph.

"That's it!" came the voice of Jack Lemmon, followed by the sound of his slamming out the door.

Next day I no longer had those brothers and sister.

Easy come, easy go. But it made me very sad.

Dock of the Bay

Chris Record, of Autodesk, had said he'd pay for an apartment I could stay in while we were negotiating. I looked at a couple of apartments in Sausalito and they were the same bleak condos as in San Antonio, though pricier.

Then I thought, 'What about a houseboat?' My assistant lined one up.

The night was perfect as the real estate agent walked us down the pier. Stars were shining and a wind was slapping ropes against aluminum masts of sailboats, parked to the south, with a romantic pinging sound.

We walked in partial darkness down a long row of what looked like houses—most of them. But they were rocking a little bit. Others were wondrous strange, especially a very tall structure that seemed to have pointy ears.* I was smitten by the romantic, wacky atmosphere of the neighborhood, somewhere between a seaside suburb and the Emerald City of the later Oz books by Neill.

* Called *The Owl*, I later learned.

'Sittin' on the dock of the Bay,' I sang, little knowing that the song had been written only two docks up, a few hundred feet away.

The houseboat neighborhood was no longer as Bohemian as it had been—it had turned to real estate following the Houseboat Wars of 1971—but the atmosphere and the views were marvelous.

I stayed.

Race Driving or Sex Workshops? (July 1988)

I wanted to take the Bondurant Racing Driver's Course, which at that time was taught in the Bay area. I was intelletually fascinated by the competitive aspect of driving: the highway is a horizontal dogfight,* and the racetrack formalizes this. I also imagined I would have all kinds of free time for that sort of thing.

---— **COINED WORDS** ———
* I believe this phrase may be my coinage.

However, my friend Joyce— the wonderful gal I'd lived with in San Antonio— was now, by wild coincidence, a madam in Corte Madera, a couple of miles north of Sausalito. She knew the score in the Bay area and strongly recommended a program called the Stan Dale Sex Workshops.*

* Now rebranded and mellowed as the Human Awareness Institute, hai.org. They have my highest recommendation.

It was a tough decision, but I chose the Sex Workshops. I called up their office and said I'd like to sign up for all four workshops. There was a pause.

"O-kay," said Nina, the secretary, slowly. I didn't know that nobody had ever signed up for the whole series at once.

The workshops were held up in rugged hills near Clear Lake, in Sonoma County. I'd heard there was a lot of nudity so I took off all my clothes, but nobody else was naked, so I got dressed again.

The Sex Workshops weren't at all what I expected. There was very little sex. It was about the heart.

Turning toward the Light

For years now I had been full of bitterness, rage and grief from the failure of my projects and my life.

I think it was at the Level Two, the second Stan Dale workshop, that I received a great gift of healing and peace. (Anyway, a calming that is the closest I get to peace.) I became much better able to appreciate other people, at least until they express their opinions. I'm working on that.

After the four Stan Dale workshops, I stayed on in the program as an Intern, a volunteer helper, for two years (the standard hitch).

It was a turn toward the light from the bitterness of my life. I became good friends with Stan Dale, and later he helped deeply in my life, flying thousands of miles to facilitate in my family matters—and he didn't charge a cent. A very wonderful man.

DEFINING MOMENTS
XANADU STORY
Dropping the Pilot (1988)

It was in third quarter 1988, I think, that I acted decisively to save the Xanadu project. Or so I thought. I did what any sensible person would do, and it was totally, disastrously, wrong.

I was told on the phone—I forget by whom— that my good friend Roger Gregory, who was in charge at XOC down south in Palo Alto, was throwing things and acting crazy. I heard that 'everybody was ready to leave,' possibly quit within a day or so.

That made it an emergency comparable to a fire.

I called John Walker, informally still head of Autodesk, and told him the situation. We agreed drastic action was called for; we summoned Roger to meet us at John's house at Muir Beach, and Walker told Roger he was no longer in charge.

(I read aloud to them the end of *The Once and Future King*, where young Thomas Malory is told he must go away and not be in the battle.)

Roger was demoted to programmer, and given a furlough away from Palo Alto to cool off.

The call to John Walker was one of the greatest mistakes of my life. I had hastily sided with (in varying degrees) the shallow, conventional, pompous and smug.

XANADU STORY

WHAT WAS REALLY HAPPENING

What I did not understand was *why* Roger was throwing things. He was throwing things because the team wanted to start over and redesign the Xanadu system on completely different principles. Roger wanted to keep his promise to Walker to get out a product in one year. He foresaw correctly that changing horses in midstream would delay the project intolerably, and that competition—somewhere—would soon be breathing down our necks.

What should I have done? I should have called Phil Salin, a people person, who had put together the Silver Agreement. But I felt I had to act decisively. Calling Phil did not even occur to me until years later.

Creative Control

It turns out Roger was *right* to throw things. There is a saying in Hollywood something like, 'The director should have a tantrum on the second or third day, and fire somebody; after that things will ve peaceful.'*

> * I heard a variant of this from Ralph, didn't realize it was standard.

Roger was trying to get a product out, and this was his way of trying to exercise creative control.

XANADU STORY
The Ent-Hill

They turned around and tried to create a different Xanadu.

With Roger no longer at the helm, the group at XOC started all over. They threw out the old design that we'd worked on so long and hard (the Tumbler system, xu88), and they started a new one.

I will call it the Ent Project. The design was based on a structure called the Ent, which I will not try to explain.

It was changing horses in midstream.*

> * As well as No One In Charge, Too Many Cooks, Second System Syndrome, and other less polite terms.

This was what Roger had been trying to prevent.

It brought disaster.

(That's Part Of It)
What would Bill Gates have said? ca.1988

I next ran into Bill Gates in Tokyo, I think on my first trip to Japan for Autodesk. He and I were both giving keynotes at the same conference at the Makuhari convention center. My keynote came first, talking about Xanadu as always.

(I had rejected his earlier advances. I saw Microsoft as catering to the shallow, conventional, pompous and smug, and their software as clumsy and obtuse. For me to go into Microsoft would be Selling Out, the fate worse than death that I had feared since boyhood. It would have been, according to my way of thinking, not just embarrassing but Immoral.)

After my talk at Makuhari, during the break before he spoke, Bill came up to me and said, 'Now I get it—Xanadu is a *server!*'

'Well, that's part of it,' I said. 'Let me give you a brochure.' But he was already walking away and did not turn around. This pissed me off.

My Own Foreign Policy, ca. 1989

I received an invitation to speak, I think for quite a bit of money, in Singapore. The letter said that the invitation came from 'the highest levels of government', obviously meaning Lee Kuan Yew, the founder of modern Singapore and then the head of state.

I wrote back that because Singapore did not have freedom of speech or the press I could not accept the invitation.

I could have done no other. I would have considered it immoral, in those days.

XANADU STORY
Great Pith and Moment, 1989-92

Shakespeare implied in Hamlet's great speech that too much thinking prevents action, and from this paralysis great doings collapse—

> "And thus the native hue of resolution
> Is sicklied o'er with the pale cast of thought,
> And enterprises of great pith and moment
> With this regard their currents turn awry
> And lose the name of action."
> *Hamlet's "To be or not to be" soliloquy*

As Hamlet warned, so it went with the Xanadu project at XOC. I saw it close up, watching the new Xanadu—the Ent project they crazily initiated— stumble for four years, the proverbial train wreck in slow motion.

In 1988, Autodesk had given me an office in Sausalito, far north of the programmers at XOC in Palo Alto, supposedly so as not to interfere with development; Roger wanted a free hand and did not want me around. My job was to publicize Xanadu and prepare for its world-wide deployment.

Unfortunately, in organizational dynamics, when you create departments you often create schism and enmity.

I would drive down to Palo Alto for the weekly meetings, but the situation was not that friendly.

I had become an outsider on what had been my project. They resented me! I did not feel welcome at the meetings. I did not trust the guys newly-hired from PARC, and they obviously didn't like or trust me.

Also I could contribute nothing. I no longer understood the technicalities, as they were based on Drexler's Ent structure (which I understood only vaguely), and various ways to house and twiddle that structure.

There followed endless deliberations and paralysis– the pale cast of thought on which the great Xanadu enterprise went awry.

~~XANADU TECH~~
WHO DOES WHAT TO WHICH

I was not a convert to object-oriented programming, and the design meetings at XOC, continually rethinking the Ent structure, did nothing to bring me around.

BACKGROUND: "Objects" are the units of a program, these days, and how to set up their relationships in a given program is now the central issue.

It turns out the relations between objects is by no means determinate. It can be debated endlessly. There are many schools of thought about the CORRECT way to program with objects.

For many hours over many months, I listened to the group argue about which part wraps what part, or inherits from it, or sends messages to it, or broadcasts, or fucks it, whatever.

The discussion seemed to go on endlessly.

And, worse, the discussions seemed to repeat. The achievements of the first year came around again as problems of the second year, as if they had never been discussed or settled. This was disturbing.

What would Laurie Spiegel have said? ca. 1989

I visited my friend Laurie Spiegel, the electronic music pioneer, in her fabulous Tribeca loft (surrounded by her marvelous antique computers). Laurie is very hip, not just about music and software and computer politics, but about the Art World. She is in general very astute.

When I demonstrated ZigZag, she said:

"*My god! You're a hard-edged minimalist!*"

That was surprising, but on consideration it sounded about right. So now I was positioned in the Art World; I had yet another set of coordinates.

(I don't know if Laurie's work is hard-edged. She may be too nice for that.)

XANADU STORY
Kudos

I was now on corporate email and hated it. The XOC guys were continually congratulating each other over work done. 'Kudos' would be the subject or the first word, and some statement of what the person had done. It was wearying, especially since I had no authority and had let go of understanding the details of the Ent system.

The XOC group also talked about interfaces, both by email and in the weekly meetings. Their ideas for interfaces appalled me. I tried to stay out of the discussion.

Varietal Sex, Varietal Marriage

In California they serve up varietal wines. They also serve up varietal sex.

The San Francisco Bay Area is known as the most liberal and flexible place in the USA for sexual tolerance– not just gay and Lesbian, but bi, group, transgender, S&M and other specialties. I arrived too late for Rajneesh's orgy cult in Mill Valley (it is not mentioned in Wikipedia that Rajneesh got to Marin County, but I heard about it from friends). More University was still functioning, where they taught the two-hour orgasm; but as in certain other cults, the full instruction was rumored to be very expensive.

Of course I wanted to have fun, but I was interested also in theoretical issues and social engineering: especially, how to set up a better sexual system for a whole society—i.e., more rational and intense than middle-class Protestantism allowed, such as open swinging—but still compatible with a happy home life and child rearing. The social engineering issues couldn't get any more layered (as witness the various religious approaches with their strong prohibitions).

But some groups in the Bay area, like the Polyamory cult and the Keristans, were working on overall sexual systems, not just satisfying individuals. I found this particularly interesting. Especially the Keristans. Like the 19th-Century Perfectionists, they set up a system of group marriage which appeared to be viable. (They also had a computer company, from which I bought a Macintosh at one point.)

But the Keristan world imploded. I happened to be at a Kerista gathering on the night they launched into their founder, Jud Presmont, with a verbal attack from all sides, hitting him with years of reproaches. Kerista came to an end and the people dispersed. (Was it because they lost the strong leader?*) But Jud and I remained good friends.

* John Humphrey Noyes, founder of the Perfectionists, said a strong leader was necessary for a radical community to work. He should know. But that's another story.

INTERACTION STORY
XANADU STORY
The Poor User

One guy at XOC wanted to talk to me in private about interfaces. He wanted to persuade me that Xanadu documents should have only one link per page! I said that was a ridiculous restriction.

"Think of the POOR USER! The POOR USER!" he said to me over and over, and tears came down his face.

Creative Control

I hoped these people would get their work done so that I could design decent Xanadu interfaces on my own, without having to listen to such inanities. I was not interested in discussions of interfaces, just in designing them singlehandedly.

What would Kevin Kelly have said? ca.1989

I knew Kevin Kelly as an amiable editor and paintball adversary, but not exactly as a deep thinker.

We were having drinks or coffee in San Rafael, and he asked how Xanadu structure kept links from breaking. I explained as clearly as I could about content stabilization and editing by pointer list.

"Weird," said Kelly dismissively.

This greatly pissed me off. (I have always considered 'weird' a very insulting word.) If he wanted to know he should have listened.

He has since written in *Wired* that he was sorry he didn't pay better attention in that conversation. So am I, so am I. His inattention led him to participate in *Wired*'s great attack on Xanadu and me in 1995.

What would Al Gore have said? ca.1989

(While in Finland I bought a fedora, because I was going to Washington, and it amused me to wear a fedora, which was the sort of hat worn in Washington when I was a boy.) I was to testify before Senator Gore's committee inquiring into the "Information Superhighway".*

> * It turned out not to be an inquiry but a publicity thing; perhaps that's what 'inquiry' means in Washington.

Senator Gore and other dignitaries looked down from a long table facing the audience. there were TV cameras and floodlights. Sen. Gore interviewed Bob Kahn, one of the key Internet guys, giving him a luxurious forum. then the lights went off and the cameras went away and it was my turn.

Sen. Gore made fun of me. I don't remember the details.

Before the meeting, I think, I asked Sen. Gore's secretary if I could meet with the senator afterwards. *"Meet with the Senator???"* she asked, AGHAST, as if my request had been to pull his pants down.

Suddenly I understood Washington.

To meet with the senator would be a vast privilege; to ask for it lightly, and with no quid pro quo, was naïve, even an insult.

Washington revolved around such meetings and around the favors and potential favors they represented. There is no free lunch, or free meeting, in Washington. That is what I learned in that split second.

What would Bob Taylor have said? (3) ca. 1990

For some reason Roger Gregory and I were asked to speak at Digital Equipment Laboratories in Palo Alto. I took celebrity for granted in those days, but as I think about it now, it was an amazing group we spoke to— Bob Taylor, now retired from Xerox PARC (who had offered me his own job thirty years before), Peter Denning of the ACM, his wife Dorothy Denning the security gal. We were there to talk about Xanadu.

I only remember one exchange. When I began my standard spiel against paper and its simulation, Bob Taylor said:

"It has wide acceptance."

Taylor had expressed it all in a nutshell, simply and laconically as usual. There it was in a phrase, the whole paradigm gap. Taylor and his minions at PARC had imposed paper simulation on the world, and they were proud of it. Never would they be able to understand the harm that had been done.

This brilliantly expressed his side in the paradigm confrontation. Abruptly I saw the chasm that separated us; I was shouting across the Grand Canyon. Everything in his world confirmed the paper view of documents-- what his bosses at Xerox needed, what the world could understand instantly, what he had been awarded for.

Taylor had famously said: 'I don't know what it will be, but I'll know it when I see it.' And it was paper simulation and fancy fonts on the screen. He was a great puppeteer, and he had chosen his puppets carefully, not hiring either Doug or me. (Doug is still in grief about losing of his team to PARC in 1974.)

The world had praised PARC's imitation of paper and fonts, and could not imagine the wavelengths of connection they were missing.

Telling Werner about Gordon Pask

What would Werner Erhard have said? ca. 1990

When I heard my eccentric friend Gordon Pask was seriously ill, I thought someone should tell Werner Erhard, especially since he was such a close neighbor. (Erhard had worked with Gordon at one time.) So I walked across the parking lot to Werner's office.

It was a fascinating place. Blackboards by the receptionist (or whiteboards, I don't remember) told of communications pending and incomplete—telephone calls and letters that needed to be replied to. It was surprising, very impressive and very effective.

Brisk but solicitous secretaries took my message about Gordon. I walked back to Autodesk.

A day or so later, I received a phone message: 'Werner has received your message and thanks you.'

That was that.

However, I was hugely impressed by Werner's up-front system of communication tracking. I told my assistants I wanted to implement the same thing, with whiteboards tracking what was going on and what had to be done (it was all so out of control). They told me firmly that such a system would make me look bad to Autodesk and they wouldn't do it. (As if anything could make things look worse to Autodesk at this point).

CINENYM STORY
movie editing

THE WRONG AVID

I'd been talking to friends at Industrial Light and Magic, Lucas' top-of-the-line special effects outfit,* where they were working on a prototype editing system. I had money at the time. They offered to sell me the editing system for $80,000, I think. I actually had the money, or thought I did, but I didn't much like what I saw. I waited.

* The main location of ILM was cleverly concealed in a mall parking lot in San Rafael at that time.

Around 1989, The Avid came out, which was the first really serious system for editing movies by computer.

I bought one.

I could have just bought the basic unit for $30,000 and been home free. Unfortunately I went wild and bought more stuff and got it on lease-purchase, a terrible mistake, which meant I had to rent it out. But that is another story.

------- A Note from the Present
They STILL haven't got movie editing linked to text and logging. Or to text control... (See my proposed interface shots, 1965.)

Finishing Slocum

~ MAKING MOVIES ~
movie editing

The first thing to do with my Avid was finish my first movie, which had languished silent in cartons for thirty years. I had recorded the sound track and spliced it in order but it was far from synchronized.

An aspiring young film editor, Nick Renbeck—I think he was nineteen, delightful kid—came from New York as an intern. I rented another houseboat for him and the Avid, and he finally put the sound track on Slocum. It's a very poor sound track but at least now you can understand the movie.

What would Douglas Adams have said? 1990

I had grown less and less able to read fiction because of the time pressure of my life—I would put a novel down on page 1 (Why should I be interested in these characters when the real world is so much more fascinating and interconnected?) But when in 1979 I saw *The Hitchhiker's Guide to the Galaxy* on a rack I had to buy it, I don't know why.

The universe, and my serendipity luck, had spoken: never did I enjoy a book more. Douglas Adams' zany wit, through which peeped his genuine knowledge of science, had me howling.*

> *I later realized that *Hitchhiker's Guide* was a sort of rewrite of *Alice in Wonderland*-- a passive protagonist goes through wacky places and marvels at wacky characters. Like Alice (and *Gulliver's Travels*), it's a kind of a social satire disguised as a fantasy travelogue, with a passive hero. It's about British society, its pretensions and obsessions—for example, speaking of 'the less fashionable part of the galaxy' and why 'bypasses have to be built' through the solar system are really jokes about 1970s Britain.

When the original BBC radio show of *Hitchhiker's* Guide came on in the late seventies, I taped every episode.*

> * Good thing that I did, too. The later re-edit of the show's audio, which I bought on CDs at the BBC in London, ruined it by speeding it up and losing the inane, meditative slowness in which its charm was woven.

Adams had not written the book first, as I understand it. *First* he had done the radio plays, with the extraordinary sound effects that he had made himself, then transcribed the radio shows into a novel.

> *Creative Control* -------------------------------
> *Creative Control* -------------------------
>
> * Legend is that he and a collaborator locked themselves into the BBC Radiophonic Workshop until they were done.

There was no one in the world I wanted more as a friend than Douglas Adams.

Unfortunately, it was not to be.

I met him gradually. Amazingly, Adams wrote me into a witty video documentary in 1988-- "Hyperland",* produced and directed by Max Whitby**. I met with Whitby in San Francisco to record my lines (he didn't tell me I had chocolate on my face, but O Well). In the final edit, I got the closing lines.***

> *Creative Control* ------------------------
>
> *For absurd rights reasons, "Hyperland" cannot be licensed for showing in the USA because of the limited permissions given by Art Linkletter and others for included content. (I get this from Max Whitby.)
>
> However, it's on YouTube.

> ** Whitby is not mentioned in the Wikipedia piece on "Hyperland", and should be.
>
> *** Actually, I had composed and rehearsed the lines in the car, intending them as show-stoppers, and it worked-- that's the way Whitby edited it.

Adams came to my talk in London on the World Tour in 1990, and then took Lizzie Davenport and me to dinner at the Groucho Club.*

> * A very stylish club for BBC types, named after a line Groucho made famous, 'I wouldn't want to be a member of any club that would have me as a member.' (This line may or may not have been written by someone else.)

I found Adams to be intense, skeptical and cynical, with deep anger-- not at all what I would have expected. (Takes one to know one, I suppose.) We had dinner a second time, and I unburdened my heart and my sorrows to him. I could tell at the end that I was too wacky for him. (Imagine! Too wacky for the author of the wackiest book of the twentieth century. O Well.)

XANADU STORY

But Adams' response was splendid when I talked about Xanadu for making writing decisions. He said: 'I've always thought that eventually all my sentences would be rearranged into EXACTLY the right order.'

What would Paolo Soleri have said? ca. 1991
   (DESIGN INFLUENCES: Paolo Soleri, when I was thirtyish)

In my early thirties, I thought of Paolo Soleri as one of the great visionary designers of our time. His imagined cities—which he dared to prototype as the experimental communities (well, residences) of Cosanti and Arcosanti-- were among the very few attempts to make a seriously different world, and supposedly attracted lovely female cult volunteers. In 1970 he had a big, beautiful traveling exhibit, which I saw at the Whitney in New York.

Twenty years later, I unexpectedly found myself drinking in the sunset with himself!-- Paolo Soleri, the great architect. Nothing like Wright with the cloak or cultman Leary in white, he was a small, polite man in a suit. He had merely arrived where I was visiting, and the hosts were busy, so there we were, just the two of us, Soleri and I, I think at a backyard dry bar in the Palo Alto sunset. The hostess brought food but they left us alone.

This is what Paolo Soleri told me:

"*The building codes killed us.*"

When Soleri had built his visionary complex of Cosanti, the city of Phoenix had no building codes that would prevent his innovations. Then Phoenix expanded, and with it the building code perimeter, making what he was doing—indeed, any innovation-- illegal; so he moved further out and built his visionary complex of Arcosanti. And it happened again: Phoenix moved out and stifled his ideas.

That is of course the way of it. Shallowness, conventionality and smugness defeat all innovation. Building codes are there partly to protect the public, partly to pad the fees of builders and unions, and partly just to make everybody live alike. Design innovations are smashed by conventionality and enforced by bureaucracy.

(Only in software, it seems, is innovation possible any more; and little of that.)

The Girl Next Door, Feb 1992

I got an invitation while I was busy preparing for an IRS audit and could hardly do anything about it. The invitation came from a visitor on the houseboat next to mine. It was printed in several fancy fonts, inviting me over for a glass of wine.

I had to take care of business and politely demurred. However, I took note of when she was leaving, and the last possible night I knocked on the door.

We went through a whole bottle of wine and laughed a lot. She was beautiful and clever. "You're too much fun," she said. I felt the same.

She did not stay over that night but did some checking on me. She was skeptical about a lot of the things I said. They kept turning out to be true.

Marlene Mallicoat was a computer veteran and a software designer. She had taught at IBM, worked as an independent software consultant, and personally designed two serious interactive software packages. Unfortunately, like most software endeavors, they had met with bad luck, typical disaster stories in the software world--

- "Suite talk" was a package to allow hotel guests to use a computer through the TV. Unfortunately the endeavor was bankrupted a sales department that spent out the budget even before the software was ready.
- "Litany," her other package, was a legal system for litigation support. It was kept off the market by an attorney who could not stop adding features to the design.

Marlene was also an organizer. Soon we were staying together, and fairly soon she decided to help me get organized; despite all the assistants and my frenzied finger-dyke attempts, there were too many accounts and too many things to keep track of.

She told me later that she planned to stay with me a year, to get me organized and on my feet. That agenda stretched out and out.

I greatly enjoyed Marlene's company, but she was not on the Bohemian side, like most women I had been involved with. She came from the conventional world (she had been with *IBM!*), but she was not stuffy and her heart was in the right place.

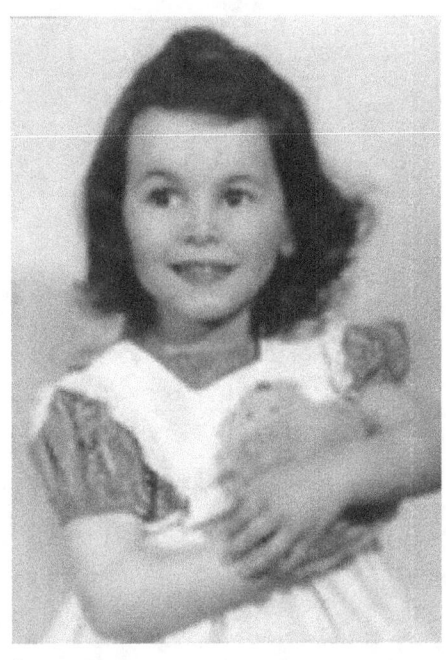

Marlene Mallicoat in youth. At nine she won the grand prize at the Oregon State Fair for her tunnel-free cupcakes. At twenty-two she was teaching programming at IBM International. Her sweetness has not changed since this picture was taken.

:

However, love came as a total surprise. While we were still living on the Sand Barge. I started singing in my sleep, and Marlene grabbed me and cried, "I love you so much!"

This surprised me. Somehow I hadn't expected this relationship to get serious. But it made me happy.

ZIGZAG STORY

When I met Marlene, I told her about ZigZag, which at the time had never been implemented. She promptly had a dream about ZigZag which I certified as "technically and spiritually correct." She is one of the few people who ever understood ZigZag from a description in words.

WHO SHE TURNED OUT TO BE

Marlene could handle accounts and logistics, figure out how to use idiotic technoid software and even fix computers. Because she was not Bohemian in style, it took me a while to recognize the obvious. We have been together ever since.

········ A Note from the Present
In this book I speak of the difficulties of collaboration. Marlene and I have been able to collaborate over the years on Xanadu and ZigZag because we love them. And each other.

Chapter 15.
THE KALEIDOSCOPE TURNS, 1992-4

The rest of this book is disproportionately short. While many things happened, many stories I could tell, many fascinating people and efforts I could describe, they were mostly not fundamental to the work and ideas of my life, and that is what this book is about.

For the most part those times wove around the old issues and hopes.

Especially the disaster of the World Wide Web.

XANADU STORY
The Great Dumbdown of Hypertext:
The World Wide Web Arrives, ~1992

> Objects in the mirror may be closer than they appear.
> *Statutory Warning*

To everyone, the World Wide Web came as a surprise. To billions of people it was a gorgeous, enlightening, magnificent new idea.

But not to the hundred people who had been trying to create something better. To the Xanadu veterans, in varying degrees, it was a shock, a dumbdown and a disaster. (I speak for those Xanadu veterans closest to me; I have not taken a survey.)

On the Xanadu team, we had always been telling each other that Xanadu was going to have competition, but we couldn't imagine what. After all, we knew more about transclusion than anyone else. If you were going to have worldwide hypertext, wouldn't transclusion be the center?

We did not recognize the competition at first because it was just too stupid. When the World Wide Web appeared, we paid no attention at first.

I assume everyone in the Xanadu gang was shown it individually, but this "World Wide Web" seemed hardly worth considering. Where were annotation and marginal notes? Where was version management? Where was rights management? Where were multi-ended links? Where were third-party links? Where were transclusions? This "World Wide Web" was just a lame text format and a lot of connected directories. Xanadu veterans considered the World Wide Web to be inane, just one of many blundering projects in this area that didn't measure up; we only began to pay attention when we saw it taking off.

It took off precisely at the geometric rate of increase I'd predicted for Xanadu in a 1988 brochure. But it took years to for us Xanadu guys to believe that this "World Wide Web" was the competition we'd feared. It was just too loutish.

(And the public thinks of the web as "technology"—like most of what's going on today, the web is not technology, it's *packaging*—like email, like Windows, like the Iphone, like Facebook. Technology is TCP/IP, text display, graphic compression... but how you put them together is packaging. *Enfilades-* now, that's *technology* :)

"Soon we'll be reading and writing on computer screens,' mid-1990s (after Mosaic and the World Wide Web came out)

In the early sixties I tried to tell everybody my vision--
    'Soon we'll be reading and writing on computer screens.
    'And there'll be new forms of publication for the screen.
    'And you'll be able to call up any document out of millions.
    'And everyone will be able to publish in this new medium.
    'And there'll be many new kinds of connection among them.
    'And you'll be able to see every quotation in its original context.
    'And you'll be able to quote without limit without permission.
    'And there'll be an automatic royalty to each author for the part they wrote.'

And in the mid-1990s, after Mosaic and the World Wide Web came out, people I'd talked to earlier would say--

'Oh, I get it, *that's* what you were talking about!' And I would say,

"*NO!* That is NOT it!"

~ MAKING MOVIES ~
BIZ STORY

Silicon Valley Story: My Parachute Rips

My plan, in case things went sour at Autodesk, was to get the hell out of the industry I hated (where nobody liked or would hire me or believed I had my special abilities) and do what I loved. I had put together my own little movie studio (i.e., a $60,000 Avid editing system and a $10,000 Arriflex camera) and I was in principle feature-capable.

As always, I thought I could do a low-budget feature that could get me into feature filmmaking. Hundreds had done that. My father had unexpectedly done it long after my own schemes of a breakthrough feature had begun. It was doable and certainly doable by me.*

> * Note that "Blair Witch Project," successful in theaters, was done for a budget of essentially zero– shot with video cameras which they returned to get their money back.

But 1992 was exactly the wrong time. Video was not yet good enough and in the new emergency, my time was too short.

I had to face up to reality: using the Arriflex would mean having to shoot double-system (sound track separate from the camera). This would vastly increase the cost and complexity and the time, the worst factor.

And there turned out to be no time. So instead of doing the feature, I just did a ten-minute comedy in video-- essentially a trailer– as a whiff of what I might do later.

DOUG AND ME

As a sentimental touch, I cast Doug Engelbart as my father. We shot Doug's scene at Roger's house. Doug's wife, Ballard, was there, as well as Marlene. We had a wonderful time at the shoot. (Doug's wife Ballard came too, with her merriment.) And I put my great friend Larry Moyer, the New York zero-budget filmmaker, in it too.

(If "The Epiphany of Slocum Furlow" was my Pagnol/Satyajit Ray period, "Silicon Valley Story" was my Preston Sturges period :)

"Silicon Valley Story" was amusing and competent, but led nowhere. At least it was kind of funny.

------- A Note from the Present
I recently put "Silicon Valley Story" on YouTube (2010). It got a straight five-star rating for the first 400 viewings, but then YouTube stopped posting stars.

What would Andrew Singer have said? 1992/2010

Andrew J. Singer had been my friend since the sixties, long before he became eminent in the industry.

When he recently saw "Silicon Valley Story", his reaction was:

"I thought Doug's appearance was one of the most blatant examples of product placement I've ever seen :-) "

XANADU STORY •⎯⎯⎯⎯⎯⎯
XOC, continued: The Collapse

Autodesk pulled the plug on XOC, which for four years had been *their* Xanadu, the tekkies' Xanadu, the Ent project.

Possibly Autodesk did this because they understood the portent of the World Wide Web sooner than anyone in the Xanadu group, since the Web looked trivial to us. But more likely they did this simply because the group had delivered nothing in all that time and money, which was certainly reasonable.

The XOC group in Palo Alto had spent perhaps five million dollars and delivered nothing in four years. (My hands were tied by the Silver Agreement; Roger would have delivered a product, but he was no longer in charge.)

XANADU STORY •⎯⎯⎯⎯⎯⎯
Fiasco Endgame

We had a big meeting, the XOC guys and I. It went very badly.

It seems the guys didn't think I deserved the publishing rights to the system; in the Silver Agreement I had given up the development and commercial rights in order to keep the publishing rights, but they felt I deserved neither of those things, nothing at all for my twenty-two years of work on Xanadu except stock in what was now *their* endeavour—but our shared fiasco.

Worse, Eric Drexler—the famously great thinker who invented the Ent, and nanotechnology—needled me at the meeting until I flew into a rage. (His wife Chris, bless her, kept trying to hold him back, but there was no stopping him.) This ended my fragile relationship with most of the XOC programmers.

A few wanted to go on with the Ent project for no pay. I saw this as fruitless, the whole Ent thing looked to me like it was over; I just wanted my trademark back, and to get back to the system Roger and the gang had designed in 1979-80.

The guys from PARC didn't like or trust me, I didn't like or trust them, and that was pretty much that.

XANADU STORY
The End of the Six-Month Joke

First it was my credo in the nineteen-sixties, then it had slipped into being joke: "Xanadu will be done in six months."

This continued to be the refrain during the long twilight of the XOC endeavor, but the six months never ended—if indeed they had begun.

No one had ever done a PERT chart or a serious attempt at planning. Jonathan Shapiro, perhaps the most realistic member of the team, finally put together enough information to make a realistic time estimate.

Shapiro's grim time estimate was this: *it would take six months to find out how long the Ent project would take to finish.*

That was the grimmest joke of all.

XANADU STORY
------- A Note from the Present
Eventually I got the Xanadu trademark back.

The code for both major Xanadu efforts— the Tumbler System and the Ent system— were put into open source (1999), under the names "Udanax Green" and "Udanax Gold." But, like most open source projects, they have languished there.*

* A noble collaborative project to document the Tumbler Project (Udanax Green, formerly xu88.1) and the Ent Project (Udanax Gold, formerly xu92) continues at Sunless-Sea.net. Unfortunately it is hard at this location to tell these two extremely different systems apart, and no mention is made of my continuing work and new versions under the Xanadu trademark— rather galling omissions.

Since then I've been deconstructing the basic Xanadu system into a lean, mean simple version that doesn't bother with far-flung transclusions. Of course it's what we should have done all along, but it didn't occur to us, and we reached way too far.

~~XANADU TECH~~
-------- A Note from the Present

In 1972, indeed, with the JOT box, Xanadu was close to a full single-user system of the local kind, like the World Wide Web. It would have been easy to add links, as a layer independent of the content, but I wasn't quite sure how, and I wanted to finish the text layer first.

In 1979, Roger and the gang figured out exactly how links and overlays on plain content should work, and that has been the design ever since.

Chapter 16.
GAIJINX*, 1994-2001

COINED WORDS
*This excellent word was coined by Eames Demetrios. "Gaijin" means foreign or foreigner(s). The hijinx of us gaijin are a perpetual nuisance to the Japanese people.

Japan: Land of Passion and Precision

There is too much to say about Japan, and I will not try here. I love Japan. The people are very smart and very idealistic. The architecture is amazing, the food is delicious, the coffee is marvelous, and everything runs on time.

The Ultimate Idealist

Yuzuru Tanaka, inventor of IntelligentPad software system, is one of the warmest and most idealistic people I have ever known. His design is elegantly simple and his diligence in keeping the project going has been awesome. He invited me to come work in Sapporo, on the northern island of Hokkaido. (Take note: Hokkaido is next to Siberia, and quite cold in winter.)

Our year and a half in Sapporo were wonderful. Sapporo is a beautiful and wondrous city with very hospitable people (though very cold in the winter), and we were glad to move to a warmer climate further south in Japan.

=== 1995 (I was 57)
Ponytail Ed

In Sapporo we acquired a new friend and collaborator, Ed Harter. Like me he was from Manhattan and like me he spoke with a New York Episcopalian accent. His grandfather had founded a little magazine I long admired, *The Monist*! Ed was very very sharp, and he also spoke Japanese.

Ed became a part of our working family, and helped smooth the way in many tricky situations of our life in Japan.

DEFINING MOMENTS
The Jackal's Curse: *Wired* Attacks, June 1995

In the annals of human friendship there have been worse betrayals: Sejanus' murder of Tiberius' family, for example. But very few. The attack on me by my former pretend-friends Louis Rossetto and Jane Metcalfe in *Wired* magazine* ranks perhaps in the top ten. (In my life I have had time to reciprocate very few of the friendships that have been offered; in Rossetto and Metcalfe I chose the worst.) The article expressed a previously unimaginable level of hatred and malice toward me and my work. It redefined my life, bringing a new depth of bitterness and grief.

> * "The Curse of Xanadu" by Gary Wolf. It can be found on line, with no correction or apology.

It was signed by a shallow, conventional, pompous and smug reporter, but I believe he was only a hired assassin, very good at his job. I prefer to call this author Gory Jackal. I personally consider him the most vicious and dishonest journalist since Goebbels, for reasons that will be clear below. But I am sure that Rossetto and Metcalfe approved every word.

One of the intentions of this book is to refute the *Wired* article with enough detail about my work for computer professionals of good will to understand the depth and malice of the article's incorrectness. What follow in the next few pages are some key points about specific charges and misstatements.

THE SNEAK SURPRISE ATTACK

The Japanese *Wired* had run a friendly piece on me, and Jane Metcalfe, by email from California, said that the main *Wired* in the States were going to do a big piece on Xanadu.

Marlene and I rejoiced: at last the world will understand our heroism, daring, design achievements and determination. Metcalfe was our friend, we thought. We told all our friends about the coming article and eagerly looked forward to it.

Then Metcalfe and her husband Rossetto hit us with un unimaginable attack-- the nastiest thing ever written about anybody, or anything, in the history of the computer field.

The article seems intended to destroy any understanding and memory of what the Xanadu project and my work have been about. It seems further intended to frame me as having caused the Xanadu fiasco at Autodesk, culminating in 1992, by strongly implying a rich twist of innuendi:
- that I am delirious and ignorant;
- that I never finish projects;
- that I was somehow responsible for the crash of the Xanadu project at Autodesk, *even though I wasn't in charge*, adding it to a hypothesized great chain of compulsive failures;
- that the Xanadu project was crazy and impossible.

The casual reader will not follow these contortions, but will nevertheless absorb a cataract of smears, nasty descriptions and distortions seemingly intended to tell the reader we (and especially I) were deluded morons.

I believe "The Curse of Xanadu" was dirty journalism with dirty intent, intended to cripple my career and destroy my life, and it did a pretty good job. (Indeed, some have said that the purpose of "The Curse of Xanadu" was to engineer my suicide; if so, they nearly got their trophy. However, I doubt that Rossetto and Jackal actually had this in mind. Whatever their hatred, even for the likes of them my suicide over the article would have been a long-term embarrassment.)

MALICIOUS MISSTATEMENTS OF NOTE

Jackal begins the article by attacking me with a torrent of vilification, hatred and slurs. His nasties include various small misstatements, gratuitously malicious –
- claiming that I drove wildly (a fellow passenger, the sober John R. Levine, asserts that it was an ordinary trip to lunch)
- implying that I offended my professors in college (I got on splendidly with all but one, and all but one of my professors in graduate school)
- claiming that my home is "full of incomplete notes and unsigned letters"— *NONSENSE!* (And what the hell is an "incomplete note"?????)

But here's the beauty of them all, later in the article:
- Jackal says of my 1960-1 hypertext ideas: "The notion of a worldwide network of billions of quickly accessible and interlinked documents was absurd, and only Nelson's ignorance of advanced software permitted him to pursue this fantasy." How's that again? I was somehow wrong to be correct??? It was too early for me to know about the possibility of world-wide hypertext in 1960, *because computer scientists didn't ???* This contorted assertion is beneath contempt.

It is important to note that Jackal does not say what aspects of 'advanced software' supposedly stood in the way in 1960. They probably still do :)

ABOUT NOT FINISHING; JACKAL'S BIGGEST OMISSION

Jackal goes on and on about my unfinished projects. (Apparently he lives in a world of perfect finishers-- a world without, say, Disney or Orson Welles or Frank Lloyd Wright, who started many projects that they did not finish.)

Do I never finish things? I do indeed have more unfinished projects than most people,* but Jackal fails to note that (by some criteria) I have more *finished* projects than most people.**

> * I made in general the mistake of publicly announcing my projects, which means they become "unfinished" in a way that solitary and secretive plans do not.
> ** See my curriculum vitae, on the web.

And here is the Jackal's biggest omission: Why do I have so many unfinished projects? (Jackal doesn't tell.) Because for fifty years I'VE BEEN WAITING FOR XANADU!

Nor does Jackal get around to mentioning why this matters so much to me--

- *The only kind of writing I want to do is in this new genre, the parallel xanalogical document.* Every book I write, smashed into paper sequence and rectangularity, goes against what I believe in and what I want to create in my life. I want what I consider the real thing. Jackal doesn't mention that.

- *Xanadu is a tool of organization and order.* The Xanadu design intrinsically allows the user to bind together parallel–
  - pages
  - outlines
  - narratives
  - threads
  - time-lines
  - versions

and other sequences. This fosters a document form of visible parallel structure,* unlike anything presently available electronically.

> * Good examples in the paper world are– • *The Histomap*, created by John B. Sparks. It is still available.

- The Hexapla of Origen, a key document in early Christianity.
- *I expect a decent text system* (Xanadu) *to speed work by a factor of ten* and help you (and me) do better work, too. I believe that having to work with today's clumsy tools is an outrageous and extraordinary waste of time. Jackal doesn't mention that either.

Are these just my personal myths and delusions and procrastinations? Maybe; but if he had just acknowledged these goals and beliefs, somewhere in his thundercloud of slurs and psychological conjectures, the piece might even have bordered on decency and balance.

OMISSION AND INNUENDO

Can hints and omissions be lies? I think so, if they are intentional and material. Consider a favorite joke that my great-grandfather, Edmund Gale Jewett, used to tell:

> Long ago on a sailing ship, went Edmund's story, the First Mate had a birthday party. The next day the First Mate read what the Captain had written in the ship's log. It said, *The First Mate was drunk last night.*
>
> The First Mate went to the Captain and asked him to remove the entry, since it would ruin his career. The Captain said, "It's true, isn't it?"
>
> The next day the Captain read in the log: *The Captain was sober last night.*

Omissions and innuendo, as in the above tale, can be technically true but contrived to deceive— i.e., lie– as much as explicit sentences.

Jackal himself points out that "the truth is a slave to a good story, and convincing lies are remembered while dry, factual refutations are forgotten." Can that have been his intention?

Moons Afar

In the last two decades I have dragged Marlene to the ends of the earth. Sometimes we would be separated– she would be in California or Japan, I would be in England or California. We would communicate by email, telephone or moonlight. Sharing the full moon from two far points on earth can be wonderfully warming.

Or when I would be in the office and there would be an earthquake, one would call the other to give assurance. Our love and connection deepened through these planetary events.

=== Summer 1995 (I turned 58)

What would Timothy Leary have said? ca. 1995

I had been in Social Relations—that is, the Social Relations Department-- with Tim Leary at Harvard. I had interviewed him then, but he didn't remember me at all. Later we were re-introduced, I think by Steve Ditlea in New Orleans, and we hit it off very well.

I became one of Tim's fifty best friends (just a rough estimate, he had so many). I stayed at his place in L.A. (I believe Benedict Canyon) five or six times, and we had several small adventures. (Once he invited me to Texas A&M University to share the stage with him, which was really fun.) I talked to him after his daughter's suicide, I was there when he clanked home with the muffler dragging from his Mercedes (it never got fixed), and I was with him the day after Barbara left.

For the record, I never saw Tim take an illegal drug except a reluctant toke from a joint *I* offered *him* (back in the eighties when I smoked pot).

Tim was extremely clever and quick-minded. He was also incredibly social and warm, but efficiently so: he could work a room fast, spent 30 seconds with everyone so they would always remember the conversation as if it had been half an hour. Everybody was welcome to drop in at his place for drinks and conversation. His wife Barbara was a fashionable lady who prided herself on looking just like David Bowie (including the crew haircut), and Tim treated her teenage son as his own.

The last time I saw him was when Marlene and I stayed at their house on a return leg from Japan, I think not long after the *Wired* attack.

Late at night, in that stay, Tim said to me something like, "I had lots of people backing me, but you were out there ALONE!" I was moved that he understood. But how did he know?

"You've contributed so much to my life," he said. I had no idea what he was referring to -- I felt it was the other way around-- and it seemed strangely as if he were saying goodbye. It turned out he was, for he died before we could see him again. Did he know he was near the end? Had he made some internal decision that his life was over, when Barbara left?

=== Fall 1995 (I was 58)

Angel of Order; Love and Consternation

Marlene and I were having fun and getting a lot done. We disagreed on many things, especially systems and arrangements. She was gradually revealed as my Angel of Order, but the forms of order often seemed to me a bit restrictive, a little too rectangular and contained.

However, while we were arguing, our hearts made a deal.

Marlene often got a look in her eye which I identified as a mixture of love and consternation. She claimed that what got her maddest was when I was "right for the wrong reasons." But that's still being right, isn't it?

Also when I knew things for no conceivable reason. For example, the Tokonoma.

Tokonoma!

In Sapporo we were visiting the family of Toshi Murata, a good friend (and Yuzuru Tanaka's former pupil), and Toshi was talking about some piece of furniture that used to be in the room. He couldn't remember the name. "Tono-", "tono-" he said, shaking his hand, trying to remember.

"Tokonoma, perhaps?" I asked.

'Yeah, that's it,' said Toshi, matter-of-factly. Marlene's jaw dropped, more astounded than I had ever seen her. How could I possibly have known an obscure Japanese word that even our host didn't remember?

Ah, but I remembered an exhibit at the Museum of Modern Art when I was in high school. They had built a Japanese House exhibit in the museum garden. Wandering inside, you could see the elegance of classical Japanese furnishings.

One stark, low piece of furniture had had a cardboard sign that said

PLEASE DO NOT SIT ON THE TOKONOMA

Who could forget that?

Marlene and the author at the Daibatsu—the Big Buddha in Kamakura, near where we lived in Japan.

Peacemaker for Kay

Kay Nishi is unique. They say in Japan that he is not very Japanese, but he isn't exactly an American, either. His unique perceptions, from both cultures, have made him an eminent computer guy in Japan.

Kay visited me in Sapporo and we became good friends. He hosted a number of Hypercoin seminars to investigate my system of micropayment.

The most exciting meeting we had, though, was based on Kay's initiative for a universal language, which he called Universal Networking Language (UNL). He called a big meeting in Tokyo and flew in linguists from all over the world for the launch of UNL.

UNL had actually been developed at a major Japanese company. It is a very interesting language initiative, offering great hope for translation. UNL represents common meanings-- everyday semantics—in a way that can be easily translated outward into natural languages. In other words, if you translate a document from a natural language *into* the UNL kernel representation, you've essentially translated it into every language, since once it's in UNL it can be spewed out as English, French, Tagalog and so on. (The outward translators are easy to build, the inward translators need help from humans.)

Kay had hoped for rejoicing and acclamation from the linguists he had assembled.

Unfortunately the reaction of the scholars was entirely different. This announcement was stepping on a lot of toes, competing with the work of almost everyone in the room. There were angry remarks from various sides.

Suddenly, for the first time in my life, I found myself in the role of peacemaker! For once having no axe to grind myself, I replied to the scholars' objections and repeatedly tried to show that this initiative was in everyone's best interest.

It was an extremely strange experience, since all my life I have found myself in adversarial situations, particularly intellectual ones, and this was the first time I was ever the one to bring calm and understanding.

I guess this was because I so much wanted to help Kay in that initiative. And also because I had no committed view on the issue, which is fairly rare.

=== 1996 (I was 58)

ZigZag at Last, 1996

For years—since first got the ZigZag idea* in 1983, at Datapoint—I had been mystified as to how to implement it. Its irregular systems of connection couldn't be handled in any software mechanism that I knew of.

> * Multidimensional lists and irregular multidimensional tables, now generically called *hyperthogonal structure.*

However, in 1996, talking to Andrew Pam, I finally figured out a method for storing the connections, and we were cooking.

ZIGZAG TECH

STORING HYPERTHOGONAL CONNECTIVE STRUCTURES

The breakthrough came when I asked Andrew what a hash database was. He explained that it was a database built from pairs of text strings— one string is an address to look up, and the other string is what you'll find when you look there.

THAT GAVE IT TO ME! I saw that we could store the connections as pairs of text strings. Using this method, we could state what cell was connected to which, and on what dimension.

ZIGZAG STORY

Now that we knew how to do ZigZag, Andrew Pam was raring to start implementing it—

INTERACTION STORY

Before starting the first ZigZag implementation, Andrew and I worked out the two-handed interface together. It works amazingly well, especially considering that we designed it before we had ever seen the software working.* We have scarcely needed to change it since.

> * This is now called the KBLANG interface (KeyBoard LANGuage). I acknowledge Andrew's considerable contribution to this interface design, his suggestions helped to unify it under simple rules.

As with JOT, this confirmed my Hitchcockian, feel-it-beforehand, approach to interface design.

Andrew had ZigZag working right away, within a few weeks.

I sat down and worked with it and played with it, creating structures in two dimensions and more.

In the first hour I saw everything I had imagined, and much more.

However, it wasn't until some weeks later—when I had a spare hour, waiting in a doctor's office in Tokyo—that I discovered how easy it was to build a family tree in ZigZag. That hadn't been in the design. It was just a consequence of its structure.

As I have said often, software shouldn't have *features* (added knobs and touches); everything should follow as *aspects* from the deep construct logic.

What would Peter Denning have said? ca. 1996

Peter Denning was an idealist who straddled two generations. He was Old Guard-- one of the first great theorists of operating systems; but he was also New Age, nibbling organic food from paper sacks.

I explained Transcopyright to him in the late nineteen-nineties and he made it the official copyright policy of the ACM,* which it remained for a few years. I believe he even used that name. However, his rewriting of the policy was fairly incomprehensible, and the ACM has now dropped the matter.

* Still on the net as "The ACM Interim Copyright Policy."

Keio SFC

After a year and a half in beautiful Sapporo, I received a surprise invitation to come to Keio University, one of Japan's top private universities. I was offered a visiting professorship Keio University's Shonan Fujisawa Campus, called "Keio SFC".

Keio SFC is a beautiful little campus a few miles out in the country from a small town where we lived. (They would have called it the Keio Fujisawa Campus, I was told, except that the initials "KFC" mean in Japan the same thing they do in the USA, and Keio did not want fried-chicken jokes.)

There are only a few departments at Keio SFC. Translated to English, they have names like "Media and Governance," "Environmental Information" and "Policy Management". No one knows what these mean, so both students and professors have wonderful flexibility to do anything. This is how academia should be. (If strange terminology is needed to eliminate borders, so be it.)

The students were wonderful and the faculty very smart. Professor Hajime Ohiwa was my special protector and mentor. He had done a wide range of projects with a lot of talented students, some of whom I got to know well.

I lectured in English, sometimes with classes as large as 400. The feedback sheets were generally quite positive, with a number of students saying "You gave me permission to think." Who, I wonder, withheld it in the first place? It's not just Japanese culture, it's the nature of educational systems everywhere.

We spent six excellent years at Keio (the maximum allowed) and were very well treated.

What would Robin Morgan have said? ca. 2006

I knew Robin Morgan when she was eleven and twelve, playing younger sister Dagmar on my father's show "Mama". She was personable and energetic and worked hard as an actress. In the summer of 1952, when I was hanging around summer stock with the cast of "Mama", she had confided in me that she really wanted to be a writer.

In the years that followed Robin became a leading feminist author. Most famously she was the instigator of the notorious "bra-burning" episode* at the Miss America pageant. Marlene and I visited her in New York.

> * Brassieres cannot be burnt, Robin points out, since they are made of polyester and wire. What she did was ceremoniously drop a bra in the trash for the benefit of the press. However, some reporter decided to embroider the episode, and that is how it lives in history.

Robin Morgan is one of the most brilliant people I know. (I hadn't noticed when she was twelve, or I would have pursued her when she reached legal age.) From my demos, she immediately Got both Xanadu and ZigZag and their future significance.

I mentioned to Robin the first time I had to fill out a form asking my occupation, when I was sixteen. I had thought a minute and put down "Poet, Philosopher and Rogue."*

> * "Know thyself."— Plato.

Robin considered this. "Poet? Philosopher? Rogue? What's not to like?"

XANADU STORY

UNDO IT MY WAY, 1996-7

On the Xanadu front, a Keio student (Ken'ichi Unnai) did something exactly my way—a text editor with version management that didn't just go forward and backward in time, but allowed you to go sideways, branching from a previous version without destroying later parts of that version. It worked beautifully.

This totally validated the design I had been carrying around for years.

~~XANADU~~ ~~TECH~~

My hypertime design allows a user to go not just forward and backward through editing steps, but sideways, allowing branching versions. Ken'ichi did the first (and so far only) implementation, and it worked perfectly, bringing up a map of branching parallel versions and allowing the user to select any point in this history, then regenerating the document at that point.

Ken'ichi's excellent client-server system used a Perl server and an Emacs client. He did a very elegant job. It is still around, though documentation may have been a bit sparse.

What would Marc Andreesen have said? ca. 1996

I spoke at Netscape before it collapsed, in what had previously been SGI's headquarters (where I had spoken) and is now Google's headquarters.

Marc Andreessen, principal creator of the web browser and co-founder of Netscape, was there to introduce my talk.

I asked if he pronounced his name the Scandinavian way, an-DRAY-yes-en, or Anglicized as An-DREEsen. He said it was the latter, and added, "I'm from the midwest; we do things simply there."

That was for me a huge insight: it was a key to him and it was a key to the World Wide Web. He saw the issue not as depth but simplicity. Marc thought of his achievement as "simple", not seeing the problems that fan out from that seeming simplicty. Whereas I have always believed that simplicity and depth could be created together.

HyperTransactions

Professor Hajime Ohiwa and his students (notably Yousuke Igarashi) implemented a number of other Xanadu features, again as a demonstration prototype.

Marlene and I were overjoyed when MITI granted a million dollars (in yen) to our project at Keio. Then we sank in disappointment when we were told that the money was already spoken for—it would go for salaries and university overhead. There was nothing extra for innovation beyond the original proposal. Ah well.

They said that 1500 pages of documentation were required for the HyperTransaction project. I protested, saying that because it was well designed, it should need less documentation. (A good design, requiring little explanation, should need as little documentation as possible.)

I was told that that the 1500 pages were a formal requirement. The documentation in such a project must be proportional to the size of the grant. This was another of the mysteries of Japan.

XANADU STORY

Under Professor Ohiwa, under this MITI grant, and with lead programmers Yousuke Igarashi and Andrew Pam from Australia, we put together a "HyperTransaction System" illustrating Xanadu-style micropayment.

It all worked. But it turned out to be just another demonstration prototype.

ZIGZAG STORY
What would Tuomas J. Lukka have said? (ca. 1999)

Tuomas Lukka had been a Junior Fellow at Harvard (sigh), and just returned to Finland when he read my piece on ZigZag, "What's on My Mind."

Lukka was extremely brilliant. He had become a celebrity in Finland when he got his PhD in quantum chemistry at the age of 20. Then he went to Harvard for the 3-year Junior Fellowship.

He was one of the few people who could understand ZigZag immediately. He wrote to me and I agreed to work with him on implementing it.

We met in Oslo and tramped around in the summer rain, talking and walking around Oslo for several hours, as I recall. (It wasn't winter.)

"ZigZag is IT!" said Lukka.

He accepted all my specs.

Lukka then proceeded to do a very fine and beautiful implementation, till we broke up over rights issues.

Wrestling with HTML

First, let me make it clear that I am in no way criticizing Tim Berners-Lee, the web's packager and founder. At some level we have very much the same ideals. He is a very honorable man, idealistic and noble, a good and decent man in his heart, endeavoring to do right, and at some level of abstraction there are ideals we both share. I like and respect him as a human being, however much I deplore what he has done.

That said, I hate HTML with every fiber of my being. It almost seems designed to prevent everything I believe in. It accomplishes the first 15% of hypertext and rules out the rest. I have wasted the last 15 years of my life trying to temporize with HTML. I am not saying I will never under any circumstances work with HTML again, but rather that I will go to the ends of the earth to try every alternative first.

For much of the 1990s, I tried to figure out what I believed in using Web formats and HTML.

We did a number of demonstration projects, such as HyperTransaction at Keio.

But there's no real way.

If you say to me that HTML5, the latest, provides a canvas on which I can project the software and interactions I want, thank you very much, there are many more hospitable canvases elsewhere.

-------- A Note from the Present

I am now completely satisfied that there is no possible reconciliation between Xanadu structure and the World

Wide Web. The only accommodation will be to implement a Xanadu client in Flash or Silverlight, and run it as an overlay window, like a banner.

People say, 'Oh, but now you can do those things in HTML 5.' I've had quite enough of HTML, thank you.*

<blockquote>* I am not saying I will never work with HTML under any circumstance, only that I will investigate every other possibility in Heaven and Earth first.</blockquote>

What hurts most is when people like my old English teacher, Warren Allen Smith, credit me in print with having created HTML. No thank you.

What would Tim Berners-Lee have said? (1999)

BACKGROUND. Around 1996, Marlene and I got an invitation from Tim Berners-Lee to dine with him in suburban Boston. We had a nice Thai dinner and then went to his home, where we argued till four in the morning.

(His wife admired my wristwatch, so I gave it to her.)

I don't know how much TBL and I communicated that night; now I suspect he didn't understand a word I said, except that I don't buy into his paradigm. It is very hard to break through a paradigm and be heard as something else than a heretic.

I don't think he gets that what I say is possible if done by entirely different methods, but of course everyone is devoted to their own particular methods.

I like and respect Tim Berners-Lee. He is iron-willed but extremely simple-minded, which helps get things done. (People are smart in different ways.)

Here is what he wrote in *Weaving the Web* (1999)—

"Ted Nelson, a professional visionary,[1] wrote in 1965 of "Literary Machines,"[2] computers that would enable people to write and publish in a new, nonlinear format, which he called hypertext.[3] Hypertext was "nonsequential" text, in which a reader was not constrained to read in any particular order, but could follow links and delve into the original document from a short quotation.[4] Ted described a futuristic[5] project, Xanadu[®[6]], in which all the world's information[7] could be published in hypertext. For example, if you were reading this book in hypertext, you would be able to follow a link from my reference to Xanadu to further details of that project. In Ted's vision, every quotation would have been a link[8] back to its source, allowing original authors[9] to be compensated by a very small amount each time the quotation was read[10]. He had the dream of a utopian[11] society in which all information could be shared among people who communicated as equals.[12] He struggled for years to find funding for his project, but success eluded him."

-- Tim Berners-Lee with Mark Fischetti,
Weaving the Web.
Harper/San Francisco, 1999, p.5.

In some way this is the best summary of my work (except for certain details). While I greatly appreciate his intention, I have added corrective footnotes. Thanks, Tim, for a kind and gracious summary within your frame of reference, and I hope someday we can reach a deeper understanding and a shared vision.

FOOTNOTES CORRECTING TIM BERNERS-LEE'S KIND REMARKS:

1. No one has ever paid me to be a visionary.

2. I don't believe I used the term "literary machines" until 1981, when I made it the title of a book. However, 1965 is when I first used the word "hypertext" in print.

3. It is vital to point out that Tim's view of hypertext (only one-way links, invisible and not allowed to overlap) is entirely different from mine (visible, unbreaking n-way links by any parties, all content legally reweavable by anyone into new documents with paths back to the originals, and transclusions as well as links-- as in Vannevar Bush's original vision).

4. Going back to the original must not be done by links but must be done by deeper transclusive means. The link mechanism, particularly the embedded link of the Web, cannot do this correctly.

5. "Futuristic" is one of those words which implies that an idea is not a possibility-- just a crazy dream, and thus only an inspiration. I believe Tim thinks he made my ideas practical, whereas I think he oversimplified them-- with today's extreme complexity as the result.

6. "Xanadu" is a registered trademark which I maintain at considerable cost, and I ask all parties to respect this by using the "®" or "(R)" symbol for the first use of the trademark "Xanadu" in each document.

7. Not "all the world's information", but all the world's *documents*. The concept of "information" is arguable, documents much less so. I believe Tim is finding his concept of pure information, the "Semantic Web", much more difficult to achieve than hypertext documents.

8. No, not a link; a transclusive pathway. The two mechanisms are entirely different. A link connects two things which are different. A transclusion connects two things which are *the same.*

9. Not authors, rightsholders. Sometimes the author is a rightsholder, sometimes not. A rightsholder is generally someone who has bought or contracted the rights from the author. While we have sentimental concern for authors, in our system of law the rightsholder can be anyone, just as the owner of land is rarely the original settler any more. Besides fairness to authors and artists, a key objective is to bring in the commercial rightsholders-- big publishers, university presses, movie studios-- who will not otherwise publish their content digitally. Many people think I am against free content; nonsense. I want to create a shared world of mixable content both free and paid.

10. No, not every time it was read (pay per view) but the first time purchased, as with a paper document.

11. "Utopian" is another synonym for "impossible", like "futuristic" in footnote 5. This shows a problem of understanding.

12. "Communicated as equals" is a gracious but confusing phrase. The author and the reader are not exactly *equal*, they occupy different roles with frequent conflict. If he means that anyone can be an author and anyone can be a reader, that has always been true (since self-publishing has always been respectable). I would say "shared a level playing field". But I appreciate the spirit of this phrasing.

Thanks, Tim Berners-Lee, for a kind and gracious summary within your frame of reference, and I hope someday we can reach a deeper understanding and a shared vision.

(I think Berners-Lee, like Gates and Jobs and the rest of them, still simply doesn't understand a word I have been saying.)

The main point is that while HTML solved 25% of the hypertext problem, it precluded solving the rest—and locked out most of what Xanadu was intended to do. The Web browser seems to have been diabolically devised to prevent everything I believe in and have been working for.

So we go on working toward another client. (Having to make it fit in a browser window is not a pleasant matter.)

=== Summer 2000 (I turned 63)
Doctor Nelson

Keio graciously invited me to get a PhD from them, waiving fees and coursework; I had merely to write a thesis (in English) and defend it (in English). This was still work, but exhilarating work, and the thesis defense turned out to be as much fun as my philosophy oral at Swarthmore.

What would Lionel Jospin have said? (2001)

I had just gotten my little knighthood from France that afternoon, and I found myself at the little palace where the Prime Minister hangs out. There were hundreds of politicians and reporters. I don't know what the overall occasion was. I shook various hands, including that of Prime Minister Jospin.

However, a little later Jospin approached me. I don't remember what he said, but it was very complimentary, about hypertext and all.

I was speechless. It is the only time ever remember being unable to say anything, pressed against the wall by his charisma wavefront. I could only nod and smile and thank him.

INTERACTION STORY
AI Bullshit (N): "Intelligent Interfaces"

> Any sufficiently advanced technology
> is indistinguishable from magic.
> – Arthur C. Clarke

Clarke's dictum, above, is one of the most unfortunate things ever said, suggesting that nobody will understand anything any more, separating the elite who control technology from the suckers who use it—undermining the democratic principle of popular understanding.

This has been gleefully accepted by the software community as: "Intelligent" means *out of the user's control.* People have overinterpreted Clarke's dictum: if it's incomprehensible, it's intelligent, right? So creating incomprehensible interfaces becomes a kind of easy actual intelligence.

A nice homey example is the monstrous package called Microsoft Word. It keeps trying to outguess what you want and correct what you intend to do. You have to spend a lot of time undoing its "intelligent" corrections. And the menus keep hopping around so that what you did last is nearest the top, making it hard to find anything.

I say, trust the user and stop trying to fool and confuse him.

Chapter 17.
SCEPTERED IDYLL, 2001-8

=== Fall 2001 (I was 64)

Fair England! Since boyhood I had thought of England as the mother country, home of Shakespeare, Shaw, Lewis Carroll, Gilbert and Sullivan; source of all the greatest movies; land of beauty and tradition. And somehow, because of the literary style in my boyhood home, I had always believed I was really English, underneath.

Once there, it became very clear that I was not. The English tend to be quite reconciled to the way things are. And their vaunted toleration of eccentricity is not what it seems.

Never-Never Land (Wendy's Domain)

In Southampton we enjoyed not only England, but the wonderful atmosphere that our dear friend and chairperson Wendy Hall had created in "her department"-- the last remaining university department that combined electronics with computer science.

It was there in the cafeteria of the Department that Marlene and I watched the World Trade Center come down, and everyone wondered in fear what new world we were entering.

DOUG AND ME ⟶

What would Wendy Hall have said? (2001)

'BUT MY DEAR, YOU ARE ONE!'

Doug Engelbart came to speak at Southampton, travelling with his sweetheart Karen. Dining at Wendy's house, we discussed their forthcoming plans for marriage. They had the license. I offered to marry them, as an ordained minister of the Universal Life Church. (I had renewed this ordination on the Net earlier that day). They thought that sounded dodgy and decided to postpone.

I made some disparaging remark about computer scientists, perhaps saying that computer scientists are like a mandrill troupe trundling uneasily through the jungle, following each others' bright tails.

'*But my dear, you are one!*' said Wendy.

I froze. *WHAT*???

I still thought of myself as a generalist and film-maker, and for years I had been furious at the pomposity and obtuseness of the computer science profession. (And, of course, *Wired* magazine made a point of saying repeatedly that I and my colleagues were not computer scientists.) Now Wendy Hall, impeccably a computer scientist,* has just informed me that I, too, am a computer scientist. If Wendy Hall says I'm a computer scientist, perhaps that makes me one. Then I thought a minute and realized she was right. What a surprise. It was an identity shock, like finding out you were adopted.

> * As I was writing this, Wendy was president of all the computer scientists (the ACM)— the alpha mandrill.

I had never wanted to be a computer scientist, only a producer-director of software, but I had worked long and hard, and fairly well, pursuing with intelligence and vigor certain technical concepts that most others refused to grasp; and I had published and published, and I had invented or discovered a few things acknowledged to be ahead of others, and I guess that carries me over the qualifying line. I'll be damned.

=== 2003 (I was 65)

Nottingham

Soon we were in England again. Helen Ashman, at the University of Nottingham, got a grant to bring me over as a visiting professor.

Nottingham wasn't at all like the movie. (Errol Flynn as Robin Hood was a hero in my boyhood.)

The Department overall was less friendly than Southampton's, but we fell into a nest of people who appreciated ZigZag.

ZIGZAG STORY

One friend, Adam Moore, a most charming and talented young northern-Irish chemist, proved astonishingly adept with the multiple dimensions of ZigZag. He did a demo of ZigZag for chemistry that is absolutely amazing.

Adam found things ZigZag would do that I never myself suspected. You don't have to know chemistry to be astounded by Adam's demo.*

*Video on line at Xanadu.com/zigzag.

Another friend, Jamie (J*) Goulding, did a great demo of ZigZag as it might work on a cellphone. (Not yet on line.)

Up the M1

While in Nottingham, I befriended a young programmer in Yorkshire, Jeremy Smith, and he worked on a new version of ZigZag that had 3D views. I drove up the M1 highway from Nottingham to Huddersfield several times for long work sessions with the lad.

ZIGZAG STORY

We demonstrated Jeremy's 3D ZigZag system at the Hypertext '03 conference in Nottingham. People found it hard to understand but it was spectacular.

=== 2003 (I was 66)

Oxford at Last (March 2004)

My senior year at Swarthmore I had planned to go on to Oxford in anthropology. This did not happen. Forty-five years later, however, I arrived in Oxford as a don.*

* As I understand it, an Oxford Don is a Fellow, Tutor or Professor at an Oxford College or Hall. My main title was Visiting Fellow of the Oxford Internet Institute, which was not a College or Hall. However, as a supplementary lagniappe, I was a Visiting Fellow at Wadham College. This meant I was a don, albeit a visiting don.

The Oxford Internet Institute has a wonderful atmosphere, almost as wonderful as Southampton's ECS under Wendy. Amiable, cheery Bill Dutton steers the Institute through academic and financial shoals while scholars of every stripe lecture on Internet topics and graduate students whirl through. It is a very nice place to be and we met a fascinating spectrum of people.

What would Jack Lang have said? ca. 2004

Jack Lang is a popular and dashing French politician, sometimes referred to as "the *real* Minister of Culture" even though he's no longer in that post.

French friends-- programmers, indeed-- set it up for me to meet with Lang. He was charismatic and clever and I liked him immensely.

I told him about transcopyright and the problems it could solve.

He was appreciative. 'I'm going to speak to the European parliament on copyright next week, and you've given me new ideas,' he said. 'I see that there could be other possibilities.'

But he didn't get, or get behind, the compelling uniqueness and power of transcopyright.

DOUG AND ME ⟶
Stay with Us, Doug (2004)

Doug Engelbart came to Oxford to speak, this time without Karen. He spoke at the OII but he wasn't in great shape.

We all went to an Italian restaurant, but as we started to sit down I asked, "Are you all right?" Doug said, "No."

I took Doug first to a clinic, then to the hospital. He had pneumonia. They checked him in and he relaxed. There he stayed for a week, then said he was ready to leave.

"But he's not ready to fly home," said the doctor.

That meant he got to stay with us! Oboy! It was a great gift. Doug normally wouldn't have had time to just hang around with us, but now he had to, and for two weeks Doug and I talked about everything.

Doug's planet is not my planet, but neither of us likes the computer planet we share, *their* planet on which we are both marooned, very much.

──── A Note from the Present
Doug had recently broken off his engagement to Karen O'Leary, and I think this undermined his health. Now they are very happily married and he is much healthier.

DOUG AND ME ⟶

What would Doug Engelbart have said? (1) 2004

Every day, for the two weeks Doug stayed with us, he and I talked at length. I explained to him issues about intellectual property, and why transcopyright was necessary, and I showed him ZigZag, and we had a wonderful time.

"This has been a real eye-opener," he said.

His last night, when he was ready to leave, we walked across Christchurch Green to a good restaurant. And as we walked, he said:

"*I'm happy!*"

Which for Doug or me, grimly frustrated as we are at the world's twisting of our ideas, was quite a statement.

Soaking Up Oxford

Our two years in Oxford flew by. The dinners at Wadham College were marvelous, with fascinating scholars and doctors coming in from every field. Oxford place is of course a great cultural Center, full of theaters and concerts and museums and lectures, and there was a stream of new friends coming through the OII, but of course our issue was always how to move forward with Xanadu and Zigzag—the two fundamental structures overlooked by the conventional computer world.

DEFINING MOMENTS
The Perfect Afternoon at Oxford, Dec. 2005

It was after-lunch coffee in the Senior Common Room at Wadham, my Oxford College. The room was exceptionally full, with perhaps thirty or forty dons, and sunlight was streaming in.

Above the chatter someone said: "Of course, Hitler and Wittgenstein went to high school together."

This was the perfect academic remark. It penetrated into every corner and the room fell silent. People moved toward that conversation, the group condensing. (Apparently it was true about Hitler and Wittgenstein, but neither Hitler nor Wittgenstein was influenced by the other. That made it trivia, rather than insight, but great trivia nonetheless .)

Now the room thinned. I found myself at the central round table, alone with an older professor.

I introduced myself.

He hesitated. "I'm... Roger Penrose," he said.

The Roger Penrose! *Sir* Roger Penrose! Discoverer of Penrose tiling, cosmologist who worked out black holes with Hawking! Thinking Penrose tiling was not unlike ZigZag, I had sent him a letter but had gotten no reply. Now he was at my mercy.

I showed him ZigZag and Adam's chemistry video. He was most interested. (He even emailed me afterward.)

It was the perfect ending to my Oxford Donship.

What would (Sir) Roger Penrose have said? Dec. 14, 2005

I treasure the email that Sir Roger sent me at 6:08 am.

"Dear Ted,

"Thanks for showing me your most intriguing way of displaying interconnections on a computer screen. I certainly hope that it catches on."

He didn't quite get the cosmology of hyperthogonal space, but it meant a lot to me nevertheless.

Chapter 18.
UMPWARD, 2006+

The work goes on.

XANADU STORY•────────
ZIGZAG STORY
Flying Documents: XanaduSpace

When my two-year contract at Oxford had ended, the question was whether Marlene and I should stay in England any longer. The answer was dramatic. A young programmer friend of ours, Rob Smith, agreed to build a 3D version of Xanadu— with ZigZag internals!

Some have difficulty understanding all the connections of Xanadu documents. I figured that a version of Xanadu in three dimensions could make the concept clearer. We held our breath. I worked with Rob, learning how OpenGL worked and how it could best be mapped to ZigZag.

Rob confirmed that ZigZag structure had indeed simplified the programming of this rather complex package.

Indeed, the prototype was sensational, and looked the way I wanted— flying pages with connections reaching into space, zooming typefaces, zooming point of view.

XANADU STORY•────────

IT'S ALL THERE,
INSIDE XANADUSPACE

XanaduSpace wasn't just a demo—the whole Xanadu system was working inside, without all the optimizations that had bogged us down in the past.

XANADU STORY•────────

STEPPING THROUGH CONNECTIONS

People have thought Xanadu is 'too complicated'—how can users find their way around so many connections?

The answer is shown in XanaduSpace. The user may step through connections one at a time, in a vivid and clarifying setting.

⋅XANADU TECH

WHAT'S WORKING INSIDE XANADUSPACE: ALL THE XANADU FUNCTIONS

XanaduSpace actually enacts successfully all the main Xanadu functions.
- it sends for content portions
- it assembles content portions into pages
- it finds transclusions by addresses
- user can step along transclusions
- it overlays xanalinks
- user can step along xanalinks

and more.

ZIGZAG STORY
ZIGZAG FOR SOFTWARE INTERNALS

In 2006, we at last made ZigZag the internal data structure of a Xanadu implementation. Rob built XanaduSpace on a fast, efficient ZigZag skeleton. This showed that ZigZag was not just a colorful interface structure for simple data, but that it could be a lean, mean and reliable internal data engine.

WORKING INSIDE:
ZIGZAG DATA MANAGEMENT AT HIGH SPEED

XanaduSpace is built on multidimensional list structures—hyperthogonal structure, or ZigZag internals. For the first time, ZigZag handles high-speed data management inside a program--
- a zzcell manages each on-screen data position

- a zzcell manages each 3-space data position
- a zzcell manages each individual shape within OpenGL

This proved my belief that ZigZag could work as an internal structure for high-speed software internals, simplifying programming, and do industrial-scale data management at industrial speed. (This one is programmed in C++.)

XANADU STORY

Rob did a brilliant job programming XanaduSpace.

Then the project gradually lost momentum. Rob thought of XanaduSpace as finished, whereas we needed consumer product. To make XanaduSpace a functioning product would require far more continuing work.

We paid a lot of money, but at way under commercial rates. Understandably, Rob felt he couldn't continue on that basis. But unfortunately only Rob could work on it because of its many levels– C++, OpenGL, ZigZag, Python, and installer packaging. Even to document this sufficiently to involve other programmers would cost far more than we had already spent.

For two years after my job in Oxford, Marlene and I stayed on there, hoping to get XanaduSpace to a commercial level, but Rob drifted on to other things and we returned to the USA with yet another prototype.

On we go.

DOUG AND ME

What would Doug Engelbart have said? (2)
(2004-current)

Doug has been having difficulty with his memory, but his mind is still great. I have shown him XanaduSpace and ZigZag several times. He is always wonderfully appreciative and his reactions are clever.

'What are you doing to publicize this?' he recently asked.

'Only everything in my whole life,' I said.

'We should hold a big meeting,' said Doug.

That is Doug's way. The last thing I want is a big meeting.

What would Donald Knuth have said? 1957-current

"I saw nothing flaky."

After the *Wired* attack I asked Don Knuth, the world authority on algorithms, if he would please go through the Xanadu algorithms with me and state, as an objective observer, whether they were based on 'ignorance' or otherwise deficient, as alleged by Gory Jackal in that foul piece.

By that time I had known Knuth for nearly forty year, in a way. (In fact we had both been first published nationally in the same journal.*) I read his first published piece when I was in college, though years later when I was aware of him as a computer professional I did not know it was the same person.

* *Mad.*

At first, shortly after the *Wired* attack in 1995, Knuth agreed to review my work, but then he changed his mind and demurred. That was about 1996. (Even though the attack was in 1995, the article still stands, smolders and throws off its stink, and probably will forever, so rebutting it by every means is no small matter to me and to the future of the Xanadu Project.)

I did not give up on Knuth, though. Uniquely in the world, he remains the authority on algorithms, and thus the unique voice to say we of the Xanadu team were not ignorant fools.

I mulled over the question of how to get a testimonial by Knuth, and finally played the big card.

I wrote to Don Knuth asking his help not as a computer scientist but *as a Christian*.

I had very mixed feelings about doing this, having been very anti-Christian at some times in my life, but there is no reason that as a generic person in distress I could not avail myself of his Christian charity. Since he has retired from email, I Fedexed him and pleaded for his help. I asked him to look at the Xanadu internals and some of my other technical work as a Christian helping a fellow man.

He called the next day and offered to help immediately, inviting me to his home on the Stanford campus.

He used to be quite macho; he has gotten much Gandhier.*

* Thanks to Karen Engelbart for this word.
―――― ~~COINED~~ WORDS ――――――――

We spent two pleasant and intense hours at his house. I showed him my visual triumphs, XanaduSpace and ZigZag; but, alas, he said visuals and interface didn't mean much to him.

What did that leave to show him? It left various data structures and algorithms, especially enfilades (the Model T enfilade that I had discovered, the tumbler enfilades of xu88 Xanadu that the other guys had developed— remember, I was trying to get vindication for the whole project as well as myself), and the internals of ZigZag.

Knuth was positive about everything I explained to him, but not, to my surprise, very impressed. The best thing he said about the algorithms was "I saw nothing flaky." Coming from Knuth, that's a pretty solid compliment, but not one that travels well; you can't take it to the bank or to the Establishment screamers at *Wired*. "I saw nothing flaky" was nothing I could publish in rebuttal to the attack. So nothing was accomplished, except for a very enjoyable intellectual conversation with a kind and wonderful guy.

I think of Knuth as a *real* computer scientist—not diverted by packages and conventions (like the World Wide Web, email and Facebook) that dominate the field today.

Thus endeth the tale.

Chapter 19.
CREATIVE CONTROL, MOVIES, SOFTWARE, AND ME

~ MAKING MOVIES ~
Creative Control
SPLANDREMICS — *Presentational Arts, Structures and Conventions*

> The difference between the right word and the almost-right word is the difference between the lightning and the lightning bug.
> — Mark Twain

> God is in the details.
> — 19th-century Shaker motto, lately reformulated as, "the devil is in the details," unfortunately.

—— COINED WORDS ——
Microtheology, the belief that God is in the details. (There's probably a better one.)

"Creative control" sounds as though it's only about art. It's about the fulfillment of any vision that needs to be done right. "Creative control" is a Hollywood term that applies everywhere. The computer world, like Hollywood, is an eternal struggle for powers of creative control.

In both the computer world and Hollywood, most people fight their battles for creative control on a small scale, for some part nearly within their grasp, but only a few people wield it massively—the moguls of old, now some like Spielberg who can do whatever they want.

In the computer world as well, creative control is wielded massively across the board by only a few— at earlier key times, by Bob Taylor, Gates and Stallman; and now by Jobs, Warnock, Ellison, Berners-Lee and Schmidt, each with his own agenda, doctrine and style.

I have striven for serious creative control on that scale and so far lost, but the game isn't over and I'm still ambitious. And I still know things about software design and electronic documents that I don't think anyone else does.

THERE HAS TO BE A DIRECTOR

I never got along particularly well with authority, except where theater was involved. I was in plays from first grade or kindergarten, I believe, and in plays it was made clear that the director was in charge. I accepted this because it was for the good of the show. Any director was better than no director; without coordination the show would be a sprawling mess.

> -------- **A Note from the Present**
> Readers may be tempted to an Oedipal interpretation here, seeing that my father became a director when I was nine or ten.
>
> However, I had come to believe in theatrical directors much earlier. I had been in plays since I was four or five, and a rather knowing moviegoer soon after, and it became clear to me as a boy that someone has to be in charge of a theatrical production or movie.* Watching my father work later simply confirmed this view.
>
> > * Aurand Harris, my second-grade homeroom teacher, was a wonderful director, and became gradually a famous and prolific author of children's plays.
>
> My views of creative control in my own work I came to entirely on my own, in fights with editors. My views of Hollywood issues I have obtained through other channels; Ralph Nelson never talked about these things.

This applies to any creative endeavor. In order for the result to make sense, someone has to make the decisions in a unified fashion.

There can only be one driver of a car, one captain of a ship; in both these cases the person who steers should also adjust the speed. And in these cases there are *only two parameters, speed and direction!* How much more complicated it is in movies, media and the presentational arts, where there are hundreds of adjustments, each impacting the rest. One person has to manage all these parts together.

In publishing this person is called the *author* (who must often give way to the next one, the *editor*). In recording this person is the *record producer*, in symphonies the *conductor*, in museums the *exhibition curator*. But in each case (at a given time) this person tries to control all the parts, blending and balancing and reworking the whole, deciding how to make it all fit together into a unified whole that the viewer can understand and appreciate.

PRESENTATIONAL ARTS ARE ALL THE SAME
SPLANDREMICS Presentational Arts, Structures and Conventions

We could say "media"; let me here say "presentational arts." The presentational arts are all the same. In writings, publications, movies, plays, recordings, one person must–
- imagine the mind of the receiving party
- contrive a presentation to the receiving party to get across ideas and feelings and connotations

Unfortunately there is no comprehensive name for this role, so I'll just say "director."

Creative Control
CREATIVE CONTROL IN GENERAL

The term "creative control" is used most in Hollywood, but it applies to all creative endeavors. Who controls the details? Who controls the final decisions?

This is an issue in movies, the presentational arts in general, and in software (even though the term "creative control" is mostly heard in the movie industry). We will make movies the main example.

Creative control is political. (The world called "Hollywood" is actually an ecological, political system for who gets creative control, a sorting-out Darwinian process; but we can't get into that here.)

THE DIRECTOR

For simplicity's sake we'll assume that one person has creative control at a time, knowing that there is always someone who wants to grab it and take it away.

For the party who has creative control at a given moment, we'll just use the term "director," though it's misleading. (Politically, this is an oversimplification; the control that movie directors have is limited.*)

> * Indeed, the term "Director's Cut" states explicitly that the director didn't get to finish a film the way he wanted.
>
> In movies, creative control is officially in the hands of the director; but the director generally serves at the whim of, and is trumped by, the producer, who can override his decisions or fire him. In the old days, the producer could be trumped by the mogul, who could in turn be trumped by the distributor (who often owned the studio, as with MGM). There are many tales of movies that were changed at the last minute by persons up this food chain from the director.
>
> Nevertheless, I will use the term "director" as shorthand for the person who is supposed to be in charge of all aspects at a given time; let the reader wink.

The director maintains overview and adjustment, from the planning phase through to the final result, carrying forward the original vision as best he can.

The vision may have many uncertainties, but the director tries to hang onto its center. James Cameron recently described the process– in this case, how he and his team populated his film "Avatar" with creatures and forest people—

```
We sought out and selected the very best fantasy
artists in the world, and turned them loose. They
promptly ran off to the horizon in all directions,
stretching the envelope far beyond what I had
imagined. I found myself in the role of herding cats,
gently coaxing them back toward the forms as I had
imagined them. But of course this was not a precise
process, for these creatures did not exist sharply
defined, but only as faint ghosts. Potentials.
Things that might be.
```
　　　　　　　　-- James Cameron, "Epilogue,"
　　　　　　　　in Lisa Fitzpatrick, *The Art of Avatar* (Abrams).

There are many political and interpersonal issues that can get in the way of the vision. People will not always do what the director says, or in the way he wants. To fight this, a director's interpersonal strategies must be diverse.* Giving orders sometimes works, but persuasion and subtlety often do more.

> * As are those of his adversaries. See the excellent book on the film industry by Lynda Obst, *Hello, He Lied*.

DIRECTORS' TRICKS

For instance, In movies and TV, the director may use many tricks to manipulate actors, and those above him.
- The wily director John Ford used innumerable tricks and stratagems to get his way; see the marvelous book by Robert Parrish, *Growing Up in Hollywood.*
- I observed my father, Ralph Nelson, playing pranks on "the sponsor's man" who was out to give him a list of changes after the dress rehearsal. Ralph's favorite trick, he told me, was to end the show with an intolerable surprise, and start his stopwatch. For instance, a 1957 episode of "Climax", in which I had a walk-on part, was a shipboard drama— which Ralph ended unexpectedly with footage of the ship sinking. In seconds the sponsor's man was there, demanding and imploring that Ralph not end the show that way. 'By the time I allowed him to persuade me,' said Ralph, 'all his notes were forgotten.'

SPLANDREMICS — *Presentational Arts, Structures and Conventions*
~ **MAKING MOVIES** ~
SOFTWARE IS MOVIES

I have long contended that interactive software is movies, a branch of cinema (not a metaphor but a literal statement).

What is a movie? Events on a screen that affect the mind and heart of the viewer.

What is software? Events on a screen that affect the mind and heart of the viewer. AND INTERACT. AND HAVE CONSEQUENCES.

So the design of software is a branch of movie-making; IT'S HOW TO REACH THE MIND AND HEART; and the principal way to learn it is not computer science, but to study your Disney, your Griffith, your Welles, and so on. Making the program loops go around is entirely subsidiary.

This brings us to the problem in software.

~ **MAKING MOVIES** ~
THE PROBLEM IN SOFTWARE: NO DIRECTOR

The reason most software is terrible is that nobody is in charge. The movie director can in principle select and change—
- the actors
- the camera angle
- the music
- the order of scenes

and so on,

All to make it look right to the user.

Who has that authority in software? A few moguls like Jobs, Warnock and Ellison.

Otherwise, software is made by *permanently delegated individuals and teams*, and judged to be successful if it fulfills a checklist—*not for how it comes across to the user.*

Most software has no director— nobody with the authority to decide and change every part—and that's why it's all so lousy.

Nobody knows this because of the Myth of Technology. Since the database is supposedly "technology" and the interface is supposedly "technology" and the organization of the website is supposedly "technology", these are delegated without recourse to people with technical knowledge and no particular presentational ability.*

> * I am not saying that technical people have *less* than average presentational ability, just average. But average is not good enough where important projects are concerned.

A nice example is the lavish website of the BBC (bbc.com). In the presentational art of radio, BBC's programs have always been superb. But the website is different. BBC's site works fine for listening on line. But trying to find anything else is a nightmare. *And management doesn't know how bad it is, because they've given final control to their trusted tekkies.* It's like that everywhere.

If movies were made that way, a movie would be finished when—
- every shot listed in the script was taken, once
- the shots were put in the right order by a clerk

but you know what a lousy movie that would make.

(And worse, there are very few programmers willing to be directed. That is a problem of the industry.)

Creative Control
CREATIVE CONTROL AND ME

> "Creative control isn't the main thing.
> "It's the only thing."
> – *sports saying, transposed*

Since college I have always had simple personal objectives for all my projects: independence and creative control. I wanted my own company, like Wright's studio or the early Disney organization, where I could do big creative projects with a fair-size staff, so as to work through others. (I dreamt of working on the scale of Wright or Disney of that day, not with today's massive staffs of Jobs and Lucas and Cameron.)

But more important than resources and staff was independence. Because unless an idea is finished right, it isn't the idea I care about any more.*

> * Someone recently emailed me that I should be happy, my ideas were all over the world. I replied that I get to say what my ideas are, not he.
>
> There are tens of thousands of companies out there based on my ideas—indeed, you might say most of the personal computer industry—but they are no longer my ideas. My ideas are the ones I get to finish the way they should be finished. Others are "interpretations," indeed often misunderstandings.

I started off well-grounded in the presentational arts, but with a dangerous early taste of creative control—I cannot bear to work on projects where the final decisions are left to others. I could never be just a team member or somebody else's 'idea man'. (For a discussion of others with this problem, see Appendix 2, "Brothers," specifically Wright, Orson and Bucky.)

> * I made one sincere attempt at such a collaboration, on the Brown University HES project, and I regret it totally. Not discussed in this edition.

I have the heart of a New York low-budget filmmaker, like Cassavetes, John Sayles, Larry Moyer— hanging onto creative control at all costs.* From 1959, I intended to make cheapo movies on my own with my own money, and get to Hollywood from there (before Ralph surprised me by doing it).

> * A number of New York low-budget filmmaker types work in Hollywood but remain true to those roots—people like Woody Allen and Tarantino.

Creative control is not just about egotism and art. It's about the integrity of ideas. Making sure that Xanadu is done *right,* above all.

HANDSHAKE DEALS WITH PROGRAMMERS

Interactive software, as I have often said, is a branch of movie-making. The problem of creative control is exactly the same in software as in movies. The way to keep creative control in a movie is to do it on the cheap. The way to keep creative control of software is to do it on the cheap.

There is no way to keep creative control in software with startup money.

That's why I still go on handshake deals with programmers— like those handshake deals that founded Apple, Microsoft, Autodesk and Google, whose founders also wanted— and managed— to keep creative control. That is why their companies achieved special success—they did not seek, or accept, backing. The only reason that Jobs and Gates and John Walker and Larry Page and Sergei Brin were able to build Apple and Microsoft and Autodesk and Google with their intelligent visions was that they got started with no backers.*

> * True, Jobs found one backer, Mike Markkula, to carry him from the Apple I to the Apple II—but Markkula trusted Jobs and left the key decisions to him. Very special case.

INTERACTION STORY
BITTERSWEET WORK WITH PROGRAMMERS

Working with programmers has been a bittersweet experience. I have almost always worked with programmers that I like and respect— I won't mention the exceptions— and some have been deep friends. About half of them have been wonderfully faithful to my designs. Others, however, often want to add their own "creative touches," which range from annoying to disastrous.

As they say in Hollywood, "Everybody wants to direct."

If a design is sprawling, changes may not be noticed. If a design is minimalist, the smallest change can be catastrophic. My designs are usually minimalist, and changes generally break the design, losing the simplicity and elegance and clarity. I will not complain here about which designs were changed.

So the slog goes like this—
- explain the general idea
- propose new mechanism(s)
- argue over new mechanism(s)
- come to gradual agreement
- write the specs
- explain the specs
- cajole and implore
- run errands for the programmer
- wait
- wait
- look at the results
- explain why it should be different

and on and on

until the program is properly finished, or (more often) simply has to be delivered.

As a producer-director of numerous software projects,* I always work from a particular vision. Working with the programmers, I would explain the vision and explore with them the technicalities that would be necessary, working out the detailed specs with them, and supervising the result according to the vision I had presented. This is essentially the same process I had used in all my media experiences before computers— immersing myself in the details of the available options and choosing. Except that programming technicalities are so much more complicated than printing or movie technicalities; the possibilities have to be discussed in stupefying detail for hours, sometimes months, sometimes conversations that continue for years.

* listed in appendix 3.

The programmers, however excellent in character and abilities, however close as friends, did not have (and could not have) the vision before their eyes that I did. Visions are hard to communicate; and once communicated, they drift. I would have to present the vision to them over and over, like Disney with his animators.

Over and over I would come up with designs which they reluctantly implemented; and over and over, the payoff has come when the programmer saw the result and was gratified— and surprised.* They imagined approximately what I planned precisely, but by following my exact instructions achieved what they did not expect, coming to see something much better than they had imagined, even though all the technicalities were in their hands. (The best example is the raving endorsements of my JOT design by Mark Miller and Jonathan vos Post, in this book around 1978.)

* As when I presented *Nothing #3* to the printer Ned Pyle.

Alas, none of my designs has so far reached the public. But will.

"WHY DIDN'T YOU FIND A BACKER?"

> As soon as you've got backers, you're on a deadly schedule. And they want you to fail, because then they get it all.
> -- *Anon.*

In my position I have had to answer a lot of questions, many extremely naïve. Those who have not tried to build things have no idea what it's like trying to get backing, or the curse of getting it.

To simplify things, let's consider the first-level backers ("angels") and the sanctified supermen of our time ("venture capitalists").

Dealing with either is taking your life in your hands, especially if you care about the outcome of the project rather than the money.

1. Backers, or "ANGEL INVESTORS"

> "You don't want angel investors.
> "Angel investors are the worst.
> "They're in your shorts and up your butt."
> -- former AT&T business analyst
> (name withheld)

> 'When I was looking to finance my film, "The Moving Finger," I found a backer who gave me a check for $30,000 in return for an introduction to the female lead. But she gave him the clap, so he tore up the check.'
> -- Larry Moyer

Many people have the notion that an inventor can find idealistic backers to fund his idea. This is extremely rare; we may refer to such a backer as an Easter Bunny Backer.

Getting backing is a dance. The guy with the project has to supply phony business plans and phony financial projections, which *everyone knows* are phony, and then the backers insult him with slogans in order to beat down his share and harshen the terms.

The first thing a backer wants is control; the second thing is the inventor OUT. Backers are not interested in elegance, power for users, destiny, literature or civilization. They just want to figure out how to get rid of you as soon as possible.

In general, having a backer means four hands on the steering wheel, and it is the backer—with less understanding of the ideas than the inventor—who wins.

2. THE MYTH OF THE VENTURE CAPITALIST

> As a rule, venture capitalists are the most shallow, conventional, pompous and smug individuals on the planet.
> -- *Anon.*

> 99% of venture capitalists give the rest a bad name.
> -- *old lawyer joke, transposed*

Venture capitalists are the most overpraised people in the world. (They can afford the p.r.)

The role now popularly called "venture capitalist" was created by the Securities Act of 1933, which was intended to protect widows and orphans from being cheated, but had the unintended effect of making it far harder for honest inventors—with no 'track record'-- to get backing. It raised the bar of registration and due diligence past the amount of money most inventors need in the first place.

Venture capitalists have a specific agenda: to take a company public and depart. That means a specific scenario:
 • After specific rounds of financing over approximately a four-year period, the company is taken public, with shares distributed to favored banks, etc.
 • The value of the company *must then rise briefly,* so that the VCs and other investors can get their money out and run.

Many inventors have been persuaded that this is the way it has to be done. But there are other, less glamorous ways to go public, and usually smarter ways to build a company—particularly if you care about the company and the product, rather than the stock price and fobbing it onto the public according to a price profile on a timetable.

WHAT ABOUT OPEN SOURCE?

What they say now is: Do it in open source! Ah, but to run a project in open source you have to like email, and you have to be one of the boys.

WHY DIDN'T YOU JUST LEARN TO PROGRAM?

Ah, you say, Nelson could have done it all if he'd "just learned to program."

In fact this is true, except for the word "just."

It was in fact my first plan in 1960-1 to program what I wanted myself, as indeed many have.* But what I wanted to do was far too sweeping for my skills and it was a million dollars too early to own a computer.

> * I made early wild attempts to do so in FAP (the assembler for the 7090).

Learning to program is not simply a threshold to cross, like learning to ride a bicycle or losing virginity. You don't 'learn to program'. You devote your life to it. It's a perpetual uphill slog and requires hours a day, every day. (See Peter Norvig, "Teach Yourself Programming in Ten Years." On the net.)

Yes, small programs in Basic or TRAC, such as I did, are easy.*

> * And would have worked for the Itty Bitty suite, had that gone ahead.

But for my deeper designs of enfilades, graphics, file management, protocol manipulation and radical internals, I would have needed a great breadth of skills honed over a long time.*

> * For example, XanaduSpace, which I did with Rob Smith, is written in layers– C++, OpenGL, Python, ZigZag for internal live data, and a layer called ZZogl, which connects OpenGL to ZigZag for dynamic control. ZigZag and zzogl were my designs, even though actually coding and debugging is still beyond my ability.

By the time a personal computer with a system language was available (in 1979– C for the 8080 by Leor Zolman), I was heavily in debt and there was no way to barricade the\

door for years to learn it. I had to support myself full time with the saleable skills I had.

From time to time I have made multiweek stabs at learning C, Perl, Java, Visual Basic, Python and ActionScript,* but there was never time (or consultation) which would let me continue. Meanwhile, deals and projects kept surfacing that seemed to promise what we needed.

> * Not to mention RealBasic, which a friend highly recommended, but which everyone reviles because of its name.

Those are the reasons. Call them excuses if you will. That I could not build my designs myself remains for me a matter of everlasting regret.

But I did what I was good at. I am a software producer-director.

Disney did not draw.

He enacted his vision through others.

As must I.

Synchronization of Agendas

My friend Kip Larson once surprised me with an astute observation: 'Marriage is the synchronization of agendas.' That's not how we usually think about it, but it's the real problem.

Creative endeavors, and business, are the same. When people have different agendas they pull in different directions, and then apart.*

> * In his epic poem, "The Hunting of the Snark," Lewis Carroll described a dozen voyagers hunting something called a Snark– and each imagined the Snark to be something completely different. This is a fmiliar situation.

Harmonizing the agendas is the hardest part. And that's why great leaders spend so much time getting people on the same wavelength.

Unfortunately, when the agenda is hard to explain, and goes into territories that others do not imagine, and no one believes or imagines what you are talking about, the going gets very tough. And should you tell them about the far consequences of what you envision? No, they have enough trouble imagining the next step.

A vision is a curse: it calls you on no matter what, sacrificing your life and everything else you might have done; it emburdens those around you; it becomes a target of doubt and ridicule; it enrages those who think it's already fulfilled.

The main purpose of this book is to find others still open to this vision and this agenda.

Chapter 20.
THE FIGHT FOR CIVILIZATION

1. COMPUTER HISTORY

> History is a myth that men agree to believe.
> *Napoleon Bonaparte*
>
> Any event, once it has occurred,
> can be made to appear inevitable
> by a competent historian.
> *Lee Simonson*
>
> Today's computer world is based on tekkie misunderstandings
> of human thought and human life.
> *TN*

"History" in the popular sense is a tale of the past that gets simpler and simpler, from which connections, depth and outliers— in other words, stories like mine— are gradually deleted in the popular mind.

I've told my own story here, with little said about what else was going on. What else happened in the computer world in those fifty years? Here is computer history as I see it, rather different from the standard picture.*

> * This view of computer history is further expounded in my book *Geeks Bearing Gifts*.

TRADITION! Computer traditions and conventions were extended and extended and never questioned.   These are:
- Lump files
- hierarchical structure
- text made of sequential characters with embedded markup
- every document is in a file (meaning that links can only point out)
- only one document per file

I believe these traditions are pernicious and blinding.

THE MAJOR STEPS OF COMPUTER HISTORY

Let's say it began with Unix, which perfected the hierarchical directory and allowed longish filenames.

• Unix, the saying goes, "made everything a file,", and so big lumps with names (files), arranged in hierarchical directories, became the nature of the world.

• Unix had a layer called the *shell*, created by Louis Pouzin, which allowed casual programming as an assembly of program pieces. Your shell program could tell different program pieces to feed results to each other. Shell scripts were taken away with the rigid "applications" in the Macintosh and Windows.

• Unix invited you to arrange programs and files in particular ways, creating a sense of order. However, the hierarchical directories run wild in most people's Mac and Windows systems, so nothing can be found except by flailing searches.

• As a counsel of despair, the new operating systems (like the Ipad) throw away any arrangement of storage and concentrate instead on searching through the user's hopeless soup.

• Xerox PARC—the guys treated as fabled heroes in all the speeches and writings– dumbed down the computer (with application prisons) and took away the user's right to program (shell scripts).

• Xerox PARC defined documents as paper simulation, and dumbed down documents (removing all connective structure). Remember, Xerox wanted to sell printers.

• The two biggest packagers, Jobs and Gates, took the Xerox PARC dumbdown of computers and sugar-coated it for the public (calling it the Macintosh and Windows, respectively). Jobs' genius was to sell the Xerox PARC package (under the name Macintosh) to people who considered themselves creatively defiant. Gates' genius was to sell a very similar package (under the name Windows) to the shallow, conventional, pompous and smug.

• Another packager, Tim Berners-Lee, took the Brown University dumbdown of hypertext (to one-way links) and put it on the Internet; two university students (Eric Bina and Marc Andreessen) put that system into the PUI (a PARC application window). Their interface was first called Mosaic, then Netscape and Internet Explorer, and the result is the World Wide Web as we know it.

These events imposed on the world a specific kind of prison, entirely of human making and unrelated to the computer underneath–
- hierarchical structure for your information, based on computer tradition. (The PARC dumbdown made the directories look like folders, but that did not affect the structure in the slightest)
- what is not hierarchical is rectangular–spreadsheet, relational database, documents
- the computer is dumbed down into a paper simulator! Documents are enforced into paper simulation–that is, rectangular and sequential structure, with trivial connectivity (one-way links). And everyone is encouraged to fiddle with fonts, which is like putting on costumes–an enjoyable form of play but with no important effect. (Fonts are used as a way of distinguishing things that should be structurally distinct.)
- paper simulation continued on the web, with only one-way connections that could not overlap
- it is impossible to show any connection between the contents of windows (my 1972 proposal for transpointing windows)
- because many people's files are hopelessly mislaid, much new software emphasizes search through a user's disorganized soup.

The public sees these as issues of "technology"–the most misleading word in the world today. Most of what the public calls "technology" refers to conventions and packages and conventions you weren't invited to choose.

People are semi-satisfied with all this because it's colorful and noisy, they can imagine nothing better, and the alternatives I have been able to show so far they cannot understand, despite all I have said and written.

So much for general computer history. What about electronic documents?

2. THE CHOICES FOR DOCUMENTS

> In the news there is no truth; and in the truth there is no news.
> *Russian proverb*

> Power corrupts; obsolete power corrupts obsoletely.
> *TN*

> No matter how you push the envelope, it's still stationery.
> *Anon.*

I asked in 1960,

How do we improve on paper?

My evolving answer was: *we can represent every possible type of connection, interactively and with animation, to clarify every possible literary structure to the user.*

But a decade later something different, something very stupid happened. The others with big money behind them *imitated paper*, which to me is incomprehensible.* And paper simulation became the backbone of today's computer world.

> * Xerox wanted to sell printers based on their copier engine, so paper simulation with fonts and page numbers fit right in. Warnock, at Adobe, made an alliance with the traditional type designers, which is why we're still stuck with "point sizes" from the 18th Century and can't incrementally thicken and modify type as we see it on the screen.

Ignoring Engelbart's work and mine, paper simulation is what Bob Taylor's group did at Xerox PARC, with projects Bravo (under Chuck Simonyi) and Interpress (under John Warnock).
- Simonyi took Bravo to Microsoft and it became Microsoft Word.
- Warnock started Adobe to commercialize Interpress, which was christened PostScript and later Adobe Acrobat.
- Then Berners-Lee put paper simulation on the Internet with HTML, creating the World Wide Web. Bina and Andreessen put this into the PARC User Interface (PUI, often called "the modern GUI"), creating the "web browser" as we know it.

Many people have thought this paper simulation was all wonderful because they didn't imagine anything else. But it did not improve the representation of documents or the organization of ideas. Instead it turned mankind's attention to *fonts*, as a cheap way of showing distinctions that should be in the structure of text.

But I see it as the victory of typesetters over authors. Like the ancient Egyptian priests, who did not celebrate life but put people's organs uselessly into canopic jars, we are sealing text into canopic jars of simulated paper (.doc files, PDFs and E-books) and pronouncing the matter handled.

Paper simulation is retrograde. Imitating paper is to me like tearing the wings off a 747 and driving it on the highway as a bus. *WHERE ARE THE CONNECTIONS?*

On the Xanadu project we sought to represent every possible literary structure and connection. Mankind deserves no less. Structures based on deeper, different documents will be far better for human life. Electronic documents should be entirely different and far more powerful.

But right now nobody seems to imagine such an alternative. You cannot put marginal notes on today's electronic documents,* let alone publish marginal notes. You cannot refer to or connect to parts of electronic documents. And on and on. This is insane.

> * There are local forms of annotation, such as on Kindle and PDF, but you can't connect the different formats.

We must be able to—
- Underline anything (not just within one application)
- Put sticky notes on anything (not just within one application)
- Annotate anything
- Make visible connections between parts of any documents, in any formats
- Re-use and combine content from all formats, RETAINING CONNECTION TO THEIR SOURCES
- Bind pages together with visible connection-lines

And much more.

I believe the world is crippled by the present system and nobody knows it. What we have is the victory of typesetters over authors— the vacuous triumph of appearance over substance, clarity and reason.*

> * Or is that the doom of our times? — the vacuous triumph of appearance over substance, clarity and reason?

To me this is not some mere technicality, not an idle musing, but the fight for civilization itself.

My central concern with Xanadu was to create a publishing system with universal quotability by transclusion, a concept I saw as vital, in the face of a great deal of shallow and dimwitted incomprehension. This seemed to me as vital for civilization has anything possibly could be.

Billions of people have been deluded to think that electronic documents can only simulate paper. It is time to show them better.

The choices are: the conventional computer world–
- Lump files lost in directories
- One-way links
- Paper simulation in canopic jars

VERSUS
- Representing the real interconnections we need to deal with.

That's worth fighting for.

3. PUBLISHING SHREDDED

Because the Web required downloading everything and did not offer enclosed presentation, the web publisher had no choice but to give everything away.

This has resulted in the proletarianization of media. The worst and the best are all free, newspapers and other information sources are being shut down, expertise is being lost, the culture is being hollowed out.

The Xanadu project always included a micropayment system for publishing—not to discourage giving things away, but to provide a clean alternative means of sale which did not restrict re-use of content—in fact, which allowed *enhanced* re-use of content—
- in any new context
- with a path back to the original
- with micropayment to the original publisher, where required

This is a win-win for everybody. (See Appendix 1.)

4. THE GRIM FUTURE

> The long gone goblins loom ahead;
> The deadly, that we thought were dead,
> Are waiting, every one.
> — Walt Kelly

In today's darkening, precarious world, are the possibilities for mankind running out?

As I write, we are in a fallen and uniquely-fragile world economy. Will it recover, or have we already reached the collapse of civilization foretold by the Club of Rome?*

> * All the simulations they ran, with different sets of premises, ended in the collapse of agriculture, government, transportation, medicine, all of civilization-- and the collapse of the human population to a small fraction of its present size. Is this inevitable? Are we there yet? Are we there yet?

The young people of the net appear to me a sarcastic rabble. They take for granted the prison walls of today's "social sites" and think they are free there. America today seems a walled garden around the arrogantly ignorant, ridiculing and shooting each other and watching soap operas.

Meanwhile the clouds and the angry gather outside.

Now the poor and angry have AK-47s, soon the poor and angry will have nukes. The history of the 21st Century may never be written. Surely the population collapse will come before that time.

But can the outcome be better? Can better document systems help us, as Doug Engelbart hoped long ago, to solve the complex and urgent problems of today? Can we ever—
- reduce the dangers of nuclear weapons?
- create peace and justice in the middle east?
- reduce pollution?
- fight poverty and injustice?
- slow population growth?
- turn back global warming?
- save the last rain forests?

And on and on.

I will not try to enumerate today's global problems. These are the "complex urgent problems" Doug Engelbart warned us about long ago, which he unswervingly sought tools and methods to solve. (Doug's work was swept aside by paper simulation and the cult of fonts.)

The Club of Rome said there was only one global problem, and they called it the *Problématique.*

Call it one problem or many-- where to begin?

I say begin with non-trivial connection tools for the mind. There is still a chance for decent document tools, enabling us to organize and annotate and connect and keep track of things by connections instead of hierarchy (conventional computing) or text strings (Google).

That may make it possible for civilization to continue. Or begin again after it crashes.

Chapter 21
UNBOWED

> I mistook a clear view for a short distance.
> — TN

> There's a saying: "In the country of the blind, the one-eyed man is king." Ah, but what about the country of the one-eyed? In the country of the one-eyed, nobody believes that there's someone who can see in stereo. In the country of the one-eyed, the two-eyed guy had better watch *himself*.
> — TN

So here we are. If you didn't enjoy the story of my life, neither did I. Like one of my boyhood heroes, Old Man Kangaroo, I did not want to live an ordinary life, but then I did not want to live the one I got, either.

Human life is so full of possibility. It is hard to know what to do. So many roads not taken might have led elsewhere better. I will not bore you with those thoughts.

I have worked long and hard to build a better world through interactive computing, and so far failed rather badly. The only design of mine that is widely deployed is the Back Button, which is trivial.

BUT STILL STANDING

> (What did you do during the [French] Revolution?)
>
> "I survived."
> — Emmanuel-Joseph Sieyès

Many did not survive the French revolution, and many, in fact, did not survive the computer revolution. We all hear about the ones who made big bucks, but not the ones who went bankrupt and slunk away.

I have survived. More importantly, I have survived without giving up, giving in, selling out, knuckling under, falling over or narrowing down.

My ideals, and my adherence to them, are untarnished. I still stand for all the principles I enunciated in *Computer Lib* and through the decades. I have never imitated anybody, though I have had many heroes.

Many think of me a clown or a pet loony, like Joe Gould or Emperor Norton. Friendlier parties perhaps think of me as a meathead on a Promethead,* a sissy on a Sisyphiïd.‡

> * A great mission to bring enlightenment, like Prometheus' delivering fire to mankind.
> ‡ A repetitive work ordeal, a torment of ponderous repetition– like the labor of Sisyphus, forever rolling a big rock back uphill.

"Then there's Ted Nelson" is a phrase lecturers use, trying to fit me into other narratives. But I don't fit in those other narratives.

I WAS HERE FIRST AND IT'S ALL GONE WRONG

I believe I clearly envisioned personal computing, personal software, text systems and world-wide hypertext—AND their psychological and commercial aspects– at least a decade ahead of anyone else.* (A much fuller list is in the Appendices.)

> * Doug Engelbart designed a great and powerful text system, but consumer deployment, rights commerce, politics, psychology, snazzy presentation and political issues were not in his picture.

―― **COINED WORDS** ――――――――
Here's a new one for the psychopathology manual: *possiplexia*, being overwhelmed by possibilities—either freezing in the face of them, like people I know, or trying to grab them all, like me.

Because of politics and overreaching, I was unable to leverage any of this.

I have had a lot of ideas and moved through various elites and had minor adventures, but so far achieved nothing. (My friends say: *think of all the people you've inspired!* Thanks a lot. I look out and see what the results have been and feel sick at heart.)

I believe I was right all along and that the others have not figured it out yet. But this gives me scant comfort.

I bear a heavy burden. Not just for myself but for the world. The pain and sorrow of my failures are with me every moment, mingled with outrage and dislike of the world the others have built. I believe this would be a far better world today, with a better future, if I had gotten traction with my ideas– very different from the conventional ideas that have so far prevailed.

But that's only so far. The story has now become an epic with a cast of billions. And this movie is not over, nor is my part in it.

I have no alternative but to go on. Like Shackleton of Antarctica, I find myself enmeshed in a harsh duty that was not the original plan. But like Stockdale– the American prisoner in Vietnam who endured by his grim optimism for the long term– I am absolutely certain that my work will be proven right eventually, and empower the world at last. The question is whether it will be in time for my serious use, and/or in my lifetime, or in time to help in the darkening future. But I will fight for it to my last breath.

Let me end on a cheerier note.

My life, and this book (I hope) have gone in what I long ago defined as "an interesting, generalized or superlative direction." I invite you the reader to try it if you dare.

UMPWARD!

APPENDICES

Appendix 1. HIDDEN IN PLAIN SIGHT: Xanadu Structure, a Deep (and I believe The True) Generalization of Literature

> The most difficult subjects can be explained to the most slow-witted man
> if he has not formed any idea of them already;
> but the simplest thing cannot be made clear to the most intelligent man
> if he is firmly persuaded that he knows already,
> without a shadow of doubt, what is laid before him.
> — *Leo Tolstoy*

INTELLECTUAL PROPERTY NOTICE.

Note that I have spent a lot of money and effort to maintain the "Xanadu®" trademark, and I ask that you respect this trademark as referring only to systems which I detail and control. (Note that trademark law requires that the trademarked goods be controlled by the trademark holder.)

If the reader wishes to implement any of these ideas, please use the term "xanalogical structure" (or, if need be, "Xanadu®-inspired").

It's often said that the best place to hide a thing is in plain sight. To which I would add: *hide it in plain sight with a bad reputation.* Then no one will see it at all.

Everybody knows about the Xanadu project and everybody sneers about it, as if the idea were ridiculous (whatever that idea might be, few seem to know) and its implementation impossible.

In fact we sought the deepest possible representation of literature with the greatest power, and I believe we found it. It is only politics and mis-maneuvering that have kept it out of the public's hands for so long. Worse, the World Wide Web has taken all the oxygen, obscuring our much deeper agenda.

**What would Phil Zimmermann have said?
(2010.01.30)**

Phil Zimmermann, creator of PGP encryption, was inspired early by the Xanadu concepts. He emails:

"How will future historians keep track of all this?" he asks. "It's so unstable. There is so much about Xanadu that is better than the web today."

XANADU HISTORY IN BRIEF

The Xanadu group sought to build a world-wide hypertext publishing system of a scope inconceivable in today's terms. Unfortunately we overreached, in two vastly ambitious designs (the Tumbler design and the Ent design). Instead of a simple single-user system (like the web), we designed in 1979 a client-server network for delivering millions of documents and also finding the re-use of content and overlays among millions of documents. Almost nobody knows what that means yet.

It was time to get simpler. XanaduSpace, in 2006-7, implemented the single-user system completely but is now stalled as a prototype. The next one is undecided.

WHAT A XANADOC IS AND HOW IT WORKS

A xanadoc is a bundle of connected pages with visible connections (which can be turned on and off), and selectable views, with animation. A xanadoc can be seen as a page simulation, but also as a cylinder, a sphere, flying snippets, or any other useful or dramatic presentation.

Screenshot of xanadoc in 3D (in the XanaduSpace prototype, a full-- though stalled-- implementation). Eleven pages of the xanadoc are shown, with visible connections between them (both links and transclusions).

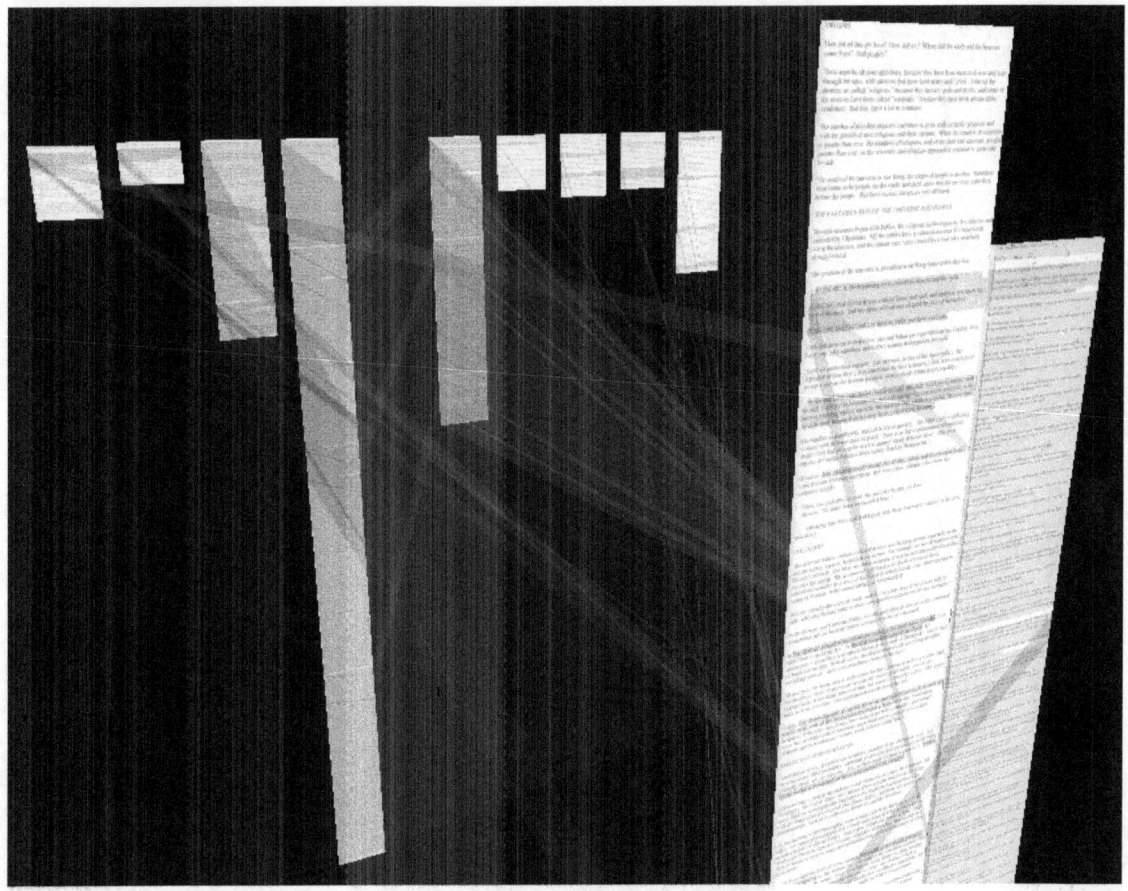

This does not have the slightest resemblance to any conventional electronic documents, and in particular it has no resemblance to the World Wide Web. (A xanadoc cannot work in a web browser, which is locked to the conventional paradigms; it is as if the web had been created to prevent everything we believed in.)

XANADOC INTERNAL DATA

The xanadoc when assembled consists of portions of content from all over, melded with independent overlays (xanalinks) from all over.

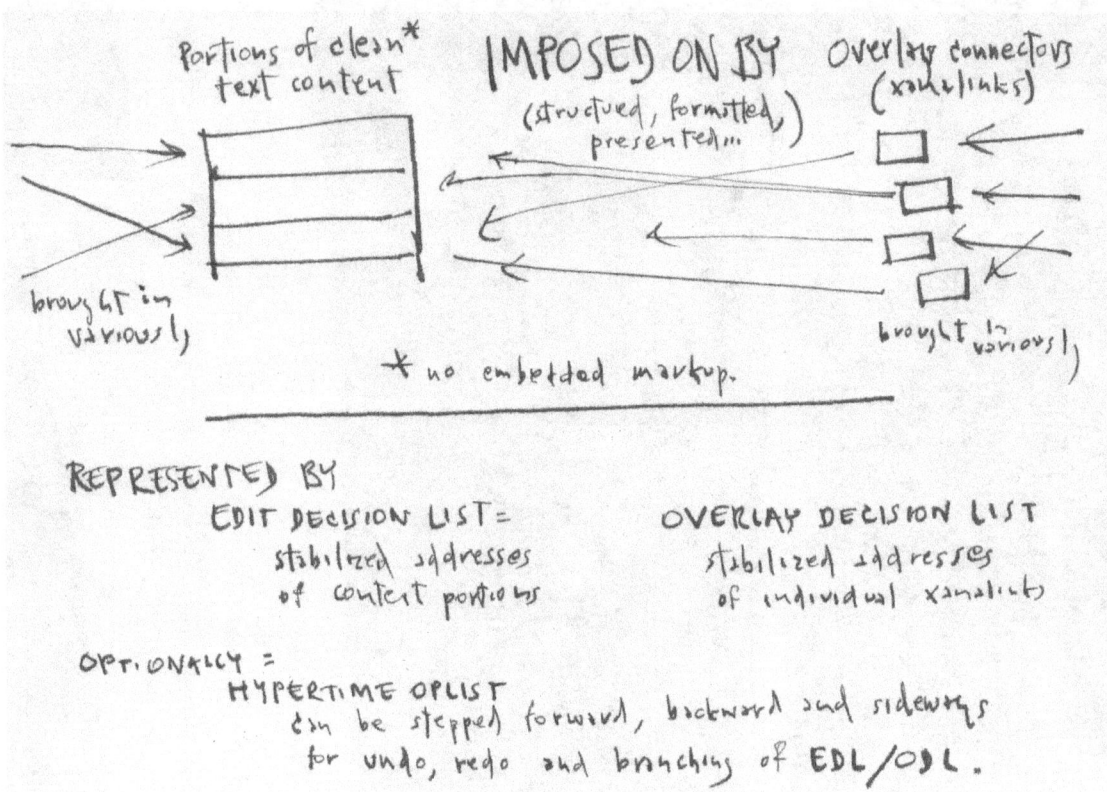

THE EDIT DECISION LIST

A xanadoc is not stored in a file,

The xanadoc is maintained and represented as an Edit Decision List (EDL), of--
   - pointers to content
   - pointers to xanalinks
   - (And optionally, a hypertime oplist, for versioning back, forth and sideways.)

It is assembled at delivery time from this list of addresses (the Edit Decision List or EDL). Internally the EDL is two lists*--
   • List of content portions to be brought in-- a selection of portions of stabilized content, untainted by internal markup, brought from arbitrary sources.

- List of overlays to be brought in– a selection of xanalinks (free-standing overlays, keyed to the stabilized addresses of the content). These are imposed upon the content to obtain structurings, interactions, user-selected views, etc.

    * We are thinking of separating these into an EDL (Edit Decision List, only the content portions) and an ODL (Overlay Decision List of xanalinks), for explanatory clarity

~~XANADU TECH~~

STABILIZATION OF CONTENT

The xanadoc consists of portions of stabilized content sent for as needed, possibly from all over, melded with independent overlays (xanalinks), possibly from all over, which are keyed to the addresses of the stabilized content.*

> * rather in the way that big messy web pages are brought in from many sources.

STABILIZED CONTENT???

The sneaky issue is stabilization of content.

The notion of *stabilized content* is not in the usual paradigm. This is content whose addresses are guaranteed to stay the same. For instance, if you wish to re-use the first sentence of the Gettysburg Address, it must be first given a stabilized address, presumably different from where you found it. (This is a political and administrative issue, not a technical one.)

This allows the same content to be used in a variety of different documents and pages.

INDEPENDENT OVERLAYS???

The notion of *independent overlays and links*, which may be sent for individually, is also entirely counter to existing paradigms.

This allows the same overlays and links to be used in a variety of different documents and pages.

XANADU'S TWO FORMS OF CONNECTION

Two completely different forms of connection are managed by Xanadu. *Note that both mechanisms are totally different from the embedded one-way links of the web.*

- XANALINKS, which specify characters in the content, connections between them, and overlays to apply. Xanalinks are downloaded and maintained separately from the content, and imposed on that content depending on their type. Xanalinks can include—
    - • formatting information, such as paragraphing and italics. Note that since formatting is not embedded, the same content can be transcluded into many different uses, differently formatted.
    - • connective information, for example connecting a comment page to the page it's commenting on
    - • interactive presentational information, for example specifying whirling snippets of text that are supposed to whirl in 3D
    - • templates to be connected to the content

  and much more

- TRANSCLUSIONS, which show the identities of content—the same content in more than one place. These are found by address comparison amongst EDLs. Transclusion allows—
    - • connection of a quotation to its source
    - • comparison of different pages side by side, showing the exact differences
    - • binding of parallel pages by identical headings

  and much more.

Both xanalinks and transclusions may be shown as visible beams, which may be turned on and off for clarity.

THE FULL DOCUMENT

A full document is then represented as—
- EDL (Edit Decision List— list of portions + list of overlay connectors (xanalinks))
- *Optional:* Hypertime oplist (change operations—see below)
- Source files of stabilized content, anywhere

VERSIONING

Conventional versioning is just undo and redo. If you redo a couple of times and make a change, the "undo" is no longer valid.

The Xanadu model is a little deeper, allowing movement not just forward and backward, but sideways to different versions.

~~XANADU~~ TECH

VARIOUS VERSIONING MECHANISMS
Previous Xanadu versions had versioning methods tailored to their complex mechanisms. Instead we are going to the author's very simple hypertime microversioning, as implemented in 1996-7 by Ken'ichi Unnai (sometimes called *OSMIC*). Unlike conventional Undo and Redo, which lose changes if another operation breaks the change, hypertime editing allows going back, forward and sideways among versions.

(And of course any two versions may also be compared side by side, with transclusion beams showing which parts are the same. So, indeed, may any other pair of documents.)

HOW IT WORKS INSIDE: INTERNAL OPERATIONS OF A PAGE

Xanadu works inside by simple content mechanisms and address comparisons.

~~XANADU~~ TECH

The internal operations for xanalogical documents are extremely simple—

- Bring in the content portions according to the EDL
- Concatenate the content portions, retaining their original addresses
- Find the shared addresses among local pages (transclusions)
- Bring in the xanalinks according to the EDL

The rest is user selection, viewing and animation. Also editing (see below).

(*Note: all these steps are fully operational in the XanaduSpace prototype.*)

EDITING

USER OPERATIONS. There are "insert" and "delete", but there is no "cut" or "paste". Instead there is *transclude*, which puts the same content virtually in another place and maintains the connection.

~~XANADU~~ TECH

Internally, the user's changes go directly to the EDL and the hypertime list. Any operation is resolved to stable content addresses; then the current version is re-generated by the EDL. Previous and parallel versions, when wanted, are generated by stepping the version through the hypertime list.

HYPERTIME OPLIST. Each edit operation is logged with its hypertime ID. This is numeric if there is no version branching, alphanumeric if

branching. It can be stepped through reversibly along any branches.

CUT - - AND - - PASTE - - - - - - - - - - - - -
XANADU AS WORKSYSTEM

Conventional electronic documents map everything to either–
- paper
- hierarchy
- rectangular diagrams (spreadsheet)

These may be appropriate or they may not. There is no reason to impose artificial systems of order.

As explained throughout this book, the cut-and-paste technique of old-- moving pieces of paper and loose notes around on a tabletop, then deciding a sequence-- has not been embodied in any available software.

Xanadu as a worksystem showing parallel connected pages, offers powerful facilities–
- flying notes can be rearranged
- outlines are parallel; transcluded headlines bind pages (showing identical headlines in other pages
- standby material (difficult to handle in conventional systems) becomes easily manipuable
- alternative outlines may be managed simultaneously

etc.

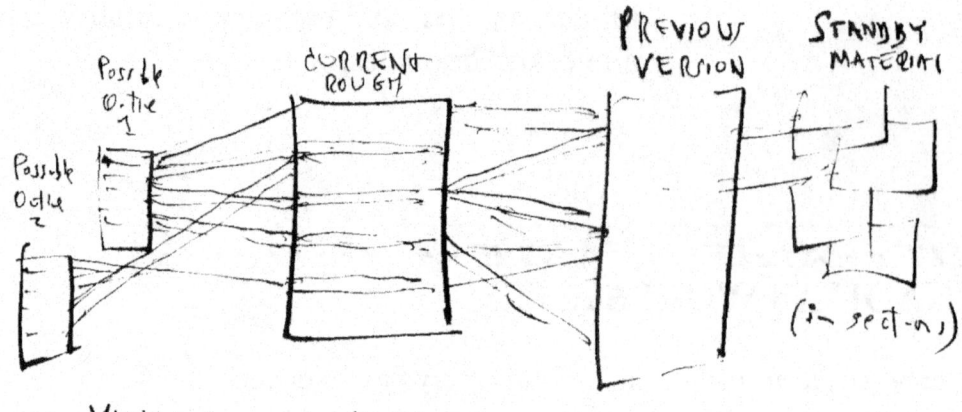

ANTHOLOGIES, WIKIS AND MASHUPS

Anthologies, wikis and mashups are essentially identical. No special formats are required: they are simply examples of xanalogical structure. (On the web they require elaborate special formats.) In addition, xanalogical structure connects each portion with its original source.

THE XANADU PUBLISHING METHOD, INCLUDING SALE

Xanadu is not just a document design. From the beginning, Xanadu was designed around a publishing method and matching systems of copyright and payment.

THE REST OF THE WORLD'S ASSUMPTIONS—
• When you publish on the web, you place whole files there for download. The contents end up in the user's browser cache and can be kept. Therefore everything has to be given away. This offers no opportunity for publishers who want to stay in business selling content.

Xanadu publishing is meant to be a win-win for publishers *and* users, allowing sale in a way beneficial to all.

The Xanadu rights model has always been straightforward. There have been variants as possibilities changed, but here is the enduring model--
- In Xanadu publishing, rightsholders may of course give away content, but may also sell it, and this sale is supported by network features.
- OWNERSHIP OF CONTENT. Content ownership by the rightsholder, defined by copyright law, is maintained at the server.
- OWNERSHIP OF COPIES. Purchased ownership of a *copy*, by a purchaser, is registered by the publisher; the publisher keeps track of what you own, down to the smallest sliver of the content. (*Note: anonymization issues are separate; this is simply the base model.*)
- Since each content portion is obtained from its original publisher, purchase (if material is not free) can be automatic when the reader sends for anything;. Purchase may be of *extremely small portions.*
- Once you've bought a portion of content, it is marked as owned by you, for your re-use. Thus you may buy a book one sentence at a time, either directly or quoted elsewhere, and always see that part without payment thereafter.
- NOT PAY-PER-VIEW: Once purchased, a sliver (or a whole book) may be re-accessed at any time by that copy-owner with no more royalty payment.

The rest of the world has now discovered our old idea of *enclosed presentation--* content which is shown but not downloadable (e.g. NewYorker.com, Google book views). That was always our model. Because the Web required downloading everything and did not offer enclosed presentation, the web publisher had no choice but to give everything away.
- Xanadu publishing uses enclosed presentation--but instead of passive enclosed presentation (as at newyorker.com, Amazon peeks), it allows the user to link, recomposite (transclude), rework the content into new documents *and publish them--* all within the enclosure-- since the reworked content will still come from the original publishers, as before.
- Enclosed presentation can reassure publishers.

Under copyright law, rightsholders cannot be compelled to join; each rightsholder would have the option of accepting this system. A publishing company would independently have to join this scheme to make their own content available in this way. But they lose nothing by it, since
- It has no effect on paper publishing, only on-line publishing
- It brings payment for all uses (except re-reading)
- It brings the opportunity for successive re-uses of the same content
- It legitimates, and makes profitable, on-line re-use.

Legally, we thus need to have a a permission system to go with the software.

TRANSCOPYRIGHT
~~COINED WORDS~~

It needed a name, so I have promulgated this copyright system under the name *transcopyright*— as a permission doctrine and as a sale method. However, it basically needs Xanadu delivery in order to work, so we're right in the problematique of getting that working.

What would Paul Brest have said? (1959-current)

In my Senior year at college I hastened to catch up with a few fields I knew nothing about. One of these was music. An amiable freshman, Paul Brest, helped me with my music homework. He married a Swarthmore gal and they went off into law.

By and by I heard that Paul had become dean of the law school at U. of Chicago, then at Stanford.

Recently Marlene and I visited Paul and Iris at their home.

I showed him XanaduSpace and explained transcoyright. Over some very good bourbon, he mulled over the transcopyright system.

"That works," he said. 'It adds up. It makes perfect sense, and everyone benefits.'

Now I know why he they made him Dean.

Test Your Knowledge!
How much of the following do you understand?

XANADU BRIEFLY DESCRIBED

(Note that all these steps are followed in the XanaduSpace prototype, which unfortunately hangs tantalizingly incomplete with no current prospect of completion.)

- Xanadu documents (xanadocs) are parallel structures with many optional views and many optionally visible connections between the pages. The user can see the connections between pages, if desired.
- Xanadu offers a radically different literary genre, where connected parallel pages simplify organization– parallel narratives, alternative versions, and much more.
- Unlike conventional electronic documents, Xanadu documents do not simulate paper except as one possible view.
- Xanadu links (xanalinks) are overlaid on the contents and may have numerous terminals, or prongs, unlike weblinks, which are mashed into the contents and have only a beginning and an end.
- Xanadu optionally shows transclusions (identities of content) made visible-- as paths between different occurrences of the same content. This can not only be used to show original context, but as binding headers between separate pages and documents, and much more.
- Xanadu is a work system, an entirely different way of writing and organizing, radically different from conventional document systems like Word, or outliners. It is intended to substitute deep overview dynamics for such barbarisms as "cut" and "paste"*

> * That is, "cut" and "paste" as redefined by the PUI, away from their true meanings as explained in this book; this redefinition was introduced to the public in 1984 under the name 'Macintosh', then adopted in Microsoft Windows and the various PUI interfaces of Linux.

XANADU ASSUMPTIONS DIFFERENT FROM THOSE OF THE REST OF THE WORLD–

- a document is not stored in a file (a deep restriction of most systems)
- a document is specified not by a URL but by an EDL (Edit Decision List) of portions and overlays to be combined
- a document is assembled as portions with overlays
- links (xanalinks or overlays) are not embedded but applied

- links (xanalinks or overlays) are free-standing entities, individually published or privately downloadable, separate from content
- content addresses are stabilized, and the same address span will always bring the same content. This involves issues of politics, policy, and caching. (We have a file type, the *permascroll*, which is a managed file whose content addresses never change, though it may be continually appended-to.)
- Any document in Xanadu may be reworked by anyone, since a new document is kept as a list of pointers, and the content is delivered separately. That new document has a new name but may be easily compared with transclusion to its original.
- a web page is basically a whole file brought in (though often decorated with numerous banners and intrusions brought and assembled in from elsewhere)
- similarly, a xanadoc is assembled from pieces of stabilized content

Appendix 2. BROTHERS

I actually have real brothers, but I'll honor their privacy here.

I have had a number of spiritual brothers, who form a part of this story for the inspirational effects they have had on me.

TIM AND DOUG AND STAN

Timothy Leary and Douglas Engelbart and Stan Dale have all spontaneously called me 'brother'. I accept this with honor and pride. (That term of praise triangulates the coordinates of my soul, and almost makes the rest worthwhile.)

DOUG AND ME ⟶
DOUG ENGELBART ESPECIALLY

Doug and I, Marlene and Karen have gotten like family. We have hung out in California, Japan and England.

ST. DOUG! The author and Douglas Engelbart on the patio of Doug's home, August 2010. Unretouched frame selected from video by Marlene Mallicoat; halo is optically authentic.

Doug and I are bound by a shared dislike of how the world has veered from what we think is right, and we overlook our differences. We have in common a rather surprising list:
- an unwavering picture of how it ought to be
- specific data structures
- specific operations
- specific visualizations
- neither of us are programmers
- we've both spent too long writing specs that aren't followed
- we both disdain 'peer review'— a waste of time when you're trying to accomplish something far wide of what the others see or understand

But Doug maintains an astonishing good humor and good will toward everyone most of the time, which I wish I could emulate.

AGNAR MYKLE

My Norwegian uncle, Agnar Mykle (pronounced Ognar Mik-leh) had a remarkable effect on me. I met him when I was twelve and was delighted by his effusive, enthusiastic personality, unlike any man I'd known before. The men in my family were reserved, each in his own way. Agnar became a role model to me: his directness and enthusiasm shaped my persona as an adult. (To a degree these are Norwegian traits, but he carried them farther.)

I first met, enjoyed and admired him in Norway when I was twelve; then he and I hung out when he visited my family in New York a couple of years later. I felt we had a special relationship.

The fact that he became the Bad Boy of Norwegian literature, and (some say) I became the Bad Boy of computerdom, is a strange coincidence that would not seem to follow from our friendship or what I responded to in him. But who can know.

STEVE JOBS

I feel I have a special relationship to Steve Jobs, though I have met him only once. I think of him as my dark younger twin. We are similar in several key aspects:
- He understands users, as do I.
- He is absolutely sure of his views, as am I.
- He is absolutely sure of his abilities, as am I.
- He is intolerant of stupidity, as am I.
- He is basically a movie director.

However, Jobs got leverage and I didn't. (His friend Woz dropped the Apple I in his lap, but not everyone would have known what to do with it. Jobs did, as I would have.)

The marvelous buildout by Woz to the Apple II was based to a large extent on Jobs' perception of the home and personal market, which few others saw. (For my own experiences with this obtuseness, see Itty Bitty story in this book, 1975-7.)

My influence on Steve Jobs? I do believe Steve Jobs based the entire style and persona of the Apple corporation on the attitude of my book *Computer Lib*—the attitude of creative defiance that I offered the reader, and that Jobs invited the Apple customers to share.*

> * Creative defiance has always been my attitude, and is the essence of Bohemianism.)

Jobs' "reality distortion field"— his cloud of ideas so often disdained by journalists— has proven to be reality itself.* But the question is, where did Jobs get these ideas originally? I believe they were pretty much set forth in *Computer Lib* two years before the Apple I.

> * As of this writing, the value of Apple— its market cap— has just passed that of Microsoft.

Jobs' perceptions have been excellent. He immediately recognized the potential of the Apple I for a market that did not yet exist, and he immediately recognized the PUI (on his famous walkthrough at Xerox PARC) as a huge and marketable paradigm shift, which he turned into the Macintosh. For the most part Jobs has selected and packaged the ideas of others, but with a superb judgment, taste and sense of style that are his alone.

TESLA

I first heard of Nikola Tesla from Andrew Singer in 1966. So strange that most people haven't heard of the man who created the modern world—but his enemy, the over-appreciated and vicious Thomas Edison, did much to destroy Tesla's reputation.

Tesla, in the 1880s, imagined alternating current running the cities of the future. He described having a sudden, unified vision whose consequences he continued to unfold throughout his working life. As part of this he invented—
- the alternating-current motors that run the world
- radio (his patents were upheld against Marconi's, though this is not well known)
- the neon light
- the guided missile

And far more.

Tesla built the first great alternating-current generator, still running from Niagara Falls. But his next, and greatest, intention was to create free power for the world by cranking up the natural electric palpitations of the earth with extra energy—attempting this from his towers at Colorado Springs and Wardenclyffe (Long Island). He planned to add energy into the earth's pulsating field that could be tapped by antennas, free, anywhere.* It probably would have worked. (The only problem: What's the business model?)

> * I am accepting the interpretations of George Trinkaus. See teslapress.com.

Overwhelmed by financial problems, Tesla retreated to feeding pigeons in Manhattan—a powerless drifter in the power-world he had created. He was supported by the electrical engineers' society for the rest of his life.

I deeply feel for Tesla. Many (including Berners-Lee and Markoff) have called my ideas quixotic and Utopian, i.e. impossible like Tesla's business plan, and many want me to go feed the pigeons like Tesla (and, like Tesla, in a world so like, and so unlike, what I tried to build). But I'm not ready for that.

THE BIG THREE: MY HERO BROTHERS OF OLD

I had a number of heroes as a boy, but three of them, I learned later, were actually very like me—Frank Lloyd Wright, Orson Welles, and Buckminster Fuller. It's not that I imitated them (except perhaps for Bucky), but that I discovered my resemblances to them in my fifties. How I'd detected the psychic resonance as a boy is a mystery.

For those readers not familiar with them—
- Frank Lloyd Wright, a visionary architect with a very long career, first built houses in stark straight lines, then in later years built buildings with strange wiggles and curves and thematic shapes. His every building, experienced within, is a fascinating and compelling space, often awe-inspiring.*

> * If you're ever in Marin County, north of San Francisco, don't miss visiting Wright's Marin County Civic Center! Be sure to look straight down on the passing cars through the strange opening.

- Orson Welles, a theatrical prodigy and innovator with an incredible voice, reached Broadway in his teens, and soon had his own theater and was performing on radio some fifty times a week. Absolute master of radio, he terrified America with a prank broadcast of a Martian invasion; then he went to Hollywood and at the age of 25 re-invented cinema. (Alas, it was downhill for

Orson from there.) For a sense of his magic I recommend the opening titles of the film "Macbeth" (1950 but with sound scarcely equaled today) and the film "The Trial", with its endless space of bureaucratic mazes.

• Buckminster ("Bucky") Fuller, a designer and philosopher, basically designed only three things but went on and on discussing the universe and everything else. Fuller designed a radical car in the 1930s (teardrop-shaped, incredibly fuel-efficient, box tube frame, driver in the middle, turn on a dime, a motor for each wheel– if malfunction, pop out the motor-wheel module and put in a spare!). Two prototypes were built but one crashed, giving it a bad name. The house he designed for mass production was equally radical– (round, corrugated-metal exterior, built-in furniture, to be lowered by helicopter onto a rotation mast!) Only one prototype was built before Bucky fought with backers, but people lived happily in it for decades. Bucky's third system of designs—and at last his financial success– consisted of geodesic domes, used for cold-war radar installations but widely celebrated (as in the U.S. dome at the Montreal World's Fair and in the molecule 'fullerene' named after him). Fascinated from childhood by the triangular pyramid (tetrahedron), Bucky combined that shape mysteriously with his philosophy of resource conservation and radical change in education. He would speak for hours, with nobody leaving.

Here are some things the four of us (Wright, Orson, Bucky and I) have in common–
- designers all
- unique and idiosyncratic talent and vision
- sweeping, extravagant, virtually limitless ideas
- unique style and unique personal visualizations
- proud to explain our unique abilities to anyone
- absolute confidence in our abilities
- very much wrapped up in ourselves and our worlds
- our agendas unflagging, independent and hard to merge with
- none of us a collaborator, though in need of assistants
- absolute insistence on independence
- absolute insistence on creative control and finishing touches
- fierce fights with those who would change our work
- a huge number of projects, many unfinished
- entrepreneurs of intermittent success
- intellectual side with broad knowledge
- excellent speakers and showmen
- excellent writers (or in the case of Bucky, prodigious writer widely-read anyway)
- flamboyant, egotistical self-promoters and/or self-publicizing narcissists
- our work inseparable from story of our lives
- very much concerned for our place in history

- out to benefit mankind (or, in the case of Orson, by entertaining and enlightening)

Most important,
- **EACH OF US SHOWED YOU SPACES THAT NO ONE HAD EVER SEEN BEFORE.**

Of course, the world is full of egotistical control freaks who promote spaces of their own devising-- notably movie directors, dictators, religious prophets. But some make the world better and more interesting, and some don't.

Appendix 3. BUM RAPS: The Accusations against Me

There are a number of outstanding accusations against me—some in print, some on the web, and some in the air. They are urban legends. If not stanched now, they will be attached to my name forever. They are—

Accusation 0. that I am ignorant;

Accusation 1. that I am lying or exaggerating about what I've worked on, or claim to have thought of early;

Accusation 2. that backers have lost a lot of money on me;

Accusation 3. that even with resources and leverage, I could not have done anything I was attempting;

Accusation 4. that the Xanadu project was an incoherent, "Utopian,"[1] "Quixotic,"[2] impossible idea.

[1] Tim Berners-Lee.
[2] John Markoff.

All these accusations are false. I will go over them one at a time.

Accusation 0. Was He Ignorant?
-- What Did He Know and When Did He Know It?
-- And How Could He Possibly Have Known?

"What did he know and when did he know it?" That's what they asked about Richard Nixon in the Watergate days. Except Nixon was trying to prove what he did not know, and I need to prove what I did know, and he was lying and I'm not.

A principal purpose of this book is to answer charges that I was "ignorant," on a spectrum ranging from the hate-prose of The Jackal to the varied fluffy inaccuracies of the well-meaning Alex Wright in a 2007 lecture at Google.* Wright's worst: "To this day he [Nelson] has no idea how to program a computer." Presentation of this absurd misstatement at Google headquarters gives it seemingly official verisimilitude.

* The title of his talk is "The Web that Wasn't", currently on YouTube.

Of course I was ignorant at the start. We all are. But walking into the computer world I was already familiar with a broad variety of media and their mechanisms (discussed below). In any medium, what you see projects from the hidden choices of the makers. I knew such choices well and loved to make them.

As soon as I saw what was possible with the computer I started making such choices.

HOW DID I KNOW WHAT I KNEW?

Why could I accurately imagine and design all this, when almost no one else did? And pursue them for so long without confirmation?*

> * I believe Freud would have called the following convergence *overdetermined*.

In particular, why could I visualize interactive screens, how they should behave and what mechanisms to put behind them, when almost no one else did in that time (and for another decade)? Why did I imagine, entirely on my own, a world of interactive computing and world-wide hypertext?

Because I'd watched men working at screens where they made things happen, in twilit control rooms at NBC and CBS. Because I'd played for years with electrical arcade games and interactive museum exhibits. (They had big pushbuttons in my boyhood.)

Because I was a project guy, a movie guy, a designer, an innovator, a troublemaker looking for a better world, a cultural radical, a fast thinker, a generalizer seeking clean generalities, a nexialist seeking new connections, and a cynical idealist in search of some totally new ideal, as yet untarnished. Because I had always sought new ways of life.

Because I knew how to put mechanisms behind desired effects. Because I knew a wide variety of media effects and their inner layers.

Media effects of those days were produced by layering of many kinds. I had an easy familiarity with how media mechanisms made effects, usually by the stacking and combination of their layers.

In all these different media modalities, the effects emerged from their inner layers in different ways; but always you built with layers— in movies[1], animated cartoons[2], "legitimate" theater[3], magic[4], photographic emulsions and darkroom work[5], printing[6], audio[7], video electronics of that day[8], arcade games and flight simulators of that day[9], museum exhibits of that day[10]. I had casual knowledge of all these mechanisms.

[1] Layerings of movies then: matte painting, double exposure, Old Technicolor and Trucolor bi-pack, masking, and (king of them all) travelling matte.

[2] Layerings of animated cartoons then: sketches, inking to cels, painting of cels, cels on top of cels, multiplane camera. Puppetoons: successive wax heads and limbs. Fantasy sound tracks (hammered home in *Fantasia*.)

[3] Layerings of theater then: blocking, timing, lighting from wings and above; dimmers, special lighting zones, scrims; flashes, turntables, treadmills, trapdoors, swinging sets and props, sound effects (and thunder sheets!); surprise use of actors in auditorium; distractions, loudspeakers, music.

[4] Layerings of magic: distraction, patter, hand passes, card forcing, view blocking, smoke, mirrors, wires, sleeves, pockets, sewing tricks, snap-away receptacles, cup and balls, Svengali decks.

[5] Layerings of photography: Kodachrome itself, with all its layers, and later Kodacolor. In the darkroom: masking and double exposure; dodging and burning; cochineal dye on negative; solarization; dye transfer printing; Flexichrome (a high-quality artificial-color layered process of that time); and good old Marshall's Photo-Oil Colors.

[6] Layerings of printing then: Two-color printing (add-on); four-color printing; tip-ins; folding tricks; cutouts, embossing.

[7] Layerings of audio then: the theremin and the Hammond organ both sandwiched their audio components; echo chambers (and later, false echo by springs); radio actors talking at once; radio sound effects, often from multiple sources and leveraging as well on audience reaction, e.g. Fibber McGee's closet; mixing of movie sound tracks; multilevel tape recording in the late forties, esp. Les Paul and Mary Ford, Louis and Bebe Barron.

[8] Layering of video electronics then: split screen, Teleprompter.

[9] Layerings of arcade games and flight simulators of that day: all kinds of buttons and lever controls; things spun and circled and zipped, and you shot at them; pinball machines already had a jangle of noise combinations; juke boxes already had lots of lights; arcade shoot-em-ups had guns with lights and electric

eyes to receive them; the LINK trainer (decommissioned from WWII in some arcades) had a 3-axis control and simulations of sound and engines.

[10] Layerings of museum exhibits of that day: models, mirrors, lighting, pushbuttons (especially pushbuttons that affected lighting, seeming to change a physically fixed scene); seemingly opaque objects which lit up inside; semi-silvered mirrors which revealed new views. And scratchy audio to accompany it, in those days generally from a worn phonograph record.

I had enjoyed all these and tried out whatever ones I could. (I had an early tape recorder in 1952.)

Because I'd read science fiction (though later when I tried to explain these things to Asimov, he cut me short). Because I knew (from history and science fiction and Hiroshima and Sputnik) that change would come.

Because I was a writer who resented having to impose false sequence and believed there could be alternatives to the structures imposed by paper.

Because I understood people's literary urges and doings.

Because I knew something about copyright.

Because I had talent and chutzpah.

Because I had total faith in my perceptions and understanding.

But most important, *because I had made movies in my mind all my life.*

Accusation 1. Did He Lie or Exaggerate?
And How Could He Possibly Have Known?
And what exactly did he think of?

I hope the appalling detail in this book, all of which I swear to be true to the best of my recollection, will clear up what I do and do not claim to have done. As stated earlier, all this can be verified from my archives*– in addition, of course, to public sources.

* As of this writing, Marlene Mallicoat is setting up an NPO for arranging some of these archives in

> hyperthogonal/xanalogical structure. Donations should be tax-deductible.

I never said I could tame wild horses, prove the four-color theorem, raise the dead, or (as some think I claimed) set up an earth satellite network.*

> * A conjectural illustration of satellites for some later period of world-wide hypertext is in *Literary Machines*. Naturally this was misunderstood. Whatever *can* be misunderstood, *will* be misunderstood.

But I have always claimed to be able to design software that is uniquely clear, understandable, simple and (sometimes) elegant.

And I took many inspired, informed initiatives on my own, in a number of computer areas, earlier than almost anyone-- and kept on with these initiatives for five years and longer, in the face of general bewilderment and skepticism, with no proof of concept from anywhere. And on since then.

EVERY ONE OF THESE INITIATIVES WAS VALID.

Here are some ideas and projects I thought of and pursued alone.

My Computer and Electronic Ideas, 1960-1

I am not saying I am the only person who thought of these things, only that I thought of them independently.

(This may be only a partial list.)

- principles of interactive software; my own theory of interaction (first called *splandremics*, later called *fantics* and *virtuality* (as well as *construct logic* and *substruction*); all these closely related to what is now called "user experience design")
  - a variety of screen tricks--
    - • selection method based on light-pen sweeps ("Zorro-language")
    - • scrolling (vertically, horizontally, diagonally)
    - • zooming
    - • menus (but not cascading menus; and I did *not* come up with the term "menu," which I found quite amusing the first time I heard it)
  - a paper for Professor Couch, in that first computer course, proposing to represent all information as dyadic relations with types. (I believe this anticipated the RDF file format by over thirty years.)

- a possible computer language, NELTRAN (I believe this specified early pieces for what become the Xanadu design)
- a possible computer language, MAN-TRAN (a system for abstraction in the social sciences, e.g. in the Human Relations Area File– from listings of attributes, looking for commonality-sets).

The Xanalogical Ideas, 1960-1

I am not saying I am the only person who thought of these things, only that I thought of them independently. Some of the visualizations may have come later.

(This may be only a partial list.)

- interactive text systems (now called 'word processing'– I did not know that Engelbart was doing it already)
- lists of items pointing to a stored original (transclusion, edit decision list)
- referential editing (editing by transclusion, now used by Wikipedia)
- fine-grained transclusion based on fine-grained referential editing
- "mashups" of content from different sources, but each portion connected to its original– a simple use of transclusion
- "wikis," or ever-changeable documents revised by many parties– a simple use of transclusion
- links, of course (Engelbart had 'em already)
- VISIBLE links between pages (still not generally accepted)

- side-by-side intercomparison of connected pages and documents, with visible connections
- version management
- version compare side by side
- intercomparison of alternatives (now called in part *decision support systems*)
- side-by-side, visibly connected pages as a new literary genre [may not have been in this time frame]
- storage of text for permanent referential use (now called in part *content management*)
- compositing of text from various sources (now called *wikis* and *mashups*–but always with paths back to the original contexts of each portion; in xanalogical structure, only the one mechanism is needed)
- undo and redo
- version management with version tree.* Later generalized (and implemented with Ken'ichi Unnai) as hypertime editing, not yet generally accepted.

> * I have recently heard that Bobrow was working on similar ideas at about the same time.

- publishing of electronic documents for public accessibility on electronic networks
- digital rights management–
  - - ownership of original content (copyright management)
  - - ownership of copy by purchaser
  - - (later elaborated as the transcopyright doctrine for on-line permission—only works with xanalogical systems)
- sale of content with micropayment (a term I coined)—later elaborated and patented as gateway micropayment for the web
- commercial plan of connection-points for user access to on-line documents (now called an *ISP*)
- commercial plan of document storage service for users (now called an *ISP*)

The Pseudo-Photography Ideas, 1961+
—now called CGI (my trademark Fantasm™)

I am not saying I am the only person who thought of these things, only that I thought of them independently.

(This may be only a partial list.)

- ray tracing
  - - " with what I called a flat map (now called "texture map")
  - - " approximating curved objects with a polytope of triangles
  - - " with automatic curvature over a polytope of triangles, with no additional parameters
  - - " with shadow
  - - " with chromium/mirror reflection
- triangular frames to be curved over to make arbitrary surfaces (I called it "fairing", a term used in aircraft and sheet-metal curvature)
- list-processing methods for projecting outlines of a 3D scene to 2D (Fantagraph)
- list-processing methods for shadow management

My Second-Stage Computer Ideas, 1962-5
I am not saying I am the only person who thought of these things, only that I thought of them independently.

(This may be only a partial list.)

(Still at this time I had no confirmation of these possibilities, except several articles I read about industrial and military uses of computers in such magazines as *Datamation, Electronics, Computers and Automation*.)

- one-handed stealth typing system (Walkie-Thinkie, still needed)
    - - five-finger typing of ASCII as Walkie-Thinkie input. (I did not know this was being implemented by Engelbart; however, his implementation was not intended to be portable or inconspicuous, as this was.)
- movie and video editing by computer (Cinenym); now called *non-linear editing*, except mine was intended to be controlled in part from a script with parallel alternatives
    - - linking of movie script and logging to video editing

My Later Computer Ideas, after 1965

I am not saying I am the only person who thought of these things, only that I thought of them independently.

(This may be only a partial list.)

- The Back Button (ca. 1967), my only widely-deployed design [OPERATIONAL; now in every web browser -- as well as Microsoft Windows windows]
- TRANSPOINTING WINDOWS (not yet generally accepted), published 1972)
- rearrangeable indexed trees for text management (enfilades), 1971-2 – later generalized by my colleagues as "general enfilade theory"
- state-diagram design of interactive systems, 1971-2
- Lollipop Notation, visual language for state-diagram design of interactive systems, 1971-2
- plan for consumer information stands ~1970-3 (tentative price list published~1977), intended to offer–
    - - walk-up workstation rental (now called an "internet café")
    - - accounts for access to document network (now called an ISP)
    - - document storage for user work, publication and reference (now also called an ISP)
- number pad used as arrow keys [OPERATIONAL, in Flapdoodle, ca. 1977]
- typeahead [OPERATIONAL], ca. 1977 in Superlanguage
- HYPERTHOGONAL STRUCTURE (ZigZag®) (not yet generally accepted), 1983-present [OPERATIONAL IN SEVERAL VERSIONS]
- transclusion-over-time diagrams, ca. 1978; rediscovered by IBM-MIT team, 1990s.
- "pivot browsing" (somebody else's new term, intrinsic to ZigZag) [OPERATIONAL IN SEVERAL VERSIONS]
- gateway micropayment for the Web (my patent no. 6,058,381, now owned by Intellectual Ventures).

- swooping of windows to line up a current connection between pages [IMPLEMENTED IN XANADUSPACE]
- triggering on changed data field in ZigZag (independently discovered-- common in relational database)
- connecting packages of cells in hyperthogonal structure (ZigZag slices) [OPERATIONAL IN TWO VERSIONS, by Jeremy Smith and Rob Smith]
- packages of cells inserting themselves amongst other cells in hyperthogonal structure (ZigZag intercalary slices)   [OPERATIONAL, by Jeremy Smith]

Accusation 2. How Much Have His Backers Lost?

Here's the legend: "Nelson's backers have lost millions." (This legend is thanks in part to Gory Jackal and the attack in *Wired*.)

How much have those who invested in me actually lost?

Zero. Nothing. Zip. Nada.

- I have had *only one investor*--referred to in this book as M.T. Flagon--and he backed out, calling the lesser sum he chose to put in a "donation."

We were building what would have been an early, if not the first, word processor for the public, the JOT Box.

First saying he would put in $10,000, he induced me to design the JOT Box, the first enfilade and the JOT interface. He then decided to put in only about $6000, a useless amount (to rent the equipment for a while), rather than the promised full $10,000 which would have bought the computer and given the product a start. He didn't lose his investment (since he now called it a donation), he threw it away. I believe he would have made a vast amount of money, but we will never know.

- What about the 1992 collapse of Xanadu at Autodesk, you ask? Weren't *they* backing Ted Nelson?

No. Autodesk invested, not in my projects, but in the company founded by Roger Gregory-- XOC, Inc.-- which had a president, a board of directors (on which I did not serve) and many stockholders, of which I was only one. I had a nice title (Autodesk Distinguished Fellow) and a nice office, but Xanadu was not my project any more, and I had no say in the development; the Silver Agreement had given away the development rights to XOC.

Due to spectacular mismanagement, as described in this book and elsewhere, XOC failed to deliver. Autodesk, and the other shareholders (including myself) lost their investments in XOC. But those shareholders were not backing me. They were investing in a corporation based originally on my ideas but giving me no chance to flesh them out.*

> * Of course, you could say most of the personal computer industry is based on my ideas, but at a greater distance.

Accusation 3. Could He Have Done It?

Here I will deal with the subtler accusation, that I don't seem like a guy who can get computer things done, in such phrases as–

'He couldn't have done it'.
'He had all those ideas, but he lacked the skills...'
'He was just a dreamer, he couldn't have actually done any of those things.'

Excuse me.

SOFTWARE DESIGNED, PRODUCED AND DIRECTED BY THE AUTHOR

I have produced and directed all the following projects with people who understood the mechanics I needed, and used their programming skills to implement my detailed designs.

- with HES team at Brown University (ca. 1967): the BACK button [and its implicit address stack], now universal on Web browsers
- with John R. Levine: SPAR system for Fretheim Chartering Corporation (interactive database program for ship chartering, (1971~2, in Levine-Eichenberger version of PDP-11 TRAC [OPERATIONAL, DELIVERED, CUSTOMER PLEASED]
- with Cal Daniels: JOT editor (1971-2), in Algol for the Nova computer [MAY HAVE BEEN operational]
- with Cal Daniels: the first enfilade (1971-2), in Algol for the Nova computer [MAY HAVE BEEN operational]
- with John V.E. Ridgway: DINGO (Display lINGO) Graphics language (1971-2), in Fortran/Assembler for the IBM 1620 [partly operational]
- with Ron Lachman: "Photography Hypergram" (1974 or 5), in the GRASS language [OPERATIONAL]

- with U. Illinois student, name temporarily forgotten (1974-5), "Fast Eddy"--minimal text editor in the GRASS language [OPERATIONAL]
- with William Barus: Superlanguage (1970s-style personal-computer language—an extended version of TRAC®), 1977 (in C) [OPERATIONAL]
- with William Barus: FlapDoodle (also called Pictrola) lo-res animation editor (1977) in Superlanguage version of TRAC [OPERATIONAL]
- with William Barus: database, invoicing and accounting system, with typeahead, for book-distribution company (ca. 1977 in Superlanguage version of TRAC) [OPERATIONAL, DELIVERED, CUSTOMER SATISFIED]
- with Steve Witham: JOT for the Apple II in Forth [OPERATIONAL AND DISTRIBUTED]
- with Steve Witham and others: demos for Datapoint management: Thunderscroll demo, Popcorn demo and Hyperhop demo, consolidated into Thunder Hop'n'Pop demo), 1981-2, in C and/or DASL [OPERATIONAL]
- with Ian McFarland: 3D zoom effect through bookshelves, 1990 [OPERATIONAL]
- with K. Ookubo: 'Tatsuno Otoshigo' zipper-list editor (in IntelligentPad and C), 1994-5 [OPERATIONAL]
- with Ken'ichi Unnai, 1996: hypertime microversioning system, sometimes called OSMIC, with Perl server and Emacs client [OPERATIONAL]
- with Ken'ichi Unnai: Spiraltime™ generalized time visualization and annotational interface (from nanoseconds to eons), in VRML; ca. 1996 [OPERATIONAL].
- with Roy Stringer: Spiraltime™ generalized time visualization and annotational interface (from nanoseconds to eons), in Macromind Director; ca. 1996 [OPERATIONAL]
- with Andrew Pam: ZigZag prototype (version Azz) in Perl, 1996. [OPERATIONAL]
- with Yousuke Igarashi, Andrew Pam et al: Hypertransaction system, ca.1988 (mostly Perl) [OPERATIONAL, DELIVERED TO MITI, ACCEPTED.]
- with Christopher Gutteridge: extensions for transquotation in the Eprints Server (2001-2), in Perl [OPERATIONAL AND WIDELY DEPLOYED]
- with Ian Heath: CosmicBook (ca. 2001-3), in C++ and Windows classes [OPERATIONAL]
- with Ian Heath: dictation/transcription system with visual looping (ca. 2001-3), in VisualBasic, C++ and Windows classes [OPERATIONAL]
- with Ian Heath: connection-line routine for transpointing windows (ca. 2001-3), in C++ and Windows classes [OPERATIONAL]
- with Jeremy Smith: Zzz version of ZigZag in 3D, (2003), in C and OpenGL [OPERATIONAL]
- with Mikhail Seliverstov: Ezz version of ZigZag in Java (2003) [OPERATIONAL]
- with Andrew Pam: The Little Transquoter; in Perl, 2006. [OPERATIONAL]

- with Robert Adamson Smith: Rzz version of ZigZag in C++, 2006 [OPERATIONAL, INTERNAL TO XANADUSPACE, below]
- with Robert Adamson Smith: ZZOGL (ZigZag OpenGL layer) [OPERATIONAL, INTERNAL TO XANADUSPACE, below]
- with Robert Adamson Smith: XanaduSpace version of Xanadu, 2006-8 (in C++, Python, ZZOGL and Rzz ZigZag) [OPERATIONAL]

DESIGNED BY OR WITH THE AUTHOR BUT NOT IMPLEMENTED

- Xanadu stands: Public hypertext service? (Gee, that's sure caught on.)
- Xanadu stands: local companies that would broker computer services to individuals. That's now called an ISP, and very popular world-wide.
- Xanadu stands: a place where a customer could rent a computer by the hour. That's now called an "Internet café."
- Xanadu stands: Selling digital storage services to consumers. That's also an industry.
- with Mark S. Miller: SKED (simple PERT system for personal use), 1977 [design]
- with Stuart Greene and others: Vortext editor design, 1981-2. [rejected by management]
- with Charles Strauss, Brown University mathematician, ca. 1966: Fantasm 3D surface-curvature function, generating curved surface from only vertex points (no splines or additional parameters).
- with 1979 Xanadu team (Roger Gregory, Mark Miller, Stuart Greene, Roland King, Eric Hill): overall paradigm and specs for world-wide Xanadu system, designed for millions of servers, billions of documents and transclusion following of arbitrary content among millions of documents. [The full Tumbler Design of Xanadu* with three enfilades was theirs, completed in the months that followed.]

    * Also referred to as xu88, and more recently Udanax Green.

- with Laura McLaughlin, 1980-81: JOT for the Apple II in AppleSoft Basic [turned out to be impossible due to undocumented gotchas in the language].

PROJECTS I INSTIGATED BUT DID NOT DESIGN, RELATED TO MY ONGOING WORK --

(This may be only a partial list.)

- Wordsearch program for IBM 360 at Harcourt Brace & World, designed by Andrew J. Singer and implemented by Singer and Mel Patrick, 1966-7 (360 assembler and JCL) [OPERATIONAL]
- by William Barus: Xanadu algorithms involving partner-crums and complementary rearrange, 1973-5) [algorithm work]
- General Enfilade Theory, extending my original enfiladic insights, by Gregory, Miller and Green, 1979-80 [ONLY LIGHTLY DOCUMENTED]. Their basic finding: enfilades (rearrangeable indexed trees) may be custom-designed for powerful search and manipulation. An enfilade has—
    - • upwardly-cumulative indexes (WIDative properties), which are decomposable, associative and composable, and may be represented in different ways
    - • downwardly-imposable arrangements (DSPative properties), which are decomposable, associative and composable, and may be represented in different ways

Their discoveries include the fact that more than one of each property may be custom-built into the same enfilade. These facts were used in the three enfilades of the Tumbler Design (xu88, also known as Udanax Green).

- virtual cell manager for ZigZag (then called GRIDL), by Mark S. Miller and Terry Stanley, in Forth, ca. 1982-3 (partly implemented)
- by 1988-92 XOC team: REdesign of world-wide Xanadu system (for millions of servers, billions of documents and transclusion following of arbitrary content among millions of documents), this time based on K. Eric Drexler's Ent structure. Design by Mark S. Miller, Dean Tribble, Ravi Pandya and many others. (partly implemented.)

* Also referred to as xu92, and more recently Udanax Gold.

Accusation 4. Was the Xanadu design ridiculous?

The legend persists that the Xanadu project, my main work for these fifty years, is a ridiculous pipe dream with only mangled, delirious pseudo-technical ideas. This is utterly false, as already discussed in Appendix 1. But the Xanadu design is counter-paradigm—
- a document is not delivered as a lump file
- paper simulation is only one document visualization
- connections are visible as straps (for instance)

and much more.

It has had many stages. However, since 1979 the Xanadu document has been--
- a series of content portions, with overlays

- represented and delivered as a list of addresses for the content portions and overlays

"The rest is presentation." See Appendix 1.

Appendix 4. The Crafting of Media
(from the catalog of the Jewish Museum "Software" show, 1970)

The crafting of media
Theodor H. Nelson

The strange revolution of our information environment has only begun; yet it has begun in such an obscured and clouded form that the public sees only various meaningless disguises.

The all-purpose machine, as von Neumann called it, has been falsely promulgated to the public as the socalled *computer*, numerical, uncompromising, demanding and intractable. It has profited certain computer companies to make "computers" and their associated techniques incomprehensible and awesome; these same companies now seem unprepared for the widespread public revulsion to this image of the computer. It has profited some computer companies to build ungainly and obscure systems for business purposes, badly related to what their business customers do; and to con the customer and his poor employees into believing it has to be that way; this keeps the hapless customer on the hook indefinitely. These same companies now seem unprepared to have their all-wisdom questioned. I would like to employ the word *cybercrud* to mean, in general, putting things over on people using computers. Cybercrud is one of the most important specialties, if not the economic backbone, of the computer field. The promotion of false or clumsy approaches to a problem as "scientific," the frequent claim that "the computer has to have it that way" —when a certain thing could be programmed very differently —are cybercrud.

We should distinguish between media and facilities. A facility is an available activity, or function, like a movie splicer or desk calculator. A medium is a set of presentation elements, and relations among them, that may be used by a person to create an object, environment or experience for someone else.

Creating media that are *organized*, then, clear and easily related to the human mind, is our task. Creating media that are focussed, or gently converging, is the delicate part. Rather than present a user with ideas and activities stretching limitlessly in all directions, a presentational system should help organize his work and attention.

This is the age of option. For instance, we may have anything we want on display screens—text or diagrams or both, moving or flickering or interacting or whatever. What do we want?

This is also the age of crunch. Ecstatic possibilities must survive various forbidding or shaping factors that might cut them down. In the design of media these include not merely economics and technicalities (such as transmission rates on phone lines), but social structure and motivation (what will the teacher put up with in the classroom? Why don't students use the language laboratory?).

Hypertexts and *hypergrams*, then, are two new species of media for the computer age: personal, dynamic, and contradictory of the heavy-handed and stupid "computer" in the

the frequent claim that "the computer has to have it that way" —when a certain thing could be programmed very differently —are cybercrud.

But the computer is an all-pupose machine, and the computer display—a screen programmed to present text and pictures somehow stored in the computer—is a universal miraculous communication tool, as Ivan Sutherland showed in the early sixties with his Sketchpad system. And computer prices, unlike other prices, go down relentlessly. Expensive as these devices may be today, within the decade small good ones will cost a few hundred, at most a few thousand dollars. As we learn to free ourselves from cybercrud, the question becomes not, "how do I relate to this sinister, demanding artifact?" but "what is the grooviest way to use this thing?" The human environment can now be wholly, wonderfully redesigned. What do we want? What do we want?? What do we want???

Until now, our media—letters, books, television—have been based on specific inventions and technical connections. But no longer are specific inventions of special importance: information may be commuted to any form, functioning networks may be built connecting any device to any other device; total trans-pluggability has come. (Imagine if you will a device with a red oval 2-inch TV screen, a set of chimes in the natural key of C, a smell generator capable of giving off most smells, and a foghorn. Should the F.C.C. authorize this combination as a broadcast medium?)

The design of media is thus in a sense a new art; before, we could tinker little with the package. I suggest the term "fantics" for the art and technology (in that order) of showing things; the crafting of media for human communication purposes is therefore its most important franchise, something like "city planning" in generality. Making things look good, feel right, and come across clearly should be a general objective.

Hypertexts and *hypergrams*, then, are two new species of media for the computer age: personal, dynamic, and contradictory of the heavy-handed and stupid "computer" in the general stereotype. Hypertext, or writing that can branch or perform, is seen in the *Software* show's "*Labyrinth*" piece, wherein the visitor may browse through a maze of writings on the screen. "Hypergrams," branching or performing pictures, will be the pictorial equivalent. Designing the detailed activities of the presenting systems is an important task, demanding technical knowledge, love and appreciation for words and pictures, and a sense of alternatives and inspiration.

The new age will not be "scientific." The word "scientific" is obsolete (except where specifying the activities and problems of scientists), like the adjectives "modern" and "streamlined." The technological imperative is a fake, computerization can take whatever form we wish it to; therefore we must learn about computers in order to wish better. As Burnham says at the end: "... *Software* makes none of the usual qualitative distinctions between the artistic and technical subcultures. At a time when esthetic insight must become a part of technological decision-making, would such divisions make sense?"

May 24, 1970

Bush, Vannevar, "As We May Think" in *Atlantic Monthly*, June 1945.
Sutherland, Ivan, *Sketchpad: A Man-Machine System*, Lincoln Laboratory, Lexington, Mass.
Nelson, Theodor H., "Getting It Out of Our System" in Schechter (ed.), *Critique of Information Retrieval*, Thompson Books, 1967.
Nelson, Theodor H., "No More Teachers' Dirty Looks" in *Computer Decisions*, September 1970.
Nelson, Theodor H., "As We Will Think", to be published.

Appendix 5. Donations

Some have said they would like to donate to further this work.

As of this writing, the nonprofit organization (suitable for tax deduction) is not yet in place.

In the meantime, donations are gladly accepted at

First Church of the Imagination
C/O MINDFUL PRESS
470 SCHOOLEYS MOUNTAIN ROAD #298
HACKETTSTOWN, NEW JERSEY 07840

The issue of deductibility is between you and the government. Talk to your accountant.

11.01.28
D28st

www.ingramcontent.com/pod-product-compliance
Lightning Source LLC
Chambersburg PA
CBHW060309240426
43661CB00059B/2705